Gospel Light's

TEACHER TRAINING
SMART PAGES

Gospel Light

How to make clean copies from this Book

You may make copies of portions of this book with a clean conscience if

► you (or someone in your organization) are the original purchaser;

► you are using the copies you make for a noncommercial purpose (such as teaching or promoting your ministry) within your church or organization;

► you follow the instructions provided in this book.

However, it is ILLEGAL for you to make copies if

► you are using the material to promote, advertise or sell a product or service other than for ministry fund-raising;

► you are using the material in or on a product for sale; or

► you or your organization are not the original purchaser of this book.

By following these guidelines you help us keep our products affordable.
Thank you,
Gospel Light

NOTE

Editorial Staff

Founder, Dr. Henrietta Mears • **Publisher Emeritus,** William T. Greig • **Publisher, Children's Curriculum and Resources,** Bill Greig III • **Senior Consulting Publisher,** Dr. Elmer L. Towns • **Senior Managing Editor,** Sheryl Haystead • **Senior Consulting Editor,** Wesley Haystead, M.S.Ed. • **Senior Editor, Biblical and Theological Issues,** Bayard Taylor, M.Div. • **Associate Editor,** Veronica Neal • **Contributing Editors,** Sally Carpenter, Mary Davis, Gordon and Becki West • **Art Director,** Lenndy Pollard, Samantha Hsu • **Designer,** Zelle Olson

Some of this material was originally published in *Early Childhood Smart Pages* (Ventura, CA: Gospel Light, 2002), *Children's Ministry Smart Pages* (Ventura, CA: Gospel Light, 2004), and *Preteen Ministry Smart Pages* (Ventura, CA: Gospel Light, 2005).

How to Use this Book

If you are a children's pastor or director,

1. Read the Straight Talk on Training section that begins on page 11 for an overview of the steps you can take to effectively train leaders and teachers for your children's ministry.

2. Skim through the Contents section to get an idea of the topics for which articles, tips and miniposters are provided. Cataloged by subject and always at your fingertips, this book (and the CD-ROM) is ready to assist you whenever your children's ministry volunteers need training in a specific topic.

3. Use the Monthly Calendar (p. 43) to plan and schedule several training events.

If you are a small-group leader or teacher,

1. Skim through the Contents section to get an idea of the topics for which articles, tips and miniposters are provided.

2. Keep this book as a handy reference when you need concise, down-to-earth information about your job as a children's leader or teacher.

Contents

Articles, Tips and Miniposters 71

Select resources from this section to use in training your volunteers. Include the articles and tips in e-mails and newsletters or distribute them as handouts. Miniposters can be displayed in classrooms or hallways, or made into transparencies for use in teacher training meetings.

Age-Level Characteristics

Articles

Building Relationships

Articles

Discipline

Articles

Learning Styles

Articles

Spiritual Formation

Articles

Storytelling

Articles

Teacher's Role and Preparation

Articles

Trauma

Articles

STRAIGHT TALK ON TRAINING

STRAIGHT TALK ON TRAINING

Sometimes children's pastors are so glad to have someone willing to lead a group that they are tempted to forego the steps that are needed to help the willing volunteer become an effective teacher. But here's the straight talk: A teacher who receives little training is unlikely to experience a fruitful ministry. Turn to the page numbers listed to get the essential information you need about how to motivate and build your volunteers.

Guideline 1: Get the Big Picture of Training (p. 13)

Plan a year-long calendar of teacher-training strategies and enrichment events that work for your church, updating the plan on a regular basis as needs and concerns arise.

Guideline 2: Make Meetings Effective (p. 18)

Plan and lead meetings that motivate teachers to attend, develop their skills and provide opportunities for team-building.

Guideline 3: Focus on Publicity (p. 25)

Make publicity a priority so that training efforts are not wasted.

Icebreakers (p. 22)

Build community among your volunteers with these fun get-acquainted activities.

Training: Tough Questions, Real Answers (p. 27)

Get the advice you need to make training happen!

Guideline 1: Get the Big Picture of Training

Just think of the many parts of a teacher or helper's job in your children's programs: leading small-group discussions, storytelling, understanding of a child's characteristics, knowledge of appropriate teaching methods, awareness of your church's policies and procedures, how to talk with children, handling discipline challenges—and more! So no matter what you call it—teacher-training, teaching enrichment, networking or orientation—the process of building up the skills of your volunteers is a significant part of an effective children's ministry.

Look at the Benefits

Some view training as something one acquires and possesses. Training, however, is actually a process whereby a volunteer improves and gains confidence in the skills they use. Training allows for growth and development of additional new skills. Training ensures vitality and freshness for the entire staff.

Consider who benefits from ongoing training opportunities. Children benefit as they participate in well-planned activities that nurture their understanding of God and His love for them. Teachers benefit because they experience increased confidence in teaching and enjoy the sense of teamwork that comes from group-training experiences. You, as the leader, benefit because well-trained teachers are more likely to enjoy their ministry experience and continue as volunteers.

A bonus benefit is that teachers are often parents who are volunteering in ministry for the first time. The skills they gain in teacher-training are often the same skills they need as parents. Therefore, training volunteers makes a significant impact in parent education.

More Than a One-Time Event

For those children's ministry leaders whose schedule is already full of endless details, it may seem that scheduling and leading even one training event is enough. However, in order for training to truly make a difference, it must be an ongoing process. Here's why:

▶ Teachers do not automatically know how to guide others in Bible learning. When left untrained, most adults tend to teach in the way they were taught, leading to very inconsistent classroom experiences for the children in your programs. Volunteers who come from an unchurched background have even less experience on which to build.

▶ New teachers need the promise of training. Having an ongoing training program will encourage new volunteers to commit their time and energy and will make the task of recruiting volunteers easier.

▶ Training that extends throughout the year enables volunteers to absorb information in manageable sections—rather than being overwhelmed by "everything you ever wanted to know about teaching children" in one training event. Teachers are more likely to put new information into practice if it is received in bite-size pieces.

▶ In any children's ministry, teacher absences will have to be filled during the year. An ongoing training plan throughout the year makes it possible for new staff members to be given the thorough training they need, instead of a haphazard, quick orientation.

▶ As circumstances and programs change throughout the year, it is easier to communicate and discuss procedural changes when a training plan is already in place.

▶ Both experienced and inexperienced teachers will appreciate the boost they receive from training meetings. Experienced teachers need fresh enthusiasm and inexperienced teachers need the practical wisdom of other teachers.

Your efforts in training will pay off as you see teachers encouraging each other, supporting one another in trying new ideas, evaluating progress, finding solutions to problems and sharing successes!

Training that Works

In order to make the most of your training efforts, focus in on these significant aspects of training:

▶ Work hard at keeping your training practical. The focus of any training, whether it is a weekly e-mail sent to your volunteers or an article posted on your church website, should be on specific ways in which the information being taught can be used in upcoming children's ministry programs. Identify at least one or two ideas they can put into practice right away. For training meetings, always ask teachers to bring the curriculum from which they are teaching. Make an effort to show how training principles relate to specific curriculum components. One of the questions that must be asked is, "How much of this training can be used by a teacher in next week's session?"

▶ From event to event and year to year, offer training that is based on the same teaching/learning philosophy. When all training events are carefully chosen to reinforce each other, you can be sure that your staff is not presented with conflicting educational philosophies and methods, and more than one age level can be trained at a time.

▶ Whenever possible, include a time in each training event that involves teachers in experiential learning. Unless a teacher tries a new skill or method, he or she will probably not feel confident enough to use it in class. Involve participants in observing and practicing the skills they are being trained to use.

New Teacher Checklist

✓ Copy of current curriculum materials

✓ Classroom policies and procedures

✓ Names and phone numbers of other teachers

✓ Class schedule

✓ Class roster (including parents' names, addresses and phone numbers)

✓ Building map with restrooms and exits clearly marked

Pre-Service Training

The first step in training actually begins when a volunteer accepts a task in your children's ministry. You can't separate recruiting and training; these elements must be linked in order to make your volunteer's experience positive. Beginnings are the most important—and probably the most risky—times for a new recruit.

▶ Consider planning a basic orientation class that presents key topics: how children learn, age characteristics and needs of children, discipline tips, small-group discussion guidelines, etc. Large churches may have enough new teachers to conduct orientation classes as part of their adult education program. Send an invitation to the orientation class to each new volunteer, and follow up with a phone call to encourage attendance.

▶ Make sure to provide a new volunteer with a current job description. When you review the job description with a new volunteer, be sure to answer the question, What are the basic things a person should do in order to succeed in this ministry? Explain why each action is important and how it will benefit the volunteer by helping him or her succeed. (For example, "It is important to prepare all materials before the session begins so that you can welcome and greet children as they arrive. Having time to welcome and greet children is a good way to build relationships with and among your class.")

▶ Schedule a time for the volunteer to observe a class or program already in progress, preferably assisting an experienced teacher several times. (See the Observation Form on p. 44.)

In-Service Training

In order to motivate and sustain interest in training opportunities, incorporate several different methods of training.

First, all teachers will benefit by attending training conferences or workshops in which their teaching skills can be improved. Both new and experienced teachers need opportunities to learn new skills, correct mistakes and expand their vision of ministry. Many churches find it helpful to plan at least two special training events each year, approximately four to six months apart.

More than one such event is advantageous because not all teachers will attend any single event and new teachers need significant reinforcement during the first year or two of service.

Depending on the size and resources of your church, you may take teachers to a local, regional or denominational convention or seminar. You may cooperate with one or more other churches in your area. Or you may plan and conduct the event just for your own staff.

If inviting teachers to attend a conference in your community or region, carefully select from possible events to make sure that the information communicated will support and enrich the philosophy of education in your ministry. The advantage of attending events outside your own church is that they often create enthusiasm and excitement about ministry.

In planning an event at your own church, consider several options for speakers and programs:

▶ An experienced public or private school teacher who can address a particular topic such as age-level characteristics, discipline tips, etc.

▶ A children's leader from a nearby church.

▶ A teacher in your church who has demonstrated effective teaching techniques.

▶ A teacher-training video that provides a discussion guide (available from curriculum companies or your local Christian bookstore).

▶ A round-table format at which several teachers share specific tips regarding a particular topic.

A second category of training is to invite teams of teachers to meet together for planning and problem-solving. Quarterly or monthly meetings of this nature keep the program functioning well and build a sense of teamwork. The advantage of such meetings is that teachers will have an extended time period to focus in on needs and concerns in their classes and programs.

A third type of training is intended for individuals. Send weekly or monthly e-mails to your volunteers that include announcements, encouragement, as well as training tips. Training articles such as those in this book can be sent via e-mail, included in newsletters or posted on your church website in a section just for volunteers. (See articles which begin on pp. 71.) You may also provide teacher-training books or videos which the volunteer may read or watch at home. In addition, you may arrange for the teacher to observe an experienced teacher in action.

Get Started

So how does a busy children's ministry leader go about getting started with a training plan (or freshening up an existing program)? Begin by evaluating the existing training in your church. Answer the following questions. (Note: If you are a new leader at your church, interview a long-time teacher or past leader to find answers to the questions.)

STRAIGHT TALK ON TRAINING

1. How is a new teacher most typically trained?

2. What training opportunities have recently been offered to the teachers in your program? How often do these training events take place?

3. Are the training opportunities instructional, inspirational or both?

4. How and when do most teachers plan together? What is done to encourage teachers to plan together?

5. What obstacles keep teachers from attending training events or planning meetings?

Use the answers to these questions as a guide to help you form a plan for training. Use a blank monthly calendar form (see p. 43) to schedule ongoing training techniques as well as several training events during the year. See the Sample Calendar on page 17 for ideas. Check dates and room availability on your church's master calendar. If your training plans are on your planning calendar from the very beginning, they are less likely to be forgotten or crowded out by other events.

Plan for a variety of events that include once-a-year teacher orientations, individual training through the use of e-mails, newsletters, your church's website, videos and/or books, age-level meetings, speakers, attendance at conferences, etc.

If you are creating a training program, it's wise not to overwhelm your staff (or yourself!) by planning a full-blown calendar of training all at once. Establish priorities such as

▶ a general teacher orientation at the beginning of each teaching term

▶ at least one follow-up meeting later during the year. (Larger churches will want to conduct these meetings by age level; smaller churches will find it necessary to meet with all teachers together, allowing some time during the meeting for teachers who teach together to meet.)

▶ a plan to orient and train new volunteers who join your staff during the teaching term, either through group meetings (in a large church) or by individual training (in a small church)

▶ a monthly e-mail providing encouragement and a training tip to all volunteers.

Every year, expand your training program by adding one or more training components (attendance at training conferences, observation at other churches, etc.).

Ideas

▶ Ask teachers to write brief examples of ways they have put teaching principles into practice, or information they have gained from a workshop or seminar, etc. Include this information in your monthly training newsletter (sent by mail or e-mail or posted on your church's website). **Tip:** Include a Teacher Challenge Devotion (see pp. 57-69) in each newsletter.

▶ When someone agrees to volunteer in your children's ministry, send a Ministry Welcome Packet that includes a list of the children with whom he or she will be working, names and phone numbers of teaching team members and one or more of the training articles in this book ("Ten Commandments for Teachers" on page 308 and "The Value of Children" on page 281). **Tip:** In the Welcome Packet, also include a gift certificate from a local coffee shop, a magnet with your children's ministry slogan on it, a bookmark, etc.

▶ After any training event, evaluate what learning occurred. Were your objectives for the event met? Have teachers acquired or improved the needed skills? If the answer is yes, concentrate on the next area of need. If the answer is no, consider how you can address the

CALENDAR

JANUARY
- Teacher training event by age level.
- E-mail teaching tip to all volunteers.
- Display miniposter in *Supply Room* and classrooms.

FEBRUARY
- Include article on prayer in newsletter.
- E-mail teaching tip.

MARCH
- E-mail Teacher Challenge Devotion to all.
- Display miniposter.

APRIL
- Teacher training event with outside speaker.
- E-mail article on Easter to all.
- Use Publicity Clip Art.

MAY
- Include article on learning styles in newsletter.
- Display miniposter.

JUNE
- E-mail Teacher Challenge Devotion to all.
- Display miniposter.

JULY

AUGUST
- E-mail article on age-level characteristics to all new teachers

SEPTEMBER
- Orientation meeting for all volunteers. Use Icebreaker ideas.
- E-mail Teacher Challenge Devotion.
- Include article on teacher preparation in newsletter.

OCTOBER
- E-mail teaching tip to all volunteers.
- Display miniposter in *Supply Room* and classrooms.
- Attend training conference. Give Teacher Training Certificate.

NOVEMBER
- Include article on discipline in newsletter.
- E-mail teaching tip to all volunteers.
- Display miniposter.

DECEMBER
- E-mail Teacher Challenge Devotion.
- Display miniposter.

need in a different way. **Tip:** If you feel that teachers need further information on a particular topic, use the contents in this book to find a topic-related article. Mail or distribute to teachers (along with a note thanking them for attending the training event).

► Take advantage of churches in your area that have effective children's ministries. Arrange for one or more teachers to observe at the church. **Tip:** At your next training event, invite the teachers who observed to report back to the rest of your staff.

► Provide a variety of training books and/or videos in a central location for volunteers to borrow. **Tip:** Give a book or video to a volunteer to preview and report on at a training meeting.

► Pair a new teacher with an experienced teacher in a mentoring relationship. Begin by asking the veteran to suggest several practical tips for success and by asking the novice to ask several questions. **Tip:** Encourage the use of e-mail for teachers to share questions and answers, as well as prayer requests.

► Post miniposters in classrooms or teacher workrooms that feature a specific training tip or a particular teaching strategy of which teachers need reminding. Change the posters frequently to keep interest high. **Tip:** Use the miniposters in this book (see Contents).

► Have teachers conduct a self-evaluation (see "Improving Your Role" on p. 42) to help them plan specific ways to improve their teaching. **Tip:** Follow up by asking teachers to share one action they plan to take.

Guideline 2: Make Meetings Effective

"Oh no, not another meeting!" How many of us have heard that response when announcing a teacher-training meeting? And how many of us have said those very words when receiving an invitation to a meeting?

There's no doubt about it, you and your volunteers are busy people who need to make wise choices in the use of time. Help your staff recognize the benefit they will receive from teacher-training meetings by planning valuable, effective meetings. (Good publicity is also a key component of effective meetings. Get information about publicity ideas and hints in Guideline 3 on p. 25.)

Sample Meeting Agenda
(60–90 minutes)

1. Welcome and Icebreaker (10–15 minutes)
Welcome participants, make brief announcements, pray and involve participants in an icebreaker activity. (Note: Refreshments may be served as part of this opening time segment, or they may be served at the end of the meeting. An icebreaker can also be an effective activity as people arrive, ending the activity with a welcome and prayer.)

2. Skill Improvement (20–30 minutes)
Involve teachers in activities and discussion to help them improve one aspect of their teaching.

3. Teachers' Planning and Sharing Time (20–30 minutes)
Provide time for teachers to focus on the next session(s), planning activities and procedures and identifying needed materials and responsibilities. Teachers share insights and concerns about the children they teach and discuss ways to meet children's needs.

4. Devotional and Prayer Time (10–15 minutes)
Using the teacher devotional from an upcoming class lesson, discuss how the Bible story or passage relates to current life situations. Lead teachers in prayer for each other, for each other's families and for the children and their families as well. (Optional: Serve refreshments.)

When Teachers Meet Together

There are three basic things that should happen when teachers meet together. While each component does not need to receive equal time, your volunteers will find benefit in each of these components.

▶ Sharing and fellowship. This important component can happen in several different ways. Refreshments, use of name tags, icebreaker activities (see Icebreakers on pp. 22-24), table discussions, devotionals and prayer times can all be used to create a sense of shared ministry among your staff. If your volunteers miss out on adult opportunities for fellowship, these opportunities for getting to know each other and building unity is especially important. Especially in large churches, but even in small churches, it is important to encourage volunteers to get acquainted in informal ways.

▶ Skill improvement. Whether through watching and discussing a teacher-training video, listening to a speaker or brainstorming ideas to meet a particular teaching challenge, teachers need to focus on one specific skill or topic at each meeting. Whenever possible, provide time for teachers to apply their learning to classroom situations. Limit the amount of time in which teachers are expected to sit and listen. Remember that EVERYONE—children and adults—learn best as they are actively involved in the learning process.

If teachers from a variety of age levels are meeting together, it is recommended that general teaching principles be presented first to the entire group. Then, divide into smaller groups by age level for discussion of ways to apply teaching principles.

▶ Lesson preview. This component of volunteer training gives your teachers and helpers time to plan essential lesson details (who will lead which activity, what materials are needed, etc.). In order for this part of the training to take place, volunteers need to have their curriculum available to look at and plan from. Encourage teachers to skim the Bible content and learning aims of upcoming lessons. Even meeting together briefly to plan one lesson will help your teaching teams work more effectively.

Ideas for Skill Improvement

Pay careful attention to what you provide for the skill-improvement component in your teacher-training meetings. New teachers will benefit the most from these activities, experienced teachers will be able to help new teachers grow in their understanding of teaching procedures and even those who teach alone will find it beneficial to talk over teaching methods with another teacher of the same or similar age level.

▶ Send an article from this book to teachers a week or so before the meeting. Ask teachers to read the article. At the training meeting, lead a discussion about the teaching methods presented in the article. Ask, "What new teaching strategies did you discover in this article? Based on the information in this article, what is one way you can improve your teaching?"

▶ Arrange for teachers to observe a well-taught class in action. Teachers sit in a semicircle in an open area of the classroom and observe an experienced teacher demonstrate a particular teaching skill.

▶ Find one or more children's ministry leaders in your area whose philosophy of Christian education and ministry is similar to yours. Establish a system in which you take turns leading workshops at each other's churches.

▶ Investigate the resources available at a local community college, university or library. Teacher-training videos that deal with topics such as discipline or communication techniques may be available for rental. Preview the video ahead of time to select the most helpful video segment(s) for your teachers to watch, and to develop several questions for teachers to discuss after watching the video.

▶ Identify people in your church who are experienced teachers in public or private schools. Invite the teacher to become acquainted with the church's ministry to children by informally observing one or more classes. Then ask the teacher to present a brief workshop on specific teaching skills that would be helpful in the church setting.

▶ Ask the company who publishes your curriculum if they have speakers or consultants who are available to speak at churches.

Tips for Success

The key to good meetings is good preparation. Good preparation includes:

▶ Carefully planning the meeting agenda in order to begin and end the meeting on time. Customize the sample agenda on page 18.

Training Event Publicity Time Line

1. Clear the date and facilities needed with church calendar and all necessary church staff and/or committees at least three to four months in advance.

2. Communicate date and topic to all volunteers two to three months in advance.

3. Publish weekly announcements in church bulletin and/or newsletters four weeks in advance. Also display posters as attention-getters showing details of the training event (time, date, location, topics, speaker, etc.). Make sure that all printed information is complete and accurate. Use a checklist to avoid errors.

4. Send an invitation to all volunteers three weeks in advance. Include a registration form for them to return, or a phone number to which they may R.S.V.P. Arrange child care, transportation and financial assistance as needed.

5. Phone or personally contact each volunteer one to two weeks in advance to confirm his or her attendance. Follow up with another contact (e-mail or mailed reminder) the week of the training event.

▶ Inviting friends or other leaders in the church to pray for you as you lead the meeting and for participants as they attend.

▶ Giving teachers preparation assignments. For example, you might ask each teacher to read a short article about leading discussion groups and share one idea from it. When teachers come prepared, they bring an attitude of expectancy and their sense of responsibility increases.

▶ Arriving early enough to have the meeting room set up and attractively arranged. Use a meeting checklist as a guide for your preparation. Set out a few less chairs than you think you will need. Lots of empty chairs creates a negative impression. Arrange chairs in a different format (semicircle, around tables, etc.) for each training meeting according to the activities you will be completing and to create interest from participants.

▶ Enlisting the support of all leaders in the early childhood division. Make sure all leaders are aware of the purpose and benefits of the scheduled meetings—and make sure the dates are marked far ahead on their calendars. (See more about publicity in Guideline 3, which begins on page 25.)

▶ Evaluating each meeting after it is completed so that you can continue strategies that worked well and improve plans as needed. Be excited about those who attended; avoid complaining about those who were absent.

Ideas

▶ Consider a variety of options in choosing meeting times: Weeknight dessert, Saturday morning continental breakfast, Sunday pizza lunch or Sunday during regularly scheduled classes (recruit a one-time team of parent helpers or substitutes). **Tip:** Schedule duplicate meetings at two different times and let volunteers choose which meeting fits their schedules.

▶ Encourage teachers to meet together informally (two or three at a time) in creative ways—brown-bagging lunches together once a week, coffee night once a month, early morning breakfast before work, meet together at one house while a baby or toddler naps, etc. **Tip:** Interview teachers to find out creative ways in which they plan together, and publish your findings in a newsletter or e-mail as a way of encouraging others to meet on a regular basis.

▶ Add an "early bird" arrival activity to a teacher-training meeting. Provide supplies and directions for teachers to make Bible learning games, prepare bulletin boards, assemble lesson materials, sing new songs, etc. **Tip:** During the meeting, teachers show what they have made. Invite other interested teachers to stay after the meeting to make similar items.

▶ Get the support of your senior pastor. Invite him or her to lead a short devotional at a teacher-training meeting, or tell a positive story about a childhood church experience. **Tip:** Announce the pastor's visit in publicity materials for the meeting.

▶ Provide a series of awards or certificates to give teachers after completing a designated number of teacher-training events. **Tip:** Publish names of people who participate in a training event in your church's newsletter, thanking them for their commitment to children's ministry.

▶ For variety and to create interest, schedule a teacher's meeting at a restaurant that has a private meeting room. **Tip:** Contribute a specified amount to each teacher's meal to make the cost more affordable.

▶ If you have meetings scheduled on a monthly or quarterly basis, schedule them on the same night or day of each month or quarter. **Tip:** Coordinate dates of training events or meetings with other ministry leaders, so that meeting conflicts can be minimized.

ICEBREAKERS

Use one of these icebreakers as a get-acquainted activity at the beginning of any training session. Continue the ice-breaker activity as long as time and interest permit. Provide inexpensive prizes (candy, bookmark, stickers, gift certificate to coffee store, etc.) for winners at the end of the icebreaker.

BEAN ME!

Preparation: Bring a bag of beans to the session.

Procedure: Distribute five beans to each person. People move around the area, asking questions of each other. The goal is to answer a question without saying "yes" or "no." If a question is answered "yes" or "no," the person who answered must give the questioner one bean. When time is called, the person with the most beans wins. (Hint: Ask true or false "get to know you" questions instead, such as, "You have three cats. True or False?" A bean is given to the questioner for each true answer. Challenge the winner to then tell one true thing about each person from whom he or she collected a bean!)

BEHIND YOUR BACK

Preparation: Provide a sheet of paper and pencil for each person. Provide one pad of Post-It Notes.

Procedure: Participants write their names on Post-It Notes as they arrive and place the notes on their backs. (Hint: If people know each other's names, they write nicknames or animal names on Post-It Notes.) At your signal, each player moves around the room, trying to copy down as many names as possible while also trying to keep others from seeing the name on his or her back. When time is called, person with the longest list wins. (Perhaps the winner's prize is to scratch the back of the person with the shortest list!)

CHAIR CHANGERS

Preparation: Set chairs in a circle for a game similar to musical chairs.

Procedure: Leader stands in the center of circle and then says, "If you're wearing (blue) change chairs now!" Anyone who fits that category must get up and move to another chair. No one can return to a chair immediately beside him or her. While others move, leader takes a seat. Person left standing becomes the new leader and continues the game, choosing a new category (have a dog, drive a car, voted in the last election, walk to work, etc.).

FILL-IN-THE-BLANK SEARCH

Preparation: Write out a session-related Bible verse or a focus statement on the board, leaving out several key words. Letter each key word on a separate color of colored index card. Cut each word card into 8 to 10 puzzle pieces and hide pieces around the room.

Procedure: Group the participants into teams. Give each team one color of index card that matches the puzzle pieces for which they will search. Team members look for and pick up pieces of their color only. When teams have found all pieces, they assemble puzzles and tell which blank their key word completes.

Four Corners

Preparation: Play this game in a room having four corners or else designate corners by setting out four chairs.

Procedure: Group stands in a large area where corners are designated. Leader calls out names of four choices (four flavors of ice cream or pizza, four kinds of pets, four kinds of shoes, etc.) and designates a corner to indicate each choice. Participants move to the desired corner to show their answers and then introduce themselves to each other. End the game by using four kinds of children's learning activities (skits, games, stories, art) as a springboard for later discussion.

Just Answer the Question!

Preparation: Write out questions (trivia questions about your church or community, questions related to nursery rhymes such as, "Over what did the cow jump? The moon.") on separate index cards. On another set of cards, write out the corresponding answer to each question, making one card (of either kind) for each person. Mix up cards.

Procedure: Distribute one card to each person. Invite those with question cards to move around the room, reading their questions aloud. Those with answer cards read answers to questioners until all questions are matched to their corresponding answers. Pairs then introduce themselves and ask each other more questions!

Group Up!

Procedure: Participants gather in an area where they can move freely. Leader calls out a number between 2 and 12 (call out numbers smaller than half the people in the group). When number is called, everyone gathers into groups of that number, introducing themselves to others in their group. (Hint: Vary this game by calling out other categories such as eye color, shirt color, shoe style, birth month, etc.)

Left or Right

Procedure: Give time for people to learn the names of all others in the group. When time is called, participants stand in a circle. Leader stands in the center. Leader points to one person and says, "left" or "right." The person pointed to must tell the name of the person on his or her left or right. If unable to do so, the person on the left or right repeats his or her name and becomes the new Leader. Continue until every name has been repeated at least once.

NAME TOSS

Preparation: Collect a beanbag or sponge ball for every 6 to 8 people.

Procedure: Divide participants into circled groups of 6 to 8. One person in each group says his or her name and then tosses a beanbag or sponge ball to another person. Second person says his or her name and tosses the beanbag or sponge ball, continuing until everyone has participated. Then increase the challenge: the first person says his or her name and then tosses beanbag or sponge ball to another person. Second person catches the item, says the name of the person who threw the beanbag or ball and his or her own name before throwing the beanbag or ball. Continue tossing and adding on to the list of names until every name has been added.

PUZZLING PARTNERS

Preparation: Gather pieces from several preschool children's puzzles, one puzzle piece for each participant. Place all pieces in a container at the door. (If puzzles have frames, set them out around the room.)

Procedure: Distribute a puzzle piece to each person. At your signal, participants move around the room to find those holding matching puzzle pieces. Each group then works together to assemble its puzzle. (Prizes could be awarded for the group that assembles their puzzle most quickly, the group that can name all its members, the group that can give the most interesting description of its puzzle, the group that can tell one thing learned at the last session, etc.)

SENTENCE SEEKERS

Preparation: Choose several sentences or Bible verses related to the session topic. Write one word of each sentence on a separate sheet of paper. Use a unique color of paper or ink to designate each sentence. Make a paper for each participant, repeating sentences or verses if needed. Mix up all papers.

Procedure: Distribute a paper to each person. People group themselves by color of ink or paper. Groups then work together to sequence words into sentence or verse order.

SILENT SIGNALS

Procedure: Each person silently chooses a number between one and four and then moves around the room repeating an action (patting another's shoulder, tapping a foot, snapping, etc.) the chosen number of times. When two people find they are doing the same number of actions, they pair up and then try to find more people doing the same number of actions. (Hint: Vary the game by using various types of actions as grouping criteria. For a challenge, try shaking hands the chosen number of times as the action!)

Guideline 3: Focus on Publicity

Generating awareness and enthusiasm for teacher-training events takes planning, but pays off in rich dividends. An event that seems "thrown together" with little advance planning is unlikely to inspire participation by your volunteers (nor by you!).

Create a mind-set of expectation for teacher-training events. When recruiting new volunteers and at orientation meetings, let volunteers know that attendance at training meetings is not only expected of them, but will be of such value to them that they won't want to miss these opportunities to get essential information and receive support and encouragement in their ministries.

In your publicity planning, never underestimate the power of personal contact. Bulletin announcements, newsletter notices and even verbal announcements do very little to motivate attendance at meetings. Clear communication of the benefits to be received at the meeting combined with an enthusiastic phone call or personal conversation will spark attendance by your volunteers.

Ideas

▶ Give each volunteer a refrigerator magnet that lists the dates of your teacher-training meetings. **Tip:** Inexpensive magnets can be made from cardstock and self-adhesive magnetic strips, or ordered through commercial printers.

▶ Create a series of "teaser" announcements to catch attention. Publish announcements in bulletins or newsletters, or send by e-mail. For example, for a workshop on discipline, publish the following announcement. "When was the last time you said, 'What that child needs is some discipline'?" Come to our teacher's meeting on September 10 to find out some discipline methods that work!" **Tip:** Vary the teaser in each announcement to keep interest high.

▶ Cut each meeting invitation into 8 to 10 puzzle pieces. Send puzzle pieces in an envelope to each volunteer. Volunteer assembles puzzle and tapes it together. **Tip:** Just for fun, send half of each puzzle to each partner of a teaching team. Partners assemble puzzles together to read their invitations.

▶ Using a permanent marker, print the details of a training event on inflated, but not tied, balloons. Send a deflated balloon to each volunteer. **Tip:** Add seasonal stickers to the balloons for decorations.

▶ Send invitations using an e-mail greeting card service. **Tip:** Periodically, ask volunteers to update e-mail addresses.

▶ Record a spoken invitation along with the training event details on an audiocassette or CD. Duplicate the cassettes/CDs and mail or distribute to volunteers. **Tip:** Include a message from your senior pastor thanking volunteers for their service and encouraging their participation in the training event.

▶ Send an invitation in the form of a coupon that can be redeemed at the next training event. **Tip:** Make the coupon redeemable for dessert or a meal, as well as for training.

▶ Send an invitation in the form of a coupon that can be redeemed at the next training event. **Tip:** Make the coupon redeemable for dessert or a meal, as well as for training.

▶ Collect a variety of door prizes or inexpensive thank-you gifts (coffee mugs, mouse pads, pens, colorful Post-It Notes, highlighters, bookmarks, etc.) to be given to teachers who attend training events. Tip: Members of your church or parents of children in your program may be willing to donate items.

► Along with a teacher-training announcement, include a brief testimonial from a teacher describing several benefits received from attending a previous training meeting. **Tip:** Ask the teacher to share a specific way in which the training helped him or her be a more effective teacher.

► To create interest in a beginning-of-the-year teacher orientation meeting, send each volunteer a colorful folder or binder with their name printed on it. Invite the volunteer to come to the meeting to receive all the essential information they will need to fill their folder or binder and be equipped for a new year of ministry. **Tip:** When preparing inserts, use different colors of paper to make it easy to find information (for example, all teacher and class address lists can be printed on blue paper, all dates can be printed on yellow paper, etc.).

► Catch the attention of your volunteers by developing creative names and logos for teacher-training events. **Tip:** Using the name and logo on all publicity will make it easier for volunteers to identify training information.

Training: Tough Questions, Real Answers

How can I get my teachers to try something new?

It is a common pattern for most people to teach the way they have always taught. The best way to encourage a teacher to try a new activity, to practice a new skill or to modify a class schedule is threefold: First, in a teacher-training meeting, give teachers time not only to learn but also to practice and role-play a new skill or activity. Teachers are much more likely to try something they have already practiced and feel confident doing.

Second, provide teachers with an opportunity to observe the new activity, skill or schedule in action. You may find that the teachers in one class are more open to making a change than other teachers. Begin with that class and invite other teachers to observe. After the observation, answer questions and then invite each teacher to take a turn leading the activity or class. If possible, observe the teachers and affirm them for their positive actions, giving a few helpful hints if needed.

Third, begin something new at the start of a new school year or new teaching term. Whether it is a new check-in procedure, a new class schedule or a new curriculum, clearly communicate to all teachers (and parents if needed) what is being changed and what benefits will result.

What can I do with a person who volunteers but does not seem to be suited to children's ministry?

This is where the application process is vital. First, be sure the person has an application on file (every volunteer should have an application on file—even if the person has been working in children's ministry for years). Then personally interview the person. If you feel you need more background information, talk with the references listed on the application. If after your church's approved application process has been completed, you still feel that he or she would not be suitable, express your appreciation for his or her interest in children's ministry and offer an alternative job that enables the volunteer to serve in a more appropriate capacity (preparing lesson materials or bulletin boards, shopping for supplies, etc.). If you feel the person needs to develop teaching skills further before you assign a job, place the volunteer alongside an experienced teacher who is skilled at training and can help you observe the volunteer. If you have no appropriate jobs for the person, talk with other church leaders to identify another area of service and then lovingly direct the person to the leader.

How can I get my teachers to arrive on time?

First, make sure that all teachers are aware of what time they are expected to be in their classrooms. (Each job description should include a starting time!)

Second, during training, emphasize the benefits of teachers' being present and well prepared when children arrive: Children feel welcome and can immediately begin learning. Also emphasize the likely consequences when teachers are not present: Children and parents feel unsure about who is in charge and chaos often erupts!

Third, permanently assign one of your helpers or greeters to the door of that classroom. This will keep children safe until the teacher arrives.

Fourth, if the teacher's lateness is a perpetual problem, talk with that volunteer and invite him or her to take a different position, perhaps preparing materials or doing other support activities that have no time restriction. Be understanding of difficulties but firm about your commitment to both the safety and the learning of the children.

One underlying issue may be that some children (other teacher's children, etc.) arrive much earlier than other children. If so, set aside an area where they can be supervised while participating in several unstructured activities (watching a video, free play, coloring, etc.) so that all teachers have the time free to fully prepare for the teaching session.

How can I prepare for last-minute teacher substitutions?

When recruiting teachers, develop a list of people who are willing to be on call as last-minute substitutes. Often, people who teach children during the week but who don't wish to teach regularly on the weekend make excellent substitutes because of their knowledge of children and experience in guiding classroom activities. Administrative leaders can benefit by substituting periodically, too. Teaching or helping in a class from time to time is essential to stay in touch with practical needs.

Provide the substitute with a copy of the schedule and lesson for the class and a list of children's names. If name tags are not already available, make them for each child to wear. Also make sure that all supplies are readily available. If you are unable to provide the substitute with the appropriate lesson plan, be prepared in advance by having a generic lesson or two planned along with the necessary supplies. Store the lesson and supplies in a "substitute" box.

One of my teachers continually says her class is difficult or out of control. How can I determine specific ways to help her?

Ask the following questions to plan ways of improving the situation:

▶ Is the number of teachers appropriate for the size of the class? You may be able to handle a group of children with fewer teachers, but the results are that teachers often spend much of their time providing crowd control or dealing with discipline problems.

▶ Are the teachers present consistently so that relationships are being built and consistent classroom procedures are being followed?

▶ Is the class offering enough variety of learning activities and thus meeting the needs of active children? Observe (help in) the class several times in order to fully answer this question. When teachers have unrealistic expectations (for example, sitting still for extended periods), problems often result.

▶ Are children being offered choices? Allowing children to make some of their own choices (which learning activity to participate in first, what materials to use, etc.) will help avoid discipline problems. Children's behavior is more positive when they are doing something they have chosen.

▶ What is the pattern of problem behavior? Does it happen only at a certain time, such as when children first arrive or during the large-group Bible story time? If so, help a teacher see ways to change procedures during the difficult time. For example, make sure teachers are present and prepared when children first arrive so that children are immediately involved in an appropriate activity, or have teachers sit among children during large-group times, so they can redirect children's attention if needed.

▶ Does a particular child need one-on-one supervision? For some children who consistently struggle with behavior, it may be helpful to ask an adult volunteer to participate in classroom activities alongside the child, building a friendship with the child and being available to redirect the child's behavior as needed.

▶ Does the teacher need additional training? It may be helpful to ask the teacher to work alongside a more experienced teacher or to participate in one or more training meetings or conferences.

All of these questions are best answered through your own observation. Then you can address the areas of need with kindness, understanding and sensitivity. You can also invite the teacher to complete a personal evaluation (See "Improving Your Role" on page 42) to help him or her identify areas of teaching that need to be improved.

How do you get teachers to come to training sessions? When is the most effective time to schedule teacher training?

Talk with several leaders and teachers to determine the best incentives and the best times for teachers in your church to meet. Some possibilities:

▶ Hold meetings on weeknights when the church calendar is relatively free of other meetings; providing dinner and child care will eliminate the two most likely excuses for not attending!

▶ Have training sessions during a time when teachers are already planning to be present (Wednesday night for Sunday teachers, Sunday meeting for Wednesday teachers, etc.). Another idea: On one Sunday during regular class time, obtain substitutes, or during a special program for all ages, hold a training session.

▶ Have a Saturday-morning brunch or a Sunday after-church luncheon and offer both food and child care!

▶ Offer the same training session at two different times. Invite teachers to choose the time that is best for them.

Refer to pages 18-21 for more information on how to schedule and lead training meetings.

We do want to use teenagers as helpers for our staff. What guidelines should we follow and how do we train them?

Many churches plan effective ways of training and using youth in their children's ministries—always as helpers and never as teachers by themselves. Here are some guidelines for setting up an effective youth helper program:

First, determine with your church staff and youth leaders the minimum age and grade level for youth helpers. Consider these other possible requirements: parents' permission to participate, regular attendance at church youth classes and worship services, attendance at a specified number of training classes and a recommendation from a youth supervisor or leader in the church. Youth should also complete a volunteer application form.

Second, plan one or more training classes for potential youth helpers that include their parents. Including parents in the classes is helpful, not only because it acquaints the parents with what their children are doing, but also because it encourages parents to follow up at home on the training.

At the training classes, provide job descriptions. Explain classroom procedures and safety guidelines. Role-play some common situations in which youth helpers serve. Emphasize that the job of a youth helper is an important task because of the way in which positive experiences influence children and because of the service youth helpers provide to the church family. Clearly state to helpers how important it is that they recognize they are there to help. Help them formulate questions they can ask a teacher to find out how best to help. Remind them that their purpose is to focus on children, not on other helpers. Set up a time for teachers to give feedback on additional training that is needed for youth helpers.

Third, limit the number of youth helpers who will be assisting in one class or with one group at a time. If there are too many youth helpers, the helpers may focus on each other rather than giving attention to the children.

REPRODUCIBLE RESOURCES

BORDERS

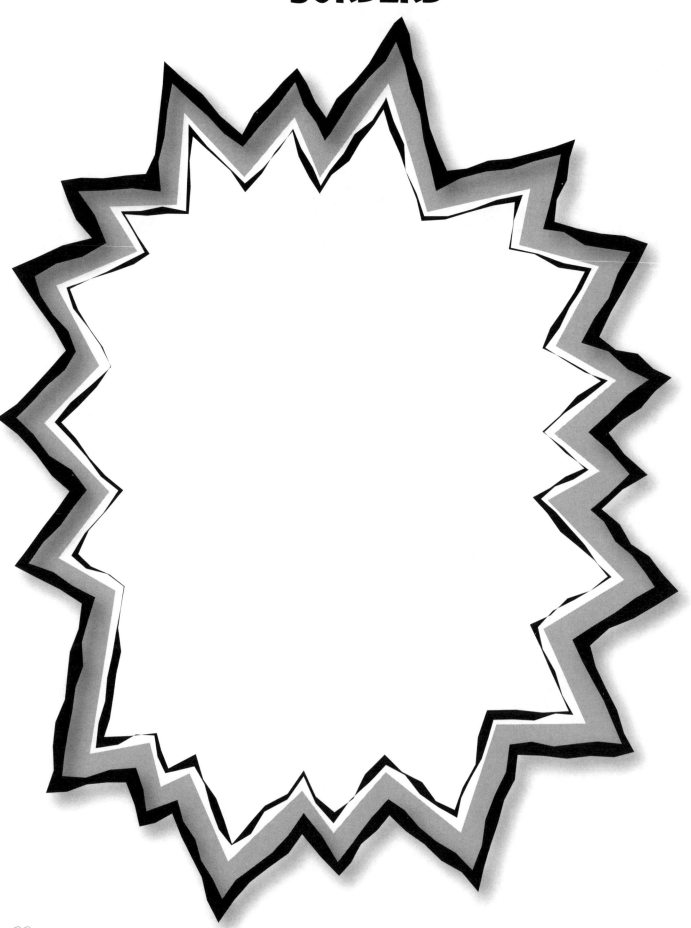

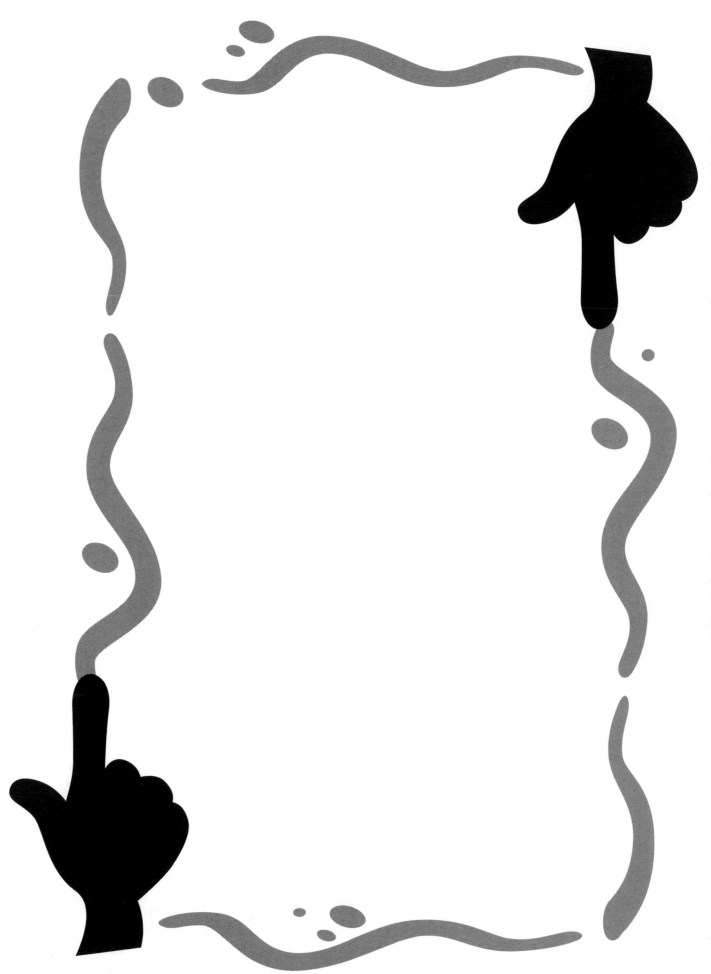

34

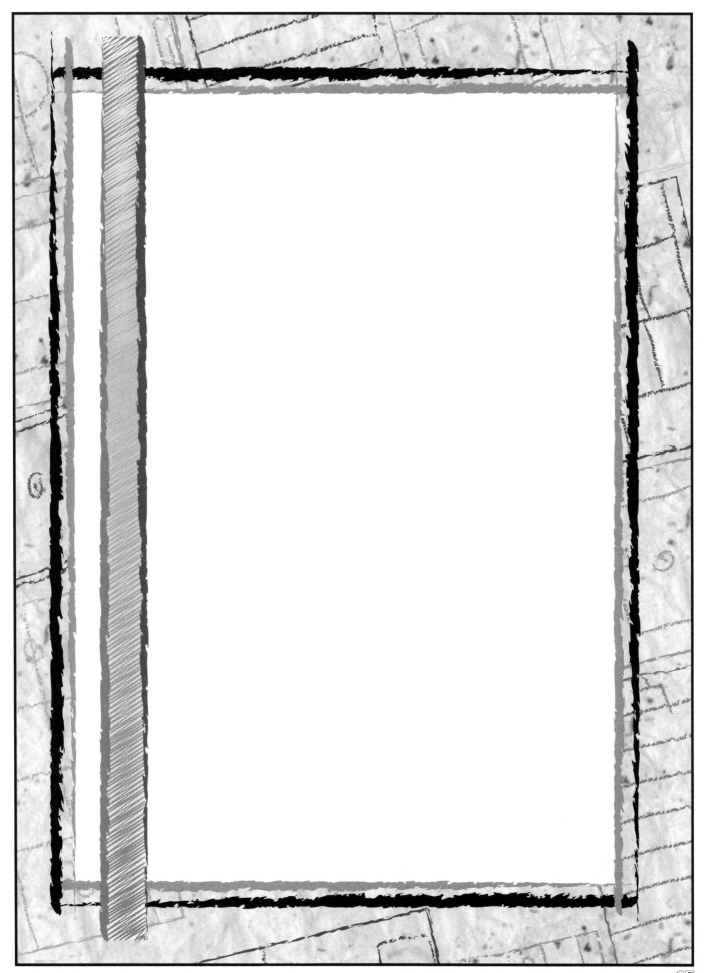

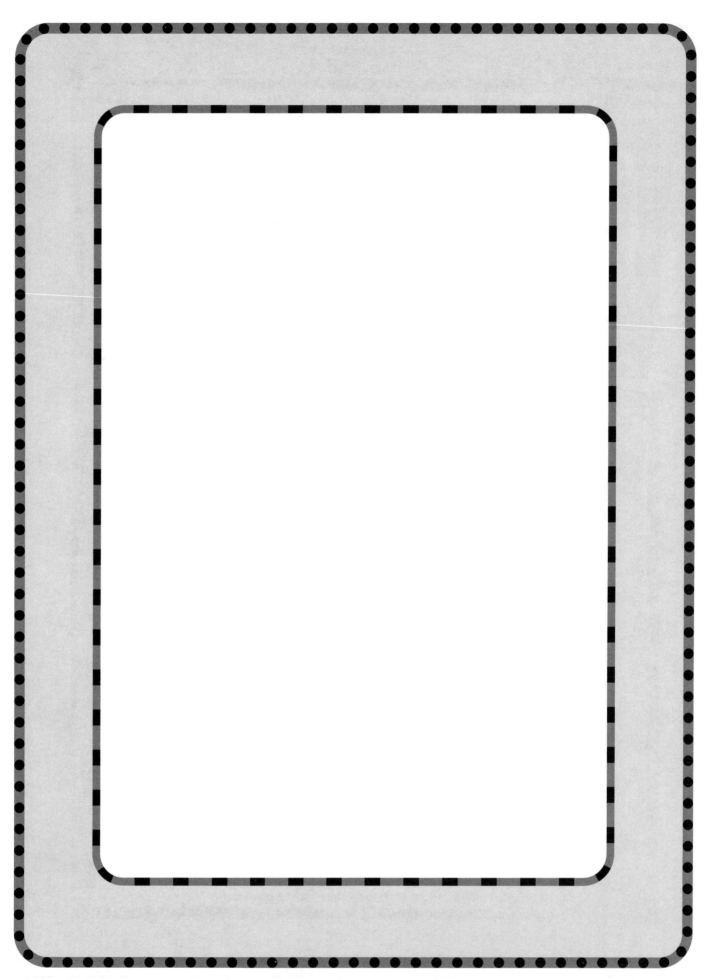

GET ACQUAINTED QUESTIONNAIRE

Child's Name_____ Birth Date_____

Address_____ Phone_____

Father's Name_____ Mother's Name_____

Siblings and Ages_____

_____

Ask children the following questions to familiarize yourself with their interests and to help you plan effective learning activities:

1. What's your favorite toy or game at your house?

2. What is your favorite pet?

3. What do you like to play outside?

4. Who do you like to play with?

5. What do you like to do with your family? With your friends?

6. Where do you like to go?

7. What do you like to do at Sunday School?

FAMILY INFORMATION SHEET

Names of Children	Birth Dates	Grades in School
1.		
2.		
3.		
4.		

(Use the back of this form if you need more space.)

Name of Parent/Guardian

1.

Attend this church? (y/n)

Address

City

Zip Code

Telephone

Home

Work

Cellular

E-Mail

Name of Parent

2.

Attend this church? (y/n)

Address

City

Zip Code

Telephone

Home

Work

Cellular

E-Mail

Mail any information from the church to:

FOCUS ON LIFE NEEDS

Check the box that most closely answers the following questions:

1 = Always   2 = Often   3 = Sometimes   4 = Seldom   5 = Never

Teaching is too often focused only on what a teacher does, rather than on what a student does in response.

Physical How often do you...	1	2	3	4	5
Monitor the room's lighting, temperature and air flow to ensure students' comfort?					
Equip rooms with appropriate furniture arranged to encourage interaction?					
Provide access for those with physical limitations?					
Social **How often do you...**					
Encourage positive relationships, avoiding put-downs of others?					
Maintain group sizes and teacher ratios that make personal attention possible?					
Seek out ways to include people besides the regular attenders?					
Plan ways for group members to interact and work together?					
Emotional **How often do you...**					
Really listen when a student is talking?					
Actively seek to make your class an emotionally safe place?					
Show respect and acceptance for a student who is upset or bored or fearful?					
Honestly share your own feelings, including times when they have not been positive?					

FOCUS ON LIFE NEEDS

(Cont'd)

Intellectual How often do you...	1	2	3	4	5
Allow students the freedom to disagree without making them feel rejected?					
Guide students to discover Bible truth, not just listen to it being presented?					
Limit the use of questions that elicit one-word (yes, no, etc.) or straight factual answers? Encourage students to compare their opinions with what the Bible says?					
Give personal guidance to students who lack the Bible knowledge of others in the group?					
Spiritual How often do you...					
Actively seek to discover each student's spiritual condition and attitudes?					
Openly share your personal spiritual pilgrimage?					
Guide students to apply Bible truth in practical ways to life situations?					
Pray regularly for the needs of your students?					
Age Level How often do you...					
Consider the characteristics of the age group you teach when preparing your lessons?					
Plan ways to accommodate different skill levels of students in your group?					
Individual How often do you...					
Know the specific interests and needs that make each student unique in your group?					
Use varied teaching approaches to accommodate the different learning styles of students?					

EVALUATING AND IMPROVING YOUR ROLE AS A TEACHER

Check each statement as it applies to you.

1 = Always   2 = Often   3 = Sometimes   4 = Seldom   5 = Never

	1	2	3	4	5
The Teacher Is One Who Guides					
I ask the Holy Spirit to help me guide my students.					
I study the Bible content and pray to apply it to my own life.					
I pay attention to the individual growth needs of each student.					
I set specific learning objectives for my class.					
I plan sessions that emphasize active learning experiences.					
I assist learning by creating a positive classroom environment.					
I plan and ask appropriate questions to guide learning.					
I am excited when students discover Bible truths for themselves.					
I evaluate each student's learning after each class session.					
I contact students outside of class to learn about their needs.					
The Teacher Is One Who Stimulates and Motivates					
I select activities that interest and challenge my class.					
I encourage students to explore and discover God's truth themselves.					
I invite students to honestly express ideas and feelings.					
I help students make plans to apply truths in life situations.					
I affirm students for evidence of positive changes.					
The Teacher Is One Who Models					
I practice specific ways for my class to put truth into action.					
I set a positive Christian example for students both in and out of class.					
I tell my students of both my victories and struggles in following Christ.					
I show students how I confess and repent when I fall short.					
The Teacher Is One Who Cares					
I know each student's name and family.					
I accept my students as they are, even when they are wrong.					
I show interest in each student by carefully listening.					
I clearly communicate the God-given value of each person.					
I pray for each of my students by name.					
I give time to each student outside of class.					
I provide practical help and friendship to my students.					
I foster a climate of positive discipline in my classroom.					
I contact absentees to show that I missed them.					

MONTHLY CALENDAR

JANUARY

FEBRUARY

MARCH

APRIL

MAY

JUNE

JULY

AUGUST

SEPTEMBER

OCTOBER

NOVEMBER

DECEMBER

OBSERVATION FORM

1. What are three characteristics you noticed about the students or this class that are important for a teacher (or other staff member) to keep in mind?

2. List three words that summarize the role of the teacher.

3. What are two ways the teacher (or other staff member) gives individual attention to students?

4. What are two ways the students are involved in discovering Bible truths and using Bible verses or passages?

5. In what ways are students challenged to put Bible truths into practice in their daily lives?

If applicable:

6. What are two ways the lead teacher keeps the session moving smoothly?

7. What are two ways the lead teacher helps the teachers to be successful in their teaching?

PARENT SURVEY

Please Let Us Know!

Please complete this form and return it to your child's teacher at church.

Thank you!

Child _____

Parent _____

As a parent, I would like my child's class to_____

_____

_____

At church my child most enjoys _____

_____

_____

My child's least favorite activity is_____

_____

_____

My child wishes that his or her class would_____

_____

_____

Special needs or allergies you should know about_____

_____

_____

PRETEEN QUESTIONNAIRE

Name _____ Date _____

1. What's your favorite thing to do every day after school?

2. What do you and your friends like to do on weekends?

3. What's your favorite music group?

4. What advice would you give to the teacher of this group?

5. What's something you'd like to know about God?

6. Who are your three best friends?

7. What three activities would you like to do for a youth group event or outing?

WORD SCRAMBLE

Unscramble each of these words. You'll find a list of essential teacher materials.

1. OLVE _____
2. PCEEIATN _____
3. TUQESSNOI _____
4. ERANWSS _____
5. MAGES _____

6. GNOSS _____
7. LICPNES _____
8. ISTROSE _____
9. UHMRO _____
10. BBLSEI _____

ANSWERS: 1. LOVE; 2. PATIENCE; 3. QUESTIONS; 4. ANSWERS; 5. GAMES; 6. SONGS; 7. PENCILS; 8. STORIES; 9. HUMOR; 10. BIBLES

If I had to choose...

Circle your answer. Then tell your answer to at least one other person.

A MOVIE
a. musical comedy
b. adventure film
c. love story
d. western

A FOOD
a. frog legs
b. grits
c. escargot
d. venison

A RESTAURANT
a. sushi bar
b. fast-food
c. Chinese
d. Italian

A SPORT
a. baseball
b. couch potato
c. boxing
d. synchronized swimming

I Remember

TELL YOUR ANSWER TO THE FOLLOWING:

1. My first big trip
2. My favorite TV program as a kid
3. My first job
4. My first kiss
5. My favorite room
6. My favorite teacher

TEACHER CONCENTRATION

Concentrate on these 14 objects for one minute. At the signal, turn over the page and list the objects from memory. You'll have two minutes.

glue

HOLY BIBLE

paint

CERTIFICATE
OF MERIT

This certificate is presented to

_____

for completion of

_____

_____
Date

_____
Signature

Congratulations!

_____

for successfully completing

_____

_____
Date

_____
Signature

Teacher Training Certificate

Presented to

_____

_____
Date

_____
Signature

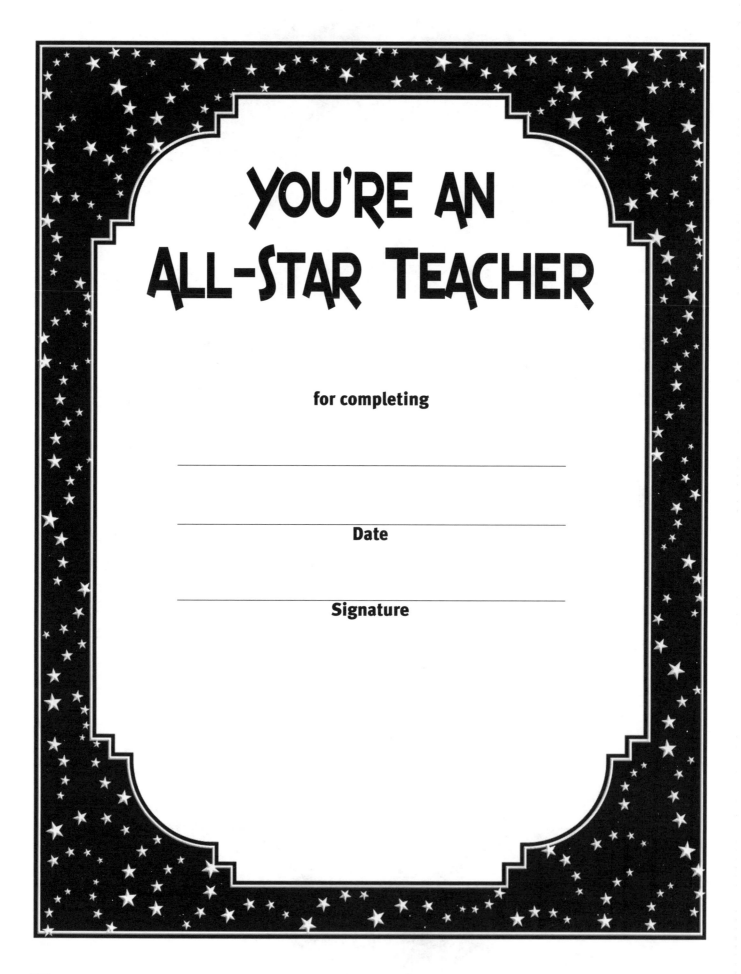

YOU'RE AN ALL-STAR TEACHER

for completing

_____

_____

Date

_____

Signature

Teacher Training Publicity Clip Art

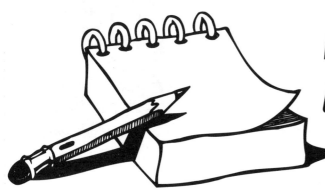

When the Teaching Gets Tough, the Teachers Get Training!

Teachers don't grow on trees, we grow through <u>TRAINING!</u>

THE ABC'S OF TEACHING SUNDAY SCHOOL

BASIC TRAINING FOR TEACHERS

Top 10 Reasons to come to our Teachers' Meeting

10. Going to a meeting is more fun than doing chores at home.

9. Your significant other will be impressed by your dedication.

8. Your kids may be asleep by the time you come home.

7. Cookies and coffee meet new nutritional guidelines.

6. You might receive the Teacher-of-the-Year award.

5. No offering will be taken.

4. Absentees are always assigned the hardest jobs.

3. You won't have to think of any excuses.

2. It's free.

1. And the number one reason to come to our Teachers' Meeting?

You will enjoy great fellowship and gain terrific teaching tips!

♥

We Train Teachers as if Lives Depended on It!

Get Your Hands on Some Practical Teaching Training

teacher (mod'l) n

1. an example for imitation or emulation.

Did you notice? Someone's following you. That's why another word for teacher could be "model."

To help you be the kind of teacher you want to be, come to our next Teachers' Meeting.

A promise to share helpful teaching ideas.

A promise to encourage your ministry to children.

A promise to start and end on time.

Nothing binds us one to the other like a promise kept. Nothing divides us like a promise broken.
At our teachers' meetings, we believe in keeping our promises.

TEACHER CHALLENGE DEVOTIONS

JOSHUA 24:15

"CHOOSE FOR YOURSELVES THIS DAY WHOM YOU WILL SERVE....BUT AS FOR ME AND MY HOUSEHOLD, WE WILL SERVE THE LORD."

People make dozens of choices every day—from what to eat (and how much) to which car to buy. Whether the choice is insignificant or a matter of life and death, the stock index, advice columns, horoscopes and talk shows all loudly proclaim "rules" (both good and bad) by which to make "the right" choices. How can we know the best way to choose?

Think about Abraham, one of the great patriarch's of the Bible. In his life, we see some choices that show he didn't always consult God first. He got into trouble several times when he "leaned on his own understanding." However, as Abraham followed God, we see that the overall pattern of his life was one of trusting and consulting God when decisions were made—despite his failures. He chose to leave Ur when there was no reason to do so except that God had told him to; he chose to believe God's promise that through his descendants, every nation would be blessed (see Genesis 12:1-9). That's quite a rule by which to live life. And in Romans 4, Paul describes Abraham's living by the rule of faith in God as righteousness! Abraham was living proof that there is no better rule for making choices than "in all your ways acknowledge him, and he will make your paths straight" (Proverbs 3:6).

Teacher Challenge: Help your students understand that there are real ways they can expect God to help them (and you) make right choices. As you teach children, describe ways God has helped you choose wisely as you have prayed, read His Word or listened to trusted Christian friends and advisors. Your living example of ways you have asked for and received His help in making choices will help your students see that pleasing God and living out His exciting promises is as wonderful today as it was in Bible times!

PSALM 119:105

"Your word is a lamp to my feet and a light for my path."

Imagine how different everything would be without the written word—no books, no signs, no newspapers or letters. In such a situation, how much information could we remember? Most of us would admit that even on a good day, we remember far less than we wish we could. And if we had no Bible and had to memorize ALL of Scripture, we know we probably wouldn't remember it all very accurately!

God, in His mercy, gave His messages to people who could write them in permanent form. His words could be remembered and reread. The written Word allows everyone with the ability to read to discover the gift of His Word for themselves. And through the writing of the Old Testament, He laid the foundation for the coming of the Word made flesh.

Teacher Challenge: As children learn to read, their understanding grows quickly. Reading may still seem to be hard work for some in your class. But help them grasp the exciting idea that reading God's Word leads to understanding of God's love letter to us!

PSALM 119:11

"I HAVE HIDDEN YOUR WORD IN MY HEART THAT I MIGHT NOT SIN AGAINST YOU."

It's happened to most of us (to some of us, more than once!). As we drive toward a place we've never been before, we realize that our directions are at home. The map we need is no longer in the glove compartment! Suddenly, the strangeness of everything around us intensifies. *Should we turn here? What was that street name?* we wonder.

But imagine that we recognize the problem and do the sensible thing—stop to buy a map, no matter how much the purchase price. We'll pay any price for that information! However, as we look at the map, we realize that the street we're on isn't even on the map! The map is outdated, incorrect and unreliable!

That's a little like life, isn't it? Spiritually, emotionally and intellectually, each of us moves through new territory every day. We are all headed for a destination to which we've never been before. Is it any wonder that people look confused, worried and unhappy? Often, a map that is touted as the solution to our confusion is held out to us. But as we study it, we realize that this map, like so many others, is not reliable. It only confuses things further! But God loves us too much to leave us wondering and wandering!

Teacher Challenge: Help the students you teach realize that God holds out a set of directions and a map, all found in one complete guidebook. It's the only reliable information for getting us through the unfamiliar territory of our lives and safely to the destination of life with Him forever! (Kind of makes you want to hug your Bible, doesn't it?)

PROVERBS 17:17

"A FRIEND LOVES AT ALL TIMES."

Jonathan and David are the Bible's classic example of friendship. The love may have been equal on both sides of this friendship, but the effects were different for each one. David, it seems, couldn't lose; he had a dear friend in Jonathan. Saul was hunting David down, but Saul's son was an openhearted, genuine ally.

David already knew he would become king, based on God's promise. Jonathan probably knew this, too. For Jonathan, God's promise meant that he would never become king. In one sense, he had nothing to gain from his friendship with David. Every bit of help he gave David took him further from the possibility of ever sitting on the throne himself. But Jonathan's love was pure and free of personal interest, born out of trust in and surrender to God (see 1 Samuel 20:13-15).

Teacher Challenge: Friendship that is free of personal interest is truly rare. But it's the kind we need to teach our students by the example of our lives! Be the kind of friend who gives each child genuine respect. Teach loving friendships by being a true friend to every child.

JOHN 3:16

"FOR GOD SO LOVED THE WORLD THAT HE GAVE HIS ONE AND ONLY SON, THAT WHOEVER BELIEVES IN HIM SHALL NOT PERISH BUT HAVE ETERNAL LIFE."

The Gospel of John tells us that God loved us so much that He sent His Son to die for our sins (see John 3:16). God's love led Him to take that most difficult and painful action, and each of the Gospels describes Jesus' suffering as He was crucified and died for us.

This is the love of a parent for his or her children infinitely perfected. God made each of us, fully knowing that we would reject Him time after time. He chose to love us even though He was fully aware of the pain this love would cost Him. This love is amazing and beyond understanding! And yet there is nothing more important for your students to understand.

Teacher Challenge: As you teach your class, remember that your students need to see the truth of the Gospel in your life as much as they need to hear it. Don't forget the needs of your students as you rush to "present the material" in the lesson. Be a mirror of God's love as you treat your students with respect, encourage them in their discovery of God's goodness and remember their concerns in prayer during the week.

ACTS 22:15

"YOU WILL BE HIS WITNESS TO ALL MEN OF WHAT YOU HAVE SEEN AND HEARD."

God is pursuing all people—even those who are not looking for Him! Consider Saul of Tarsus who was zealous to protect his religious traditions. Taught by the famous Gamaliel, Saul became a Pharisee whose passion was "breathing out murderous threats against the Lord's disciples" (Acts 9:1). But even while Saul made havoc of the Church, he was spreading Christianity like wind spreads fire—he just didn't realize it!

Jesus interrupted this zealous, misguided man. He gave the fire-breathing Pharisee an experience that got his full attention and turned him completely around! Saul was now eager to share the powerful way Jesus had intervened, brought Saul to Himself and made him zealous for the truth.

Teacher Challenge: As you pray for your students this week, take time to think about each one. Each student needs to meet Jesus in a life-changing way! Jesus may not knock any of them down in the middle of the road, but He longs for each one to know Him personally. Be ready to tell your own marvelous story of how Jesus called you. Whether Jesus came to you quietly or dramatically, your students need to know how He has made a difference in your life. Share your experience in a way your students will understand. Sharing your relationship with Christ through prayer and teaching, as well as through personal testimony and living God's love before them, will enable your students to more easily recognize Christ's pursuit of their own lives.

ROMANS 10:14

"HOW, THEN, CAN THEY CALL ON THE ONE THEY HAVE NOT BELIEVED IN? AND HOW CAN THEY BELIEVE IN THE ONE OF WHOM THEY HAVE NOT HEARD? AND HOW CAN THEY HEAR WITHOUT SOMEONE PREACHING TO THEM?"

"More is 'caught' than is taught." We may hear that often and think immediately about the children who observe us. But pause for a moment to remember: what did you "catch"? What still echoes in your heart from childhood? Each of us absorbed enormously powerful attitudes and patterns as children. As we watched adults respond to life, we were shaped unconsciously, sometimes before we could speak. It's the way we all learned what life was about.

Who was your favorite teacher as a child? Can you remember the person's name? What's more, can you recall anything that teacher said? We seldom remember the exact words of any teacher. As teachers, we may be amazed and perhaps a little disturbed when we realize that!

So what made that teacher unforgettable? See if you can list some of the reasons. It probably wasn't lesson content—it was what you "caught" from that person. Was that teacher an adult who believed in you? One who saw—and said—that you were able, worthy of love and encouragement? Who was excited about what they were teaching, and let you know it was safe to be excited and happy, too?

Teacher Challenge: Ask God's help to be an unforgettable teacher. It's not only good teaching, it's God's way. Don't let anxiety over getting through your curriculum blur your vision. God can give you the power to love each child in your class and see each one as a real person, the way God sees. It's the love that they "catch" from you that will plant the truths about God deep into the hearts of your children.

PHILIPPIANS 4:19

"My God will meet all your needs according to his glorious riches in Christ Jesus."

In the Garden of Eden, God provided for Adam and Eve's every need (see Genesis 1—2). They had a perfect place to live, all they needed to eat and important work to do. Even when they sinned, God promised to meet what had so recently become their ultimate need—the need for salvation from sin. God promised as early as Genesis 3:15 to send a Savior who would take care of the problem of sin itself and mortally wound Satan.

Today, through Jesus the promised Savior, God meets all of our needs. We discover by His tender care that He deeply loves us and that He is completely able to deliver on His promises. Not only does He know us intimately, He also knows what we need—even when we ourselves are confused and unable to understand what is best for us.

Sometimes the biggest need we have is to remember that God knows. God knows about the insensitive remark that cuts us, the longing for rest and peace or for something to do that matters in life. God knows our deepest longings and promises that as we delight ourselves in Him and commit our way to His will, He will meet our dearest desires (see Psalm 37:4-6).

Teacher Challenge: God knew Adam and Eve; He knows you and each of your students. Because of His great love, He longs to hear from us and fellowship with us, even as He meets all our needs, "according to his glorious riches in Christ Jesus" (Philippians 4:19). Commit your way—and each of your students—to His marvelous care today!

COLOSSIANS 3:13

"BEAR WITH EACH OTHER AND FORGIVE WHATEVER GRIEVANCES YOU MAY HAVE AGAINST ONE ANOTHER. FORGIVE AS THE LORD FORGAVE YOU."

Think about forgiveness for a moment. First, forgiveness flows from God to us, unworthy sinners. By God's grace, we are declared free from sin's penalty when we give ourselves to Christ. We become forgiven and free for eternity!

Then, because God forgave us, as His children we now have the ability to forgive others. That may sound impossible to you today! You may be holding a hurt as huge as Esau's hatred of his brother Jacob (see Genesis 27). Seeking revenge for an undeserved hurt may sound like a reasonable solution to you! But when you forgive the person who hurt you so deeply, you not only live out God's love, you gain the real benefit. For in forgiving others, you are freed from the hurt that can be fostered by unforgiveness in your own life.

Teacher Challenge: Clear the slate in your own life of any unfinished forgiveness business. Then you'll be able to sensitively understand and respond to the issues about forgiveness present in the lives of your students. Remember, this teaching of forgiveness is opposite from what they may see demonstrated by others around them. The young hearts of the students in your class need to understand how they can take steps to receive and give forgiveness. And they'll learn best from a living example—you!

COLOSSIANS 3:23

"WHATEVER YOU DO, WORK AT IT WITH ALL YOUR HEART, AS WORKING FOR THE LORD, NOT FOR MEN."

Think about the familiar story of Noah in the ark. What must living on the ark have been like? Take a few moments to imagine. Hundreds of animals, many of which were predators in the wild, were living nearly on top of each other! In this close atmosphere, every day must have been an endless cycle of feeding, cleaning and exercising each animal.

Noah, who'd come into this adventure by faith and obedience, trusted God and worked with all his might. He knew that if God wanted these animals to survive, He would, at least temporarily, calm the otherwise strong natural instincts of the animals. Every species survived the ark well.

Teacher Challenge: God still intervenes in our circumstances. Is the space in your classroom inadequate? Are the children crowded or restless? Is the equipment worn? Give your best effort and trust God for every need in your class, no matter how small. He wants the best for each child you teach! He can bring calmness and love as well as providing for every material need. Trust Him, expecting Him to help with the challenges you face. He will!

1 TIMOTHY 2:1

"I URGE, THEN, FIRST OF ALL, THAT REQUESTS, PRAYERS, INTERCESSION AND THANKSGIVING BE MADE FOR EVERYONE."

Many times we look at prayer as simply focusing on lists of requests. But prayer moves far beyond mundanely reciting our concerns when we become aware we are speaking to the One who truly loves us and the God we are addressing is infinitely more powerful than our circumstances.

Remember the encounter of Jairus and Jesus? When Jairus begged Jesus to heal his daughter, Jesus was ready to help. Even though He was interrupted, even though the girl died, Jesus went to her to bring her back to life (see Mark 5:21-43). This story of Jesus' great love and power reminds us to ask for His help in every situation.

But God doesn't always answer prayer in ways we expect. Sometimes God says, "No, I have something better." Other times He says, "Wait awhile." These answers can seem like they are not answers at all! Perhaps the hardest "unanswered" prayers to understand are those for things we believe are good. We pray for someone to be healed, and the sickness remains. We pray for reconciliation in a family, and divorce still occurs. We all face the very difficult struggle involved in trusting God's power and goodness, even when it seems that He doesn't really care.

Teacher Challenge: You can help your students best in these moments by admitting your own questions ("I don't know why God did not make your grandma well"), while confirming your own trust ("I do know God loves your grandma and was always with her while she was sick. And God can make something very good come out of all our sadness.") Affirm God's power and goodness with your students.

JAMES 1:22

"DO NOT MERELY LISTEN TO THE WORD, AND SO DECEIVE YOURSELVES. DO WHAT IT SAYS."

I planted the seed . . . but God made it grow" (1 Corinthians 3:6). This is how Paul described what happened when he taught the Word of God to the Corinthians. God gives us His Word so that we can grow as His children. Through our faith in Christ, God provides His Spirit to help us understand His Word and His will for us (see John 14:26; 1 Corinthians 2:13).

Read over the parable of the sower in Luke 8:4-15. This parable describes hard soil that is hostile to a seed's penetration and growth. We are warned not to develop hardened hearts and attitudes that make it difficult for God and His Word to penetrate. God wants to soften our hearts so that His truth can be planted and grow in our lives.

The parable also describes soil in which rocks and thorns choke the plant as it attempts to grow. This, too, is a warning: God wants to clear out the obstacles that prevent His truth from growing and flourishing. He wants us to put Him first so that other distractions don't stifle His work in our lives. God wants us to lead healthy, productive lives that bear the fruit of His Spirit (see Galatians 5:22-23).

Teacher Challenge: To help your students develop soft hearts that are open to God's guidance, encourage them to memorize and internalize His precious Word. Guide them to think it over carefully and do what it says. Memorize Bible verses with them. As you plant these seeds, pray that God will nourish them so that your students blossom into the people He wants them to be.

ARTICLES, TIPS AND MINIPOSTERS

BILINGUAL TEACHING

America is a land of immigrants. In recent years, even rural communities have welcomed newcomers from different nations. Some of these immigrants who come to church may speak only their native languages, or a limited amount of English. The language barrier can present a challenge for the English-speaking classroom. Through patience and effort, English-speaking teachers can make the new students feel welcomed as they adapt to their new home.

"Bilingual" refers to a person who is fluent in two languages. In American churches, this may be English and Spanish, English and Korean, English and Tagalog—the possibilities are endless! It can also refer to a classroom or church service where two languages are used.

"ESL" stands for English as a second language. In addition to their native tongue, these people learn English. Children of immigrant parents often master English rather quickly; however, in the meantime these children struggle to understand a strange language.

Also, a person may be able to speak a second language but not read it. An ESL child may be able to follow simple verbal directions in English but not read from an English Bible. A child often understands spoken English better than he or she can speak or read it. If you have several ESL children in your class, you may find their understanding of English is at different levels. If so, give verbal information to the child with the best English skills, so he or she can help the others understand.

Get help. Try to find at least one bilingual teacher, assistant or translator for your class if you have ESL children. The role of this person is to assist ESL children with directions and activities rather than translating the entire lesson word for word. Being bilingual does not mean a person is skilled at rapid, accurate translation.

Use visual aids. Although visual aids are useful for any classroom, they take on special importance with ESL children. Every child can understand pictures and photos. The visual aids give children a focal point during discussion and storytelling. Be sure that the visual aids contain mostly pictures and few words. Pantomimes and puppets are also good ways to present a story to ESL children.

Provide written materials for school-age children. ESL children will be happy to read along with the rest of your class, or you may provide classroom materials in the child's native language. Some bilingual church members may be able to translate student pages, if necessary. (Note: The American Bible Society offers Bibles in many languages.)

If a translator is available, you may wish to provide a list each week with the Bible verse, key lesson points and directions for activities in the child's native language. This list can be on a poster, written on a chalkboard or presented as a handout. When writing a second language, pay attention to special characters and accent marks which could change the meaning of a word.

Learn the language. Take the time to learn a few phrases, greetings and directions in the second language so that you can communicate with ESL children. Over time, add to your vocabulary as you talk with children and their parents. If you fail to learn correct pronunciations, don't panic. ESL children will find it humorous!

Involve the students. ESL children can easily complete art projects, play games and sing songs. As you give instructions, demonstrate your actions. Find out what customs the ESL children have for Christmas and Easter and incorporate these into your class.

As ESL students become more proficient in speaking English, encourage them to become involved in class discussions. Don't push children past their comfort zone or beyond their speaking abilities, yet provide a safe place where they can practice their new language. ESL children may make mistakes as they learn English, but avoid the temptation to correct their speech. Repeat or rephrase what they said correctly and thank the child for participating. Your friendly smile can communicate your care for the child just as much as your words.

CHARACTERISTICS OF TWOS

"Aren't all two-year-olds alike?" The answer to that question is both yes and no! Every child develops in a unique way. At any given chronological age, children's developmental differences will vary greatly. But some basic developmental guidelines can help you become both a better observer and a more effective helper.

Physical

Twos are able to walk, climb, scribble on paper, build block towers, fill a container with small objects and turn pages in a book. Although large muscles are fairly well developed, twos often stumble and fall. They move all the time! Small muscles are not yet well developed. Twos are often in the process of being potty trained. They enjoy simple songs with movement and large-muscle activities and need room to roam as well as quiet-time activities.

Cognitive and Emotional

Twos have a short attention span, and they learn best through using all their senses. A two is often eager to do things without help and uses "no" frequently as a way to define his or her separate identity. Twos may say many words and some simple sentences and recognize their names in print. Twos enjoy retelling a story or activity, which increases their sense of mastery.

Social

Twos have very little concept about other people's rights or feelings. "MINE!" is a favorite word. Using distraction and redirection works far better than reasoning when there are disputes. Twos play mainly by themselves or play next to but not with other children. Get on their eye level. Talk about what you see them doing to help them know you notice them and love them.

Spiritual

Twos can learn that God made everything, that God cares about them, that Jesus is God's Son, that the Bible is God's special book and that Bible stories are true. Talk and sing about God often.

CHARACTERISTICS OF THREES

Physical

Threes have increased small-muscle ability, can unlace and remove shoes and unbutton clothing, draw pictures and name the people and items which they draw. They build more complicated block structures and are usually completely potty trained. Threes enjoy stringing big beads, putting together simple puzzles and playing with dough, as well as singing songs and hearing simple stories. They may begin to use scissors.

Cognitive and Emotional

Threes may be able to write part of their names and can usually identify colors and repeat simple rhymes and songs. Threes begin to imitate and pretend. They can wait for short periods of time and may show more sympathy for others.

Social

Threes may interact with other children more as they play, although sharing and taking turns are still not habitual. Give good eye contact at eye level and be sure to show you see, hear and love them.

Spiritual

Threes can understand that Jesus was born as a baby and grew up to do kind things, that God is good and that Jesus loves us, and that the Bible tells us right ways to act. Threes understand more about God's love and nature through loving actions than through spoken words.

CHARACTERISTICS OF FOURS

Physical

Fours begin a period of rapid growth. Coordination catches up in both small and large muscles. They still need a great deal of space and time to explore and enjoy the creative process.

Cognitive and Emotional

Fours begin to ask why and how. Their attention spans are still short, but they can concentrate for longer periods. Fours may often test the limits of what is acceptable behavior.

Social

Fours begin to enjoy being with other children in group activities. They want to please adults and usually love their teachers. Give each child a chance to feel successful by helping in some way. Provide ways they can sing, pray and talk together.

Spiritual

Fours begin to understand more about Jesus: that He is God's Son and that He made sick people well when He lived on Earth. Fours can also be taught that the Bible tells us ways to obey God and that we can talk to God in prayer.

CHARACTERISTICS OF FIVES

Physical

Fives are learning to tie their own shoes, to cut with scissors successfully and to draw pictures that are recognizable to others. Girls move ahead of boys in development. Coordination has usually become excellent.

Cognitive and Emotional

Fives are often able to write their own names, copy words and letters and may even read some words. Fives can talk accurately about recent events and speak understandably. They love to learn why, still seek adult approval and love to discover for themselves through play and experimenting. Encourage them to think by asking what-could-happen-next and how-could-you-solve-this open-ended questions.

Social

Fives enjoy extended periods of cooperative play, usually with one or two others. They enjoy group activities and need to feel that they are seen and heard. Need for attention may cause them to act in negative ways. Give attention before negative actions occur. Give good eye contact at eye level and be sure to show you see, hear and love them.

Spiritual

Fives are the most likely to respond by talking about the Bible story or Bible verse, and some children will understand that being kind as Jesus was is something they can do. Some children, especially those from Christian homes, may be interested in becoming members of God's family. Help them feel confident that God hears their prayers and that God wants to help them. As with all young children, they think literally and concretely and cannot understand abstract ideas like "Jesus in my heart" or "born again."

The most important way we teach young children about God's love is to show them! As we get on their level, listen to them, encourage them and make them feel secure, they begin to link God's love with the joy, excitement and security they feel from you.

Helping Children Fold, Tape, Cut and Glue

To help children successfully complete some of the activities suggested in your curriculum, a few basic skills are required. These skills—folding, taping, cutting and gluing—must be learned. And as you know, not all children learn at the same rate. Read these suggestions for a variety of ways to help children learn to succeed at these four tasks.

Folding

1. Before giving paper to a child, prefold paper as needed and then open it back up. Paper will then fold easily along the prefolded lines when child refolds it.

2. Score the line to be folded by placing a ruler on the line. Then draw a used ballpoint pen with no ink in it along the ruler's edge. The line will fold easily into place.

3. Hold the corners of the paper in position to be folded. Tell the child to press and rub where he or she wants to fold the page.

Taping

1. An easy solution for the problems of taping is to use double-sided tape whenever appropriate. Lay the tape down on the paper where it is needed. Child attaches the item that needs to be taped.

2. If double-sided tape is not available or is not appropriate, place a small piece of tape on the edge of a table or shelf. Child removes tape and attaches it to paper.

Cutting

1. Cutting with scissors is one of the most difficult tasks for any young child to master. Provide scissors that are the appropriate size for young children and designed for both right-handed and left-handed children. (Purchase at educational supply stores.) All scissors should be approximately 4 inches (10 cm) long and should have blunt ends.

2. Hold paper tightly at ends or sides while child cuts.

3. Begin to cut paper for child to follow. Child follows cut you have begun.

4. Draw simple lines outside actual cut lines for the child to follow. This will help a child cut close to the desired shape—though it will not be exact.

5. Provide scrap paper for child to practice cutting.

Gluing

1. Have child use a glue bottle to apply a spot of glue to a large sheet of paper; then child presses a smaller piece of paper onto glued area.

2. Provide a glue stick for the child to use (available at variety stores). Take off cap and roll up a short amount of the glue stick for child. Child "colors" with glue stick over desired area.

3. Pour glue into a shallow container. Thin slightly by adding a small amount of water. Child uses paintbrush to spread glue over desired area. This idea works well when a large surface needs to be glued.

4. To glue a smaller surface, pour a small amount of glue into a shallow container. Give each child a cotton swab. Child dips the swab into the glue and rubs on desired area.

5. When using glue bottles, buy the smallest bottles for children to use. Refill small bottles from a large bottle. Adjust top to limit amount of glue that comes out. Instruct child to put "tiny dots of glue" on paper. Clean off and tightly close top of bottle when finished. Have several paper towels ready to clean up any spills or excess glue.

Remember not to expect perfection. Accept all attempts at accomplishing the task. Specific and honest praise will encourage the child to attempt the task again!

INCREASE THE CHALLENGE FOR KINDERGARTNERS

In any group of children entering kindergarten, developmental maturity might range from that of a three-year-old to that of a seven-year-old. This is neither good nor bad—it simply *is*. Every child develops at his or her own unique pace. Because of such differences, teachers need to be ready to either simplify or expand activities in such a way that every child gains understanding, competence and feelings of success.

At some point during the kindergarten year, many children's minds seem to suddenly kick into high gear. Fascinated with learning, they ask wonderful questions that show they are thinking deeply: "Where is heaven? Why does the water look blue? What makes your brain think?" These children are eager for greater mental challenges. Here are basic ways to expand activities and increase the challenge, keeping every child excited and involved!

Thinking Skills

Any activity, at any moment, can be given an increasing level of challenge.

▶ Invite children to observe a Bible story picture and then categorize. "What is the same about these people? What is different?" "What other fruits are the same color as these apples?" "How many sheep do you see in the picture?" "How many horses with brown spots do you count? How many goats have black tails?"

▶ Invite children to find common characteristics either in something or someone observed. "Who else is wearing red?" "Where is another person in the picture who is wearing a sweater?" "What are Arcelia and I wearing that is the same?"

▶ Stop at various points when reading a Bible story and invite children to predict what they think will happen next. To expand the prediction work, invite children to make up endings to the story or draw a picture of what they think could happen next, or invite children to suggest outcomes if a character did something different. "What would have been different if Jesus had told the blind man to be quiet?" "What if Samuel had not asked Eli what he wanted?"

▶ Begin an open-ended story. Invite each child to take a turn contributing one or two sentences. You may also show a picture and ask children to tell what they think happened before the picture or what they think might happen next. Such simple activities challenge and sharpen thinking skills.

▶ Change an item of your clothing slightly and challenge children to detect what was changed.

▶ Play charade games of any kind. Charades help children to learn the nuances of body language and think of ways to communicate without words.

Word Skills

Take advantage of children's natural curiosity regarding words and reading in the natural situations that arise during class time.

▶ When children are asked to name people whom they can help, print the names on a large sheet of paper.

► As part of a prayer time, ask children to name items for which they are thankful. Print each word on a large sheet of paper. "Read" the list aloud after each child has contributed.

► If children in your class are beginning readers, print the words of a Bible verse on separate cards. As each word of the verse is said aloud, give an child the appropriate card. Then ask children to place the cards in order.

► Label classroom items, so interested children may read the names.

While it is impressive when a young child can recite a Bible passage, memorization is no guarantee of understanding. Adult approval for memorizing will likely make a child feel successful but may also send the message that Bible words are just phrases to be spoken, not God's Word that gives direction to our lives. If children are to memorize Scripture, it should be a verse whose meaning you can make clear. Help them understand what they are repeating. If you are not able to make the ideas in the passage clear to the children, perhaps that passage should be left for later!

Since a kindergarten-aged class usually contains children not yet reading, children in the process of learning to read and beginning readers, incorporate activities that include children at any skill level. Give children books to "read" to each other (whether or not the actual words are read); let them listen to recordings of a story while looking at books that contain the same words. These kinds of enrichment will help to span the gap in reading skills among children.

Number Skills

Counting anything is fun for kindergartners!

► Count the blocks, the crayons or the toy cars.

► Measure items with a measuring tape or measuring stick.

► Use Post-it Notes to cover and then uncover items in a picture.

► Bring a scale and weigh a variety of items.

► Invite children to sort manipulative items (small building blocks, large beads, plastic animals, etc.) into a variety of categories, or create patterns in the way items are placed on the table or floor.

Include these challenges in such a way that children feel it is simply good fun. They are learning far more by these simple experiences than we can classify! Don't, however, test them later or expect right answers.

The heart of these expansion ideas is not so much achieving specific educational goals as much as it is stimulating children to explore and discover, keeping their involvement high. Most of all, make learning challenges fun! Don't pressure children to perform. Simply play with them, give out information and remind them of God's love for each one. Express your gratitude to God for the abilities He gave them!

TEACHING A GROUP OF TWOS THROUGH FIVES

There are times when one class of preschool-aged children may range from two years to five or six years of age. It's important for a teacher of any class containing such a large developmental span to be well prepared! Such varied levels of development require that a teacher tailor some activities so that each child learns best at his or her own level of development.

To a degree, younger children will enjoy being with the "big kids" and will be attracted to the activities in which older children are involved. Generally speaking, however, the younger the child, the more easily he or she will be distracted. Therefore, the younger child needs more direct, firsthand activity for effective learning. So that all activities need not be set at the level of the very youngest ones, divide the class into older and younger groups as time and helpers allow. If materials are used with older children that are not suitable for use by younger children, provide careful supervision at all times.

Use the activity center method. Keep at least one helper or teacher with each group to observe and talk with children. As you rotate these groups through the centers, let every child work at his or her own pace. Keep in mind that younger children have shorter attention spans and are likely to move between activities more frequently. Older children will be able to focus longer.

If some children don't stay in their age-related groups, don't panic. Such a natural adjustment is probably best! As teachers and helpers get to know each child, they can be observant as children interact. They will then be better able to adjust members, times and activities for any group as needed.

Plan to use activities that are open-ended. When children are all expected to produce the same craft item, the activity will require a great deal of adult intervention (and result in a great deal of adult frustration!). Instead, give children creative materials and let each one work at an individual level. Engage children in conversation about the process of what they are doing. "Tell me about your picture." "I see lots of dots on your page. What color are your dots?" "Which kind of dough is softer? Which one do you like best?" Talk about colors and shapes you see, what the child seems to be enjoying, etc. Especially in a class of mixed ages, don't focus on activities where a finished product is the goal. This avoids comparison (older ones have already heard this kind of thing from even older children) and eliminates frustration.

Many early childhood activities can be stretched to fit different ability levels. For example, if making a collage of magazine pictures, a two-year-old may have finished after gluing two or three pictures, a three-year-old may want to cover the entire paper, a four-year-old may want to trim the pictures before gluing and a five-year-old may want to dictate captions for each picture. Wise teachers of mixed ages will choose activities that will provide each age level with successful participation.

During Bible story time, having at least one teacher and one helper for each group makes it possible to schedule two story times. Even better, keeping the story time as an activity center through which groups rotate makes it possible to tailor the story to each particular group. This way, all children are taught the Bible story on their own level. If this is not possible, involve older children in telling the story. Invite them to answer questions and tell details that they want to share from the story. This not only gives older ones a sense of helpfulness and importance, but it also gives the teacher a chance to gauge what children do or do not understand about the story.

As with any other adjustment, ask for God's wisdom in the situation. Look for creative ways to see the matter of age span as a benefit, instead of a problem. Your attitude of accepting things as they are and your relaxed calmness will help each child sense God's love for him or her. As each one works at his or her own level, all ears will be open to the words you say about God and His care.

INSIGHT INTO PRETEENS AND PEERS

Emotional Characteristics of Early Adolescents

▶ **Early adolescents are subject to mood swings.** These sudden changes are confusing for teachers, as well as for the child. The preteen's mood jumps dramatically between love and hate, happiness and fear, interest and boredom. These mood swings influence every area of the preteen's life, from their relationships to their desire to attend church.

As significant adults working with early adolescents, we need to remember that these kids have little control over their emotions. We must be patient with preteens who seem to over-react emotionally to any given situation. They may laugh one minute and cry the next. It is not their fault that their changing environment and changing chemistry collide and create wide swings in how they feel about themselves, their peers and their leaders. Our job is to help the preteen learn to respond or act appropriately *in spite* of his or her emotional state.

▶ **Early adolescents can, however, control their actions and words.** It's possible, but it's not easy! They need consistent training from loving, calm, patient adults to learn to react appropriately in spite of how they are feeling.

▶ **Preteens are angry.** Anger is one of the most common emotions that emerge in the life of the early adolescent. This anger comes from a variety of sources, including fatigue, feelings of inadequacy, rejection or uncertainty. There is always a reason for anger and for anger being expressed inappropriately by early adolescents. They must be taught skills and have modeled for them patterns for processing feelings of anger positively.

▶ **Preteens are fearful.** Their fear comes in the form of worries. They have increasing demands upon them in every area of life, and they have anxiety about being able to perform to an acceptable level, as they desire to please both their peers and their parents or teachers.

Nonacceptance and rejection are the early adolescent's biggest worries in life. The preteen is constantly evaluating whether he or she is fitting in and receiving approval. Things like report card grades and peer criticism are vital to the preteen's self-evaluation process.

▶ **Preteens are often threatened by competition.** One day, they will seem to love competition; the next, they hate it. It has a lot to do with whether or not they win! Almost everyone loves competing if they are so good at something that they are assured a victory, but not many of us like losing. Competition points out even the most minor of chinks in our armor, and preteens are already too self-critical.

▶ **Early adolescents have a love of humor.** These kids will enjoy jokes and leaders who can see the lighter side of life. Humor should be included in every part of the ministry for preteens. Make your classroom a fun place to be.

Humor must never be used as a weapon, though. It must be used in a mature manner. No child should ever be the subject of the joke. You may get a good laugh, but you will lose the child. Even those kids who seem to be able to handle it and who laugh along with you are not normally laughing inside.

▶ **Preteens are private.** Although at times it appears that they will never stop talking, during the later years of early adolescence, kids will develop private areas of their lives that they do not want to share with anyone else, especially not with authority figures. These private areas include their fears and questions about themselves and their peers. Great care must be taken during group discussions to show respect for the privacy of preteens. Allow some freedom in choosing discussion topics and never pressure preteens to divulge personal information.

▶ **Preteens need encouragement, support and unconditional love.** Give kids strong, frequent affirmation. Because the preteen is constantly changing and experiencing conflicts and emotional upheavals, he or she needs to be reassured over and over that at least one significant adult loves and accepts him or her.

Social Characteristics of Early Adolescents

▶ **For the preteen, peers are incredibly important.** Early adolescents are greatly influenced by their peers. As kids begin to break away from their families and express individuality and independence, they immediately reach out to surrogate families to fill the void.

Their fear of nonacceptance leads them to want to look like, act like and talk like others their own age. The group is all-important! Failure to achieve a certain status of belonging in the group can result in an introspective self-pity for the preteen.

▶ **Early adolescents are self-critical and critical of others.** Early adolescents feel awkward. They often wonder if they are good at anything. They wonder how their intelligence and athletic ability compare with others. Failure or poor performance in any area, whether it be sports, academics or other observable indicators of intelligence or physical prowess, is sure to cause a crisis. A facial blemish, big feet or wearing the wrong brand of clothes can cause a crisis. In addition, the fact that they are surrounded by critical peers who are typically quick to point out these differences causes preteens to become increasingly critical of themselves (to fit in with what others say about them) and others (to get the critical glare off themselves).

Because of this tendency toward being overly critical, set a positive example of being accepting and nonjudgmental. Plan activities in which preteens can feel competent. This will help them balance out the harsh criticism they levy against themselves.

▶ **Preteens need good friends of the same gender.** Early in the preteen years, kids often do not like members of the opposite gender. This is the age of buddies and best friends. It is not only normal for preteens to feel close to a same-gender peer, but it is also a must for building a foundation for positive relationships with members of the opposite gender later in life. Any fears about such a relationship being a precursor to a homosexual orientation are misplaced. This is a healthy stage of the preteen's development toward social maturity.

▶ **Later in early adolescence, friendships develop with members of the opposite gender.** This is one more area of transition for the preteen. Because of this change, we believe it is important to make at least some of your small-group activities coeducational so that you can help kids learn how to relate appropriately to the opposite gender.

▶ **Early adolescents are seeking independence and autonomy from parents.** Although preteens want to feel separate and independent from their parents, they still need and truly desire adult guidance and emotional support. Provide experiences that allow gradual acquisition of the desired independence. Giving preteens too much freedom will result in chaos and insecurity. Discouragement and depression may be the outcome. Give appropriate ways for kids to be in charge and to experience success in standing on their own two feet.

▶ **Preteens are increasingly concerned about their physical appearance.** Preteens are typically overly aware of their own bodies and the changes that may or may not have begun to occur. In fact, one could say they are obsessed with their physical appearance. This is another area in which preteens feel they must do anything in order to fit in. Externals, like clothing and physical beauty, become a measuring stick that they believe will make the difference as to whether or not they are accepted.

▶ **The preteen does not enjoy anything that seems like work.** This seems contradictory at first, since they love to be needed. If the task is presented correctly, washing cars, doing dishes and babysitting will all seem like exciting challenges. It's when they become routine tasks and take on the drudgery of a job that preteens tend to lose enthusiasm.

PHYSICAL AND SPIRITUAL GROWTH OF PRETEENS

Physical Characteristics of Early Adolescents

▶ **The rate of growth and changes in preteens vary widely.** This variation is seen between individual preteens and between the genders. In general, girls will grow more quickly and oftentimes will be taller than boys during the early adolescent years. Although the timing may differ, the experience is similar. Growth in each individual rapidly accelerates before pubescence and decelerates after pubescence.

▶ **Growth comes in spurts.** Sudden spurts of growth cause the preteen to be awkward and clumsy. Bones grow faster than muscles, leaving the child's new bigger and better body uncoordinated. Hands and feet mature before arms and legs. Legs and arms grow faster than the trunk and are often the source of growing pains.

▶ **Sudden growth causes fatigue.** Just as in younger children, this sudden growth creates fatigue in early adolescents. Their bodies are working overtime to grow and change and they are left with low energy and a greater need for sleep.

▶ **Early adolescents are very physical.** They like to be active and move about constantly. Outside activities are popular at this age, because this environment allows for large-muscle movement and loud, boisterous activities.

▶ **The preteen is bombarded with hormonal changes.** The early adolescent's life is complex. The onset of puberty causes a flood of hormones into the body. New hormones affect the child physically, by causing dramatic growth and physical changes. They also affect far more than the child's body. The raging hormones dramatically affect the early adolescent's emotions.

Intellectual Characteristics of Early Adolescents

▶ **Preteens are very curious and, therefore, also quite distractible.** Attention span continues to increase with all of the preteen's activities, but the most impressive advances are in problem-solving activities. Preteens are capable of making judgments and are quickly developing the ability to use hypothetical reasoning, a product of formal or abstract thinking. Their brains function best when they are stimulated enough to cause the child to focus on the issue at hand.

▶ **Preteens are beginning to move from concrete to abstract thinking.** They are able to reason much more than ever before, but they still may have trouble with symbolism. Kids who have attended church for years will start to question their beliefs as they continually seek to understand and personalize their faith on deeper cognitive bases.

While the brain and neurological system are almost fully developed at this point in life, the preteen's practical experience is lacking. The child is, therefore, unable to solve adult problems in appropriate, mature ways. He or she simply lacks the experience necessary to acquire and evaluate the data needed to process the situation. This is one reason that preteens must still have adult guidance and should not be given more responsibility than they are ready to handle.

▶ **Early adolescents have little concept of time.** Deadlines have little meaning to the child. Deadlines for deposits and registrations are not heeded unless the communication somehow gets to the parents. Be prepared for kids to be late!

▶ **Preteens' interests are in the present and in the real and the practical.** In large part because preteens lack the concept of time, they are most interested in what they can see, touch, hear, taste, smell and do—here and now. Learning activities and lesson applications need to focus on what the preteens can experience and put into practice immediately.

▶ **Preteens enjoy activities that include writing, drama or painting.** These kids enjoy expressing themselves in creative ways. Look for ways you can include these activities in your class.

Moral and Spiritual Characteristics of Early Adolescents

Spiritually, early adolescents are very open to a personal relationship with God. As the student shifts from a parent-given faith to a personalized faith, it may appear that he or she has become interested in spiritual things for the first time. This transition sometimes causes the casual observer to assume that children cannot make significant spiritual decisions. In reality, children can make incredible decisions for God, but they must rethink them and reown them as they transition through early adolescence.

During early adolescence, students' consciences become more fine-tuned—especially about the behavior of others. They are extremely aware of the fairness and honesty of the adults around them. They will constantly evaluate the values of their parents and teachers. However, they may be more relaxed about their own behavior. For example, their own cheating in school or shoplifting is rationalized and makes sense to them while they are quick to condemn others who do the same things.

Fairness is extremely important to preteens. When adults are inconsistent, they are quick to point out, "That's not fair!" They have a sense of justice that must be satisfied, especially by the teachers and parents in their lives.

WHAT TO EXPECT FROM CHILDREN IN GRADES 1 AND 2

Physical

These children are growing rapidly. Younger first graders may be physically more like preschoolers, while the ones moving toward third grade have hit a new level of physical maturity that shouts, "I'm not a little kid anymore!" Although these children may be expected to sit in school at this age, they still need frequent opportunities for movement during every class session. Small-muscle coordination is still developing and improving. Girls are ahead of boys at this stage of development.

Teaching Tips: Use activities that involve simple folding, cutting and writing skills. Always offer drawing in place of writing for those who struggle with writing. Give them frequent opportunities to change position and to move around the room or outdoors. Vary the kinds of activities to help keep attention high and discipline problems to a minimum.

Emotional

Children are experiencing new and frequently intense feelings as they grow more independent. Sometimes the child finds it hard to control his or her behavior. There is still a deep need for approval from adults and a growing need for approval by peers.

Teaching Tips: Seek opportunities to help each child in your class KNOW and FEEL you love him or her. Show genuine interest in each child and his or her activities and accomplishments. Learn children's names and use them frequently in positive ways. Smile frequently.

Social

Children this age are greatly concerned with pleasing their teachers. Each child is struggling to become socially acceptable to the peer group as well. The Golden Rule is still a difficult concept at this age. Being first and winning are very important; taking turns is hard! This skill improves by the end of the second grade. A child's social process moves gradually from *I* to *you* to *we*.

Teaching Tips: Provide opportunities for children to practice taking turns. Help each child accept the opinions and wishes of others and consider the welfare of the group as well as his or her own. Call attention to times when the group cooperates successfully and thank children for ways you see them sharing, taking turns, etc.

Cognitive

There is an intense eagerness to learn! Children of this age ask many questions. They like to repeat stories and activities. Their concept of time is limited. Thinking is here and now rather than past or future. Listening and speaking skills are developing rapidly; girls are ahead of boys. A child tends to think everyone shares his or her view. Children see parts rather than how the parts make up the whole. They think very literally.

Teaching Tips: Consider the skill and ability levels of the children in planning activities. For example, some can handle reading and writing activities while others may do better with music or art. Use pictures to help them understand Bible times and people. Avoid symbolic language, which often confuses them. Use a variety of activities to keep brains alert and functioning at optimal levels.

Spiritual

Children can sense the greatness, wonder and love of God when given visual and specific examples. The nonphysical nature of God is baffling, but God's presence in every area of life is generally accepted when parents and teachers communicate this in both their attitudes and their actions. Children can think of Jesus as a friend but need specific examples of how Jesus expresses His love and care. This understanding leads many children to belief and acceptance of Jesus as personal Savior. Children can comprehend talking to God anywhere, anytime in their own words and need regular opportunities to pray. They can also comprehend that the Old Testament tells what happened before Jesus was born and the New Testament tells of His birth, work on Earth, return to heaven and what happened in God's family on Earth.

Teaching Tips: The gospel becomes real to children as they feel genuine love from adults. Teachers who demonstrate their faith in a consistent, loving way are models through which children can understand the loving nature of God.

WHAT TO EXPECT FROM CHILDREN IN GRADES 3 AND 4

Physical

Children at this level have increasingly good large- and small-muscle coordination. The girls are still ahead of the boys. Children can work diligently for longer periods but can become impatient with delays or their own imperfect abilities.

Teaching Tips: Give clear, specific instructions. Allow children as much independence as possible in preparing materials. Assign children the responsibility for cleanup.

Emotional

This is the age of teasing, nicknames, criticism and increased use of verbal skills to vent anger. At eight years of age children have developed a sense of fair play and a value system of right and wrong. At nine years children are searching for identity beyond membership in the family unit.

Teaching Tips: Here is a marvelous opportunity for the teacher to present a Christian model at the time children are eagerly searching for models! Provide experiences that encourage children's creativity. Let all children know by your words and by your actions that "love is spoken here" and that you will not let others hurt them nor let them hurt others. Make your class a safe place where children feel accepted, where they are comfortable asking hard questions and where they may express their true feelings without fear of teasing.

Social

Children's desire for status within the peer group becomes more intense. This often leads to acting silly or showing off to gain attention. Most children remain shy with strangers and exhibit strong preferences for being with a few close friends. Many children still lack the essential social skills needed to make and retain friendships.

Teaching Tips: This age is a good time to use activities in which pairs or small groups of children can work together. Create natural opportunities for each child to get to know others and to take on greater responsibility.

Cognitive

Children are beginning to realize there may be valid opinions besides their own. They are becoming able to evaluate alternatives, and they are less likely than before to fasten onto one viewpoint as the only one possible. Children are also beginning to think in terms of "the whole." Children think more conceptually and have a high level of creativity. However, by this stage, many children have become self-conscious about their creative efforts as their understanding has grown to exceed their abilities in some areas.

Teaching Tips: Encourage children to look up information and discover their own answers to problems. Provide art, music and drama activities to help children learn Bible information and concepts. Encourage children to use their Bibles by finding and reading portions of Scripture. Bible learning games are good for this age and children are often eager to memorize Bible verses. Help children understand the meanings of the verses they memorize.

Spiritual

Children are open to sensing the need for God's continuous help and guidance. The child can recognize the need for a personal Savior. There may be a desire to become a member of God's family. Children who indicate an awareness of sin and concern about accepting Jesus as Savior need clear and careful guidance without pressure.

Teaching Tips: Give children opportunities to communicate with God through prayer. Help them understand the forgiving nature of God. Talk personally with a child whom you sense the Holy Spirit is leading to trust the Lord Jesus. Ask simple questions to determine the child's level of understanding.

What to Expect from Children in Grades 5 and 6

Physical

Children have mastered most basic physical skills. They are active and curious and seek a variety of new experiences. Rapid growth can cause some 11-year-olds to tire easily.

Teaching Tips: 10-year-old boys will still participate in activities with girls, but by 11 years of age they tend to work and play better with their own sex. In your class provide some time for children to be grouped by gender, and some time when genders are mixed. This is a good age for exploration and research activities. Use active, creative ways to memorize Bible verses.

Emotional

Children are usually cooperative, easygoing, content, friendly and agreeable. Most adults enjoy working with this age group. Even though both girls and boys begin to think about their future as adults, their interests tend to differ significantly. Be aware of behavioral changes that result from the 11-year-old's emotional growth. Children are experiencing unsteady emotions and often shift from one mood to another.

Teaching Tips: Changes of feelings require patient understanding from adults. Give many opportunities to make choices with only a few necessary limits. Take time to listen as children share their experiences and problems with you. If your class includes sixth graders who are attending middle school, realize that these children are greatly influenced by their peers. They may show signs of low self-acceptance and need your care and support more than ever.

Social

Friendships and activities with their peers flourish. Children draw together and away from adults in the desire for independence. The child wants to be a part of a same-sex group and usually does not want to stand alone in competition.

Teaching Tips: Children no longer think aloud. Keeping communication open is of prime importance! Listen, ask open-ended questions, and avoid making judgmental comments to help them feel that it is safe to share freely.

Cognitive

Children of this age are verbal! Making ethical decisions becomes a challenging task. They are able to express ideas and feelings in a creative way. By 11 years of age many children have begun to reason abstractly. They begin to think of themselves as adults and yet at the same time are questioning adult concepts. Hero worship is strong.

Teaching Tips: Include many opportunities for talking, questioning and discussing in a safe, accepting environment. These are good years for poetry, songs, drama, stories, drawing and painting. Give guidance in a way that does not damage children's efforts to become thinking, self-directed people. Be aware of children with difficulty in reading. Plan other ways for them to gain information and be sensitive if asking children to read aloud.

Spiritual

Children can have deep feelings of love for God, can share the good news of Jesus with a friend and are capable of involvement in evangelism and service projects. The child may seek guidance from God to make everyday and long-range decisions.

Teaching Tips: Provide opportunities for children to make choices and decisions based on Bible concepts. Plan prayer, Bible reading and worship experiences. Involve children in work and service projects.

WHO ARE THESE PRETEENS—AND WHAT DO THEY NEED?

Preteens are filled with uncertainty. Everything is changing and all at one time! No wonder our students sometimes seem like they are on a roller coaster of emotions. And no wonder we, as leaders and teachers of early adolescents, have a difficult time understanding who these students are!

Early adolescence is perhaps the most misunderstood period of human development in our society today. Even professionals are finding this age group to be a difficult one to research and define. In fact, only in the past 20 years have psychologists and educators recognized the existence of this specific, identifiable period of human development. We now understand that early adolescence is that period of transitional development that exists between childhood and adolescence. It typically lasts from age 10 to age 14. And it involves the transition from concrete thinking to abstract thinking, from a child's body to a young adult's body, from emotional dependence to independence, and from primary focus on parents and family to interaction with peers.

For too long, we have treated preteens as immature high school students or hard-to-handle elementary kids. This developmental period does not belong to either childhood or adolescence. These kids are not between two stages of life. They are traveling through a specific, identifiable, wonderful period of transitional growth and maturation.

Early adolescence is unique—it is different from childhood and from later adolescence. To try to make it part of one or the other is a mistake that creates problems and ignores the incredible potential of these great kids!

Kids Are Growing Up More Quickly—Or Are They?

The casual observer will conclude that preteens and young teens are maturing faster than they used to. Their bodies seem to be blossoming at an earlier age. They are involved in far more sophisticated activities, social interactions and issues than previous generations. Their world is confronting them with much more serious problems and questions than we had to address at their age. They know more than their preteen predecessors did.

But are they truly maturing, or are they being forced to grow up before their time? While their bodies are advancing at earlier ages, are their emotions and cognitive arenas keeping pace?

Socially, emotionally and mentally, kids are being exposed to more mature material but may be no more ready to deal with it than we were at their age. The fact that they are being forced to deal with all of this does not mean that it is good for them or that they are ready for it. The world of the early adolescent is more complex and they are more socially aware. But what many do not realize is that the preteen's skill development does not match this level of sophistication. Their social contacts have pressured them to act like adolescents before they become adolescents.

What Do Early Adolescents Really Need?

▶ **The needs of early adolescents—according to them.**

What do preteens want? We can learn a lot about their perceived needs by listening to the questions that they ask us at church: Are we going to have a snack? Who's coming? What are we going to do now? What did you say? Do we have to?

We may wish that preteens would ask: "What Bible verse can we memorize today?" or "Is there a needy person in our group that we can show love to right now?"

But these aren't the issues foremost on most preteen minds. Their questions show their felt needs:

▶ Food! Food is both a felt need and a real need! Kids are a lot easier to work with when their stomachs are full.

▶ Friends! Preteens want to know "Who's coming?" because relationships are central to their existence. They want to be around peers by whom they feel accepted. Friends are a must. Our style of ministry needs to maximize development of relationships.

▶ Fun! They want to know what they're going to do, because they want to have fun playing and being active with their friends. They also want to be sure that they won't be embarrassed by an activity that makes them feel awkward. Preteens demand fun, so a certain amount of our ministry must be devoted to entertainment.

▶ Focus! Early adolescents want to be the center of attention—but only in certain ways. They desire to be noticed by their peers and the significant adults in their lives. So some of the things they say and do at church may simply be to get the attention they desire.

Although it is important to be sensitive to the likes and dislikes of our students, we must avoid building our preteen ministry solely on what the kids say they want or on what we assume they want. Just as we would not consider parenting children by meeting the children's every whim, we should not design our classes and programs with only the desires of the kids in mind. We must carefully craft our preteen ministries according to the desires of the kids along with what we know kids need and what we know will help them grow spiritually—needs that even the kids may not be able to express or understand.

Age-Level Tips

Have you noticed how children are bursting with curiosity? "Let me see!" is a familiar plea! It also means, "Let me touch, smell, hear and move!" Firsthand learning experiences are the "meat and potatoes" of a child's learning. A child needs to discover through hands-on experiences that God loves and cares for him or her.

Repetition may bore an adult! However, repetition is one of the most important ways a child learns. Repetition gives a child the assuring sense that "I know what comes next!" Even through the elementary grades, children enjoy activities in which they already know the correct response—it makes them part of the group! Use repetitive chants, songs and responses that make everyone feel successful.

Provide skill toys appropriate to children's varied levels of development. Watch carefully to see that a toy provides challenge but not frustration. Success is more closely related to a child's fine-motor development than to chronological age. Some children will need puzzles with only three or four pieces. Each piece should be a whole object (cat, ball, etc.). Others will enjoy the challenge of puzzles that are part of a whole object.

"I," "me" and "mine" are words often used by two- and three-year-olds. Don't expect a child to miraculously understand or act upon words such as "share" and "take turns"! Be the planter of ideas: When you see a child sharing, put words to what just happened. **Linc, you let Kurt look at the book with you. You shared the book. Thank you. That's what God says to do!**

Never shame a child for not sharing. Instead, model sharing behavior yourself. Put words to your actions, as well: **I'm sharing my crackers with Linc, Kurt, Destiny and Ella. I'm glad God gave me friends so I can share!**

Children need to move! When adults see this intense desire to move as somehow undesirable, don't forget that this is the way God wired children. A child will become frustrated, inattentive and disruptive if expected to sit still for long periods of time. Give children of all ages plenty of chances to move, stretch and use their bodies!

Expect very young children to use blocks merely by carrying them or by stacking several and knocking them down, usually playing alone or near another child. Only as a child matures is he or she interested in cooperative block play. There is a complex set of social patterns yet to be learned. It's more likely that four- and five-year-olds would build a larger structure together. Six- and seven-year-olds will create elaborate structures together and use them to play out many imaginary roles.

Age-Level Tips

In this high-tech world, picture books make a great high-touch activity center. To make the book center a favorite, you'll need a warm, interested adult at the center who enjoys reading, talking and asking open-ended questions! Younger children need only a few books with clear pictures and not too many words. (Adult books with clear pictures of birds and animals or wall calendar pictures work well, too!) For elementary children, include more advanced picture books from the library. Given permission and the model of the adult, they'll soon be reading on their own or to younger children.

Recognize that the younger the child, the less likely it will be that he or she will sing along with you. Younger children often participate by listening. To involve older children in a song, invite them to add a clapping pattern, use rhythm instruments, make motions or call back words. Even non-singers will join in!

First and second graders are beginning to care about what other children think of them. Many children at this age feel that they have no friends. They are struggling to develop their social skills and find ways to make friends. On the other hand, being first is still important to them as they move from the "me" stage to the "we" stage. Treating others with kindness or taking turns may still be difficult. Acknowledge and encourage the steps you see children in your class taking toward cooperating and sharing.

When a young child wants to try using scissors, first hold the paper while the child tries to cut or begin a cut line that the child may follow. Do notice whether or not the child might need left-handed scissors. And do not expect preschool-aged children to be able to cut elaborate shapes.

When you encounter children who are uncomfortable playing with dough, using paint or any "messy" activity, understand that some children have been told not to get dirty. Provide paint smocks (men's short-sleeved shirts put on backward). Also, try making dough from Ivory soap flakes and water. It can't get a child dirty!

Children sometimes "go blank" even after excitedly raising a hand! If a child cannot seem to think of an answer, invite him or her to choose someone to answer the question.

Here are tips for groups that contain both readers and non-readers: Group at least one reader into each small group or team. If using cards with words on them, number the cards in order as well; add shapes to corners of cards that need to be matched. If words are to be written, clearly print them where children can easily copy them. A child who does not want to write may draw a picture or dictate ideas to an adult who can write. Invite children to write words as they sound them out; then invite each one to read his or her own work rather than puzzling over spelling!

Sing

God's Word to plant it deeply in a young child's life.

A child's brief attention span gets even more brief in a large group where the child is expected to sit still and listen.

A Child's View of the World

Each generation faces its own unique challenges. Children today are growing up in a world different from the environment their parents knew. Yet children still process information and deal with life in predictably childlike ways. Understanding how a child sees the world today will help us meet the child's needs.

Characteristics of a Child's World Today

1. A child's world is sometimes scary. Children now live in a post-September 11 and post-Columbine world of fear and danger. Some children enter their school buildings through metal detectors and past police officers. Even at school, children are no longer safe from guns or drugs. A child may live in a neighborhood plagued by gang violence. Child abuse and abductions are common headlines. While most children will never experience such extreme tragedy, even small communities are not immune from calamity. The church should be a safe haven where a child feels protected.

2. A child's world is full of information. With cable TV, MTV, the Internet, magazines, video-cassettes and DVDs, children are exposed to a wealth of information, including material too sophisticated for young minds. Fashion styles, fads and music change at lightning speed. What's in today is out tomorrow and impressionable children struggle to be cool and acceptable. With this media exposure, children are tempted to talk, dress and behave like adult or teenaged role models in ways inappropriate for their age. They mimic adults without understanding their actions. Although a child may try to act mature, his or her young mind is still that of a child. The church can minister to children by providing a sanctuary from the constant barrage of news and peer pressure that can overwhelm them.

3. A child's world is techno-savvy. DVDs, CDs, video game systems, cell phones, computers and other technology are a way of life for today's children. Even preschoolers can load and turn on a VCR. However, this high-tech lifestyle may often result in low-touch relationships, as children communicate more through instant messaging and cell phones rather than face-to-face encounters. The church is an "unplugged" place where cell phones are turned off and the focus is placed on children's experience of genuine, firsthand relationships.

4. A child's world is egocentric. "It's all about me." The younger the child, the more deeply the child is the center of his or her universe. Infants use this survival technique to command the parent's attention and get food or care. Even to children of elementary age, the most important time to a child is what is happening to him or her now. Children are unconcerned with long-ago events that occurred to other people, and they have little awareness of the future. A 2,000-year-old book about a faraway land with strange customs is meaningful only as far as it directly affects the child's life today. The church can be a place where adults model and teach how to move beyond self-centeredness to identify and respond to the needs of others, as well as to live out what the Bible teaches.

5. A child's world is full of imagination. Children love fantasy and make-believe! They relish hearing stories and playing creatively. Children are constantly active and have short attention spans. They are just beginning to develop their ability to reason logically and are unable to make sense of complex doctrinal arguments. The wise church helps children learn through activities that engage their bodies and all of their senses as well as their minds.

6. A child's world is diverse. No community is homogenous anymore. Children have friends and classmates of all races and ethnic backgrounds. They know schoolmates with physical and cognitive challenges. There is no longer a one-size-fits-all model of family life. Children may live with two parents, one parent, a stepparent, a relative, foster parents, parents of different races or same-gender parents. The church classroom is a place where children of all backgrounds can learn and play together because every child is valued and loved.

Tips for Communicating Between Their World and Ours

1. Know the children. With such diversity among students, it's essential for teachers to know about the children's home lives, especially those who come from difficult situations and need extra care. Teachers may also want to pay attention to the music and media fads that interest students so that they know why a child dresses like the latest pop star or is fascinated by a particular sports figure.

2. Listen to children. Children love to talk about themselves and share their interests and concerns. A student with a troubled family life needs a caring adult role model. All students are more likely to remember the teacher who lent an empathetic ear more than the story the teacher told during class. The relationships built at church will last a lifetime and keep a child involved in the church family.

3. Praise the children. Sunday School is perhaps the only school children attend where they are not graded or given a test! The emphasis in Christian education is not in getting the right answer but in getting a right relationship with God in Jesus Christ. A child may not remember long Bible verses or make the prettiest art project, but he or she will remember the teacher as a loving adult. Look for the positive in each child. Effective teachers at church find ways to affirm and support their students.

A First Day Welcome!

Can you remember how it felt the last time you met a roomful of people for the first time? Recalling those feelings will help you know how stressful the first day of class can be for a young child. There are, however, some ways to help a child feel welcomed and know "This is a good place to be!"

A Welcoming Environment

Your classroom is a silent partner in any child's learning experience. It can help or hinder, delight or depress! Take time to walk through your room. View it through a child's eyes. (Get down on your knees to get a child's perspective!) Are the tables and chairs a comfortable size? Is the room light and bright? What do you notice first? Are visual aids at eye level for children? Is there a clean, comfortable place to play on the floor? Space to move freely? Does anything in the room encourage you to explore? List ways to improve the space, if needed.

Get-Acquainted Activities

Create a welcome display by printing each child's name on a sheet of construction paper. (Keep blank papers handy for guests.) Attach the papers to a bulletin board or large sheet of paper mounted on the wall. Provide a variety of fun stickers for children to put on their name papers. You may also cut pictures from catalogs or magazines that illustrate activities children will be doing (block play, dramatic play, art activities, etc.). Add these pictures to the welcome bulletin board. Talk about the pictured activities so that children know what to expect in the classroom.

As children enjoy activities on the first day, move around the room with an instant camera. Take a photo of each child, as well as photos of children playing together in small groups. Attach photos to a bulletin board or use them to mark cubby or shelf space for each child. Display group photos at eye level for children to enjoy. This creates a sense of being included!

Invite older children to bring an item from home to share on the first day. This provides a comforting object to hold as well as something for each child to talk about and help children get to know each other.

First Day Reactions

Sometimes children are overexcited on the first day. This can result in needing to use the bathroom more often, wetting or vomiting. While these small emergencies may be a trial to you, it's important that you respond calmly, kindly and with understanding. A child needs to know he or she is accepted, no matter what!

Keep a small stock of both boys' and girls' clothing in several sizes in case a child needs clean clothing.

Always show children where the bathroom is for the first few sessions. If a child wets, respond positively. "It's OK. We'll clean you up now. Remember, you can tell me any time you need to go to the bathroom. I'll be happy to take you right away."

BUILDING TRUST IN THE CLASSROOM

Imparting information is only part of what the effective teacher accomplishes in classes at church. Establishing an atmosphere of trust and love that makes the child want to return is just as important. Why do children gather at church instead of learning about God from a book or video? Because only in a communal setting can children and teachers build the Body of Christ and form friendships that last for years. Some adults who grew up in a church fondly remember the church teacher or camp counselor who made them feel valued.

Teacher-Child Relationships

Trust. As the teacher, you have the opportunity to be someone whom children can count on to be present on more than an occasional basis. Children need to feel that they can talk to you in confidence and without ridicule or criticism. Children expect that what you present in class is accurate and useful.

Attitude. Children like teachers who are positive, upbeat, confident, cheerful, friendly and willing to help. Leave your personal problems at home and give children your undivided attention.

Fun. As responsibilities set in, adults tend to become serious and preoccupied. While the subject matter you present in class is serious in nature, the atmosphere of the class does not have to be dreary. This doesn't mean that you have to act silly or let chaos reign in the classroom. It means that you can enjoy games with your children, find joy in their discoveries and maintain a happy classroom environment.

Acceptance of feelings. Listen and empathize with the feelings of the children in your class. Children respond to situations with emotions rather than rational logic. Their reactions may seem childish because they have not learned how to control their feelings or how to think through situations. While you need not agree with everything a child says, you can be a sounding board and a sympathetic ear.

Acceptance of ideas. Adults are often self-critical and self-censoring. Children are freer to express wild and crazy ideas. Encourage children to think aloud and ask questions. Children are more involved in learning when they feel that their ideas are accepted. One way to encourage brainstorming is to ask open-ended questions about opinions instead of facts ("How did the lame man feel when he could walk again?" "How do you think David felt when he heard King Saul's threat to hurt him?") Questions with more than one right answer are less threatening to children because they don't feel that they will make mistakes in their answers.

Enabling questions. Allow children to make choices instead of telling the child what to do. Instead of saying "Put the paint back in the cabinet," ask, "Where do we put the paint?" Ask children what phrases or slogans best summarize the lesson's Bible truth. Children like to feel they have an important role in the classroom.

Praise and affirmation. Every child wants to feel like the most special child in the world. Compliment and encourage children frequently, mentioning specific actions you have observed. The more children feel valued, the more they want to participate in learning and feel that God accepts them.

Nonverbal signs. Use body language to show acceptance. Sit at the children's eye level and avoid hovering over them. Nod and lean forward when a child is speaking. Smile frequently!

Touching. Due to concerns over child abuse, touching can be a difficult issue in educational settings. While you don't wish to appear cool and aloof, neither do you want your well-meaning gestures to be misinterpreted. Children sometimes have crushes on a teacher of the opposite gender. Placing a hand for a few seconds on the child's upper arm, shoulder or upper back can be appropriate to express concern. Hold a child's hand when leading the child across a room, as part of a game, in a prayer circle or if the child is scared. Brief hugs are fine when you and the child have developed a trusting relationship over time. A child may be uncomfortable if you continue touching him or her for a long time or too frequently. It is always safer to have two adults present in a classroom at all times.

Child-Child Relationships

Trust and security. In many churches, children don't know each other. They go to different schools during the week and may live in distant parts of the city. The children won't automatically get to know each other, much less develop relationships of trust. Start by having children learn their peers' names (name games are fun) and something about each other (pets, hobbies, siblings, sports, favorite performers or TV shows). Maintain a safe place where children won't be hurt and their belongings won't be stolen.

Group activities. A good way to develop friendships is through group work. Children bond when they have a common goal or problem to solve. Have children work in pairs, trios and small groups using skits, music, games and cooperative art projects. Be sure each person in the group has a task and is not left out. One person from each group can share the group's discovery or project with the rest of the class. Acknowledge the contributions of each child.

Sharing. Children learn about each other by sharing their heritage and interests. Invite children to demonstrate music, food or artwork from their home life. Children also enjoy bringing an item from home with spiritual importance in their family (heirloom Bible, gift cross, Scripture sampler, devotional book, etc.).

Prayer. During class prayer time, encourage children to pray for each other. This may be uncomfortable or threatening at first. Model sentence prayers for children to hear and imitate. As children feel comfortable in telling things for which they are thankful and/or their concerns, invite other children to pray for them. Children can say together, "Thank You, God," when someone describes something for which he or she is thankful.

Meeting the Needs of Children

Children don't arrive at the classroom with a blank slate. They have physical, emotional and social needs that can interfere with learning. They bring "baggage" of what has happened to them outside of class that can distract them from learning. Think about ways you can begin to recognize and deal with such needs so that the child's mind is free to learn.

The Child's Needs

Spiritual needs. Every child needs a relationship with Christ and to know that his or her sins are forgiven. Sometimes this important goal is lost when you struggle to provide for all of the student's other needs. At times you may need to step back and evaluate the ways in which this spiritual goal is being reached. Look for opportunities to share with children appropriate examples of how being a Christian has helped you. Invite children to tell what they know about becoming members of God's family. Listen to their responses to observe when a child indicates readiness to become a member of God's family. Pray for each child and ask God to give you wisdom in discerning his or her spiritual needs.

Physical needs. A child may have a difficult time focusing on learning if he or she is hungry or uncomfortable. Make sure that the classroom temperature is not too hot or cold, the air is not stuffy or smelly, the outside noises are not too distracting and the chairs are not too hard or wobbly. Clean up and brighten the room to make a pleasant learning environment. If children arrive without breakfast, provide granola bars, fruit, bagels or juice. A church located in a low-income neighborhood may want to sponsor a free meal program or a food pantry. The church may also need to provide clothing for children without warm coats or shoes.

Safety needs. Children need to feel secure and safe from harm. Establish an atmosphere of trust and love so that children feel comfortable in class. Follow your church's written procedures to protect children when they are picked up after class, being aware of restraining orders and not releasing children to noncustodial parents. Make sure there is an area in your classroom where children's belongings can be left without being stolen or destroyed. Let children know that you will not allow bullying in your classroom.

Social needs. Children want to be with those who love, affirm and accept them. They want friends and need to feel part of the group. They don't want to be ridiculed, criticized or ignored. Be sure that all children are included in class activities. Provide team-building and trust-building exercises. Let children pray and sing together to form community. Demonstrate acceptance of a child who may appear to be different in some way. Your caring actions will teach more about God's love than your words.

Children want to feel important and respected. They want their contributions to class (singing, reading, art, discussion) to be valued and welcomed. They like their artwork displayed, their photos on the bulletin board and their names listed in the church newsletter. They like to hear the teacher say, "You did a good job!" A child who does not feel valued will be more likely to withdraw from the class and unwilling to participate.

Special Concerns

Sometimes children will tell you about a special concern or worry; most often, however, they will not. Without prying, make an effort to learn about students' everyday lives and be sensitive to children's emotions. Some children clearly express their feelings; others are quiet and moody. Some children with ongoing emotional needs or who are experiencing difficult times in their lives may need you to be nearby for support.

Family problems. Children are affected by the problems faced by their family members: an older sibling facing trouble with the law, parents getting a divorce, parent dealing with unemployment or financial difficulties. Even a normally happy event, such as moving to a new house, going to a new school, the birth of a new sibling or the remarriage of a parent can cause stress and anxiety. You can provide support, comfort and love. In extreme situations, you may need to intervene. (Note: If you see signs of possible physical abuse in a child, notify your supervisor and follow established procedures.)

School situations. A student may have difficulty at school with low grades, a dislike for the schoolteacher, no friends, encounters with a bully, etc. Parents may demand that their child achieve high grades. Children may be overburdened and tired from too many after-school activities. Children want to feel popular among their classmates. There may be peer pressure to start dating or to have a "boyfriend/girlfriend" even among elementary-aged children. Students may feel pressure to buy expensive clothes or toys. Some children may even be approached by street gangs recruiting for new members. All of these concerns can prevent a child from concentrating in the classroom.

Emotional needs. A child may be dealing with an illness or disability that prevents him or her from functioning at peak efficiency. A child may have ADD/ADHD, depression, a mental illness or a learning disability. A child may be shy and find it difficult to socialize with other people. Some may have deeply rooted feelings of inadequacy or rejection. Some students come to class with "chips on their shoulders" and uncontrolled rage.

Intellectual needs. There are children who truly want to learn as much as they can. They are fascinated by the Bible, eager to serve God and willing to work hard. However, they feel discouraged and hindered by the students who don't share their interest. The effective teacher may need to find additional learning experiences for such children to keep their interest high.

You can do much to help meet students' needs. However, realize that you cannot solve every problem, make every student's life perfect, force people to change or make every situation right. You can forgive yourself for your human limitations, do your best to minister to your students and turn all things over to God. When you show that you are secure in your faith in God, your students are encouraged to also be confident of God's care in their own situations.

RELATIONSHIPS TRANSFORM LIVES

When we adults are focused on the details of getting through a class session, it can be easy to forget that no matter how good our activities or how important our point, nothing transforms a life more effectively than building a relationship. In fact, relationship is the very reason Christ died and rose—that we might live in relationship, first with God the Father through Him and then with each other by the power of His Spirit! Relationship is the essence of God's Kingdom.

Three Reasons to Care

▶ On any given day, a child who enters your classroom may be under tremendous stress. Even a young child may be dealing with situations such as a recent move, a new baby-sitter, death of a pet, lack of food or shelter, divorce or even child abuse. Attention from parents may be limited. We never know where a child has been emotionally and spiritually.

It is imperative that *every* child be given loving acceptance, hugs, smiles and genuine interest! Often the child with the most negative behavior is the one who needs the greatest measure of loving acceptance and positive interest.

▶ School settings generally cannot make up for a lack of relationship at home. Most teachers are overburdened and must focus on the group, rather than individual children. But we have the opportunity to minister to young children simply through seeing each one as a real person made in God's image. As we use each child's name, as we touch, talk and encourage each one as a person worthy of our respect and love, children absorb information about what God's love looks like, sounds like and feels like.

▶ Coming from different neighborhoods, children in a class may not know each other well. We can minister to them by gently helping them learn how to build relationships with other children in a safe, loving environment where relationship is valued highly. Children need to know that at church, people love them and love each other. These are people whom they can love freely and safely. There is no better place to begin building unity in the Body of Christ than here!

Three Benefits of Caring

▶ We are giving the child a model to imitate. Paul instructed in 1 Corinthians 11:1, "Follow my example, as I follow the example of Christ." Our job is to show, rather than tell, what it means to live as a follower of Jesus. As we are transparent with children, they will get to know us. They will begin to unconsciously identify with and imitate Christlike character, beliefs and values. Our smiles, our touches, our hugs and our gracious reactions to surprising situations teach more effectively what it means to live as a Christian than even good curriculum or excellent activities.

▶ As we help children get to know and appreciate each other, we are also leading them to experience the Church, the Body of Christ. Children have the chance to know firsthand that believers in Jesus live and work together as a team, living in sympathy and harmony, instead of competition.

▶ We benefit by getting to know young children! Not only do we become better teachers by understanding their needs and feelings, but we also have the delightful privilege of seeing the world through their fresh and unspoiled eyes! We often gain surprising insights that help us better understand Christ's desire that we come to His kingdom as little children.

Three Ways to Show You Care

Make it a rule in your classroom that these three behaviors welcome every child:

▶ Conversation and attention to what the child says at his or her eye level

▶ A kind touch on the shoulder

▶ A genuine smile that says, "I'm glad to see you today!"

The job of welcoming children should be assigned to the same helper or teacher each week so that children who have difficulty separating from their parents will have the opportunity to build a relationship with a friendly adult. Don't leave this important job unassigned. When children feel welcomed and are given a choice of activities as they enter, they will play and work together better and will more easily learn to obey God's Word in real, practical ways!

WELCOMING THE NEW CHILD

An effective class builds strong bonds between its students; however, this bond may be so tight that a new child can feel unwelcome. Students and teachers used to seeing the same faces each week may give a new child the feeling that they consider him or her an intruder. Teachers need to be extra attentive to the needs of new children, for their presence gives the class the chance to practice what they have learned!

The new child is already feeling uncomfortable walking into the class. He or she may have just moved into the area or the parents may be looking for a church home. The child may also be from an unchurched family cautiously trying out the church or a one-time guest in town to visit relatives. Your challenge is to make the child feel at home and invite the other students to welcome the new child.

Good preparation and a warm welcome will help make a visitor comfortable and eager to return another time. For a child not raised in the church, the routines of Sunday School and other church programs can be strange. Love, attention and guidance will ease their fear and discomfort.

A Good Beginning

Warmly greet each visitor and introduce yourself as he or she enters the classroom. If parents bring the child, introduce yourself to the parents as well. Ask the parents if the child has any special medical needs. Tell the parents when the child's class will end and invite the parents to attend an adult class or worship service. (Note: Some churches provide a central check-in place where visiting children are registered.)

Visitors may feel self-conscious if they are the only ones with name tags, so avoid using name tags unless every child wears one. Invite parents to stay for a short time if the child is having difficulty leaving them.

Take a moment to introduce the visitor to one or two buddies of the same gender. Introduce these children as the ones who will help the new child find his or her way around the room and guide the visitor in the class routine. The new child will feel that he or she has at least one friend already!

During Class

Invite a visitor to participate in class activities, but don't overdo the attention. You may be tempted to gush over a new child, but keep in mind that visitors don't like to be pointed out or given undue attention.

Because a new child may feel uncomfortable sharing books with strangers, always have extra activity sheets, Bibles and other class supplies on hand.

Your students may be used to lining up in a certain way or sitting around the table in the same chairs. To make it easier for newcomers to fit in, have a "visitor's spot" always available. This is an empty chair reserved for guests and a place in the line where newcomers can stand. A new child won't want to compete with other students for a place in line or a chair.

Allow the visitor to participate in discussion as much as he or she wishes, but don't expect it. A new child won't know what has been taught in previous sessions and may know little about the Bible. Avoid calling on the visitor to answer a fact-based question; however, an open-ended question ("How do you feel . . .") can be appropriate. Call the new child by name, but avoid referring to him or her as "our guest" or "the visitor" after the initial class introduction. The child doesn't need a constant reminder that he or she is not one of the group.

Be attentive if the new child needs help; however, don't hover over him or her. If the guest needs assistance, move near the child and speak quietly so as not to draw attention. A new child may not be able to find verses in the Bible, so help the child and the child's buddy find passages.

An unchurched child may feel awkward during prayer time. Indicate that it's all right for children not to be an active participant: "Now it's time to pray. That's when we talk to God. Some of us might want to pray aloud. Others of us might pray silently. Some of us may want to listen to other people pray. Whatever you choose is fine."

After Class

Be sure a visiting child leaves with all his or her belongings. Nobody wants to return to church to go to the lost-and-found office! If parents are late to pick up the child, stay with the child until they arrive. Never let a child wander through the building alone. Greet the parents as they arrive, and briefly mention an activity that the class enjoyed. Thank the parents for bringing their son or daughter to your class and let them know you look forward to seeing the child again. Inform parents about any routines related to children's programming at your church (children attend worship services for the first 10 minutes and then leave for age-level activities, children's choir or midweek club meeting, etc.). Within a day or two, send a postcard to the guest, thanking him or her for visiting your class.

HELPING PARENTS AND CHILDREN SAY GOOD-BYE

When some young children (especially in a class with two- and/or three-year-olds) enter a classroom and leave their parents behind for the first few times, chaos can ensue! What are some ways to make separation easier?

Allow Time and Acknowledge Feelings

Always remember (and gently remind parents) that when a child cries at separation time, it is not necessarily a problem. Young children *should* prefer their parents to a stranger! A child needs time to become familiar with you and the other adults in the class. This adjustment period is usually fairly brief, especially if teachers and helpers commit to teaching every week. Your calm reassurance of both parents and child will make the separation easier all around.

Say words that show you understand. "I know you are having a hard time. I know you'll miss your daddy. I know it's hard when your daddy leaves. He will be back soon." Help a child know that you recognize and accept his or her feelings.

Know that every child handles transitions differently. Some will cry again when it's time to leave! If a child is under stress (a parent is ill, parents are separated, a parent is gone a lot, etc.), he or she is more likely to be clingy and afraid. A child's anxiety may return from time to time. Just when a child seems comfortable with separation, he or she may revert back into anxiety. This is not a failure on anyone's part but simply a normal part of growth that is best dealt with calmly.

Establish a welcoming routine. Sing the same welcoming song every week, repeat the same poem or tell the child interesting things you'll be doing in class. Encourage a parent to tell the child that he or she will return: "I'll be back after you've played with toys and listened to a story." Then be ready to involve the child in an interesting activity. With a routine, children know what to expect, and separation should become easier.

Try These Tips

▶ The same person should greet an anxious child each time and involve him or her in an activity.

▶ Talk calmly to the child, even if he or she is crying loudly. Your gentle, soothing voice will help the child begin to relax. Communicate calmness and comfort by your words, voice and body posture. A young child will then be likely to relax as well! Singing softly to a young child is also very relaxing.

▶ For some children, too much contact too soon with a stranger results in more fear. Take time to talk further with the parent, so the child sees that the parent trusts and accepts you. If a child is obviously frightened by your attention, use indirect interaction. Begin an activity. Talk about what you are doing. As the child becomes involved, talk directly to the child.

▶ If the anxiety is severe, invite a parent to stay for a while, instead of coming back to check on a child repeatedly. (Checking back can amount to four or five good-byes, upsetting the child each time the parent leaves!) When a parent stays, try having him or her leave for five minutes and then come back for the remainder of the session. Over several sessions, increase the length of each absence until the child and parent are comfortable with separation.

▶ Send a picture of the teachers home with the child or visit the family to increase familiarity. Remind parents that when they bring their child each week, repetition and familiarity help to keep separation from becoming a weekly problem. Tell parents about a specific activity or other child the child seemed to enjoy. Encourage parents to talk with the child about coming to "build with the big blocks" or "play with your friend Madeline," rather than just "coming to church."

HELPING THE YOUNG CHILD MAKE GOOD CHOICES

When the adult makes all the choices (what color paper to use in an art activity, where each person sits at the table, what game to play, etc.), the adult is also the one doing the most learning. In order for children to truly be learning, they must be more than passive receivers of information. Giving children repeated opportunities to make choices provides many benefits, not only to the child, but also to the adult.

The Benefits of Making Choices

Making choices helps a child develop a sense of independence. This is not independence from authority and direction but independence that produces responsibility, allowing the child to make good choices. Never allowing a child to make a choice can be harmful, now and in the years to come. If a child is always looking for someone else to make decisions, he or she can become a pawn for a strong authority figure to lead astray.

Making small choices, such as which color crayon to use or whether to build with blocks or play with the dress-up clothes, can actually help prepare a young child to make life's larger decisions. Because the child eventually must "choose . . . this day whom you will serve" (Joshua 24:15), we must help children develop wise choice-making skills. The child who is rarely allowed to make decisions may find it harder to make the ultimate decision of responding to Jesus Christ.

A child develops a sense of responsibility through making choices. A responsible person is one who makes a choice after having fully considered the consequences of that choice. Learning to be accountable for choices made will help the child in making responsible choices.

Allowing children to make some of their own choices will help you avoid discipline problems. Children's behaviors are more positive when they are doing something they have chosen. In contrast, when a child is told to do something he or she doesn't want to do, he or she becomes unhappy and usually will let everyone know it.

Allowing a child to make choices tells the child you believe he or she is capable of making a decision. Your trust is an essential foundation for a child's healthy development.

How to Present Choices

Limit the number of choices to two or three, and be firm about behavior that is not an acceptable option. "Would you rather build with the blocks or glue pictures? It is not time yet to play outside."

Offer choices that are not mutually exclusive. "Which book would you rather look at first? The book about friends or the one about animals?"

Comment positively about the different choices children make. "Abby chose yellow paper for her collage and Andrew chose black. Each of us can choose a different color."

TEACHING ABOUT DECISION-MAKING

Adults often view themselves as the persons with the right knowledge and correct answers to give to uninformed children. As a teacher, you may think that it's easier and quicker to tell children what to do and how to think than to teach children how to make decisions for themselves.

There are many things that a child cannot control: who is in their family, where they live, what their parents' occupations are or which school they attend. Still, children do have a surprising number of choices that they make daily. The choices they make now will help them learn how to make significant decisions for the future. Mentor children by giving them practice in making appropriate choices.

Why Teach Children About Decision-Making?

To develop responsibility. Today, a child's biggest decision may be what kind of cereal to eat. As an adult, he or she must choose a career, a spouse, where to live, how to vote, and how to serve God and humanity. Making small choices now will give a child knowledge and experience which builds into greater ability to make important decisions later in life.

To develop confidence. A child who is not allowed to make little choices now will not feel that he or she can make good decisions later on in life. A child who is told constantly what to do can be easily swayed by other people. Children may later be resentful or angry about the choices made for them. A child without experience or confidence in decision-making may make bad choices based on rebellion, emotion or lack of information.

To teach independence. A child will not be under the guidance of his or her parents forever. At some point the child must set his or her own course, start a new family and possibly move far away. Making good choices now will help a child move into mature independence.

To facilitate good behavior. Discipline problems can be averted when children choose what they want to do from among options you provide. Letting children make small choices in class will give them ownership of their learning and maintain their interest.

To make godly choices. A teacher can lead a child to God but the child must make the decision of discipleship for him- or herself. You cannot force a child to live the Christian life. By making good choices now, a child will be more likely to choose a lifestyle pleasing to God when he or she is older.

How Do I Teach About Decision-Making?

Plan age-appropriate choices. Children can begin by making small choices (write or draw their answers to questions, which section of a mural on which to draw, etc.) and be given increased responsibility as they grow older. Don't burden children with decisions beyond their experience and knowledge.

Be supportive. If a child wants to color a picture with only black and brown markers, that's OK. Children may not make the best or most rational decision, but affirm them as long as their choice is not disruptive, is not harmful to themselves or others or is not morally wrong.

Role-play. Older children can act out scenarios where they pretend to be in difficult situations, such as when they see another student cheating on a test. Act out different endings to the situation and discuss the best choice.

Provide active learning. Obviously, children are too immature to completely govern their lives. However, in the classroom, children will be more interested when they have some control over their learning. Allow children the opportunity to make choices in class:

► Choose between two activities prepared in the classroom.

► Choose the colors and materials for art projects.

► Select which Bible verse to memorize.

► Decide which part to play in a Bible story script.

► Decide on a team name for a game.

► Select a service project for the class.

► Design a banner or a logo for the class T-shirt.

With active learning, be sure that all the students have an opportunity to make decisions. Be careful that one or two strong-willed students don't intimidate the more quiet children.

Experience consequences. When students make a less-than-perfect choice and it causes no physical or emotional harm to them or their peers, let them experience the consequences. Adults who constantly protect a child or cover for a child's mistake will not let the child learn the actual results of behavior. If a child is constantly late to class, don't wait to start a fun activity. If two children constantly distract each other, then tell those children they will need to be separated for a while. When children see that their behavior has consequences, they learn to make better choices.

Distinguish between good and evil. Modern society expects each person to decide what is ethically and morally right for him- or herself. But to make good moral choices, children need to know what God expects! While God allows people to choose their actions, His established behavior standards never change. Teach children what God expects from His children.

Use biblical examples. The Bible shows the consequences of good and bad decisions. The Israelites chose to worship an idol and God punished them. Mary chose to give birth to Jesus and helped bring salvation to the world. Use Bible stories to show child what great things can happen when decisions are made that honor God.

Building Relationships Tips

All of us long to feel that we matter to someone. If we expect the children we teach to show love, then we must be sure they feel our love for them! It is only as they receive love that they then can learn how to show love. As you pray for each child, ask God to make you alert to ways you can show love to him or her. Then do!

Here are five steps to demonstrating love to a child: Place yourself at the child's eye level. Look at that child with kindness. Use the child's name often as you speak. Ask open-ended questions (questions that cannot be answered *yes* or *no*) about things that interest that child. Listen twice as much as you talk!

When you are in a classroom with other adults, temptation is great to catch up on news while children seem to be absorbed in an activity. Resist the temptation! Being available to the children instead of chatting with the other adults sends kids the message that to you, they are the top priority. Such honor and attention reaps eternal benefits!

Remember the words *acknowledge* and *encourage*. Every child (and every adult!) thrives on knowing that you see and appreciate him or her. **Jordan, I see you built a tower. You stacked the blocks yourself. Thank you for doing good work!** Your words, your facial expression and body language will tell the child that he or she has value in your eyes!

When talking with children, show the same kindness and courtesy you would show adults. When we interrupt a child's conversation, we show a lack of consideration and model just the kind of behavior we don't want children to imitate! Before you speak, ask yourself, *Would I talk that way to a grown-up friend? Would I use that tone of voice?*

All children need to feel a sense of belonging. As you talk, always use inclusive words such as "we," "let's," "our church," and "all of us."

A child who asks, "Will you do this for me?" may be feeling pressured to do things perfectly. Remind children, **In our class, it's OK to make a mistake. It's part of learning!** Help the child figure out how to accomplish the task. Try responses such as, **That does look tricky. Let's work on it together.** When a child does make a mistake, show complete acceptance. Focus on the positive. **That's OK. We learned something. Let's clean it up together!**

Make this a personal rule: In every session, with every child, I will take a moment to focus on, listen to and encourage something I have noticed in that child. It can be as simple as saying, **Ali, I see you were careful not to hit Bono when you moved. Thank you. That is a way to be kind!**

Building Relationships Tips

Every child needs to feel safe and loved in your classroom. If a child seems to be quiet-natured, don't call the child "shy." (The child may try to live up to that label!) Don't insist that every child talk in a large group. Because there is often a great deal of attention focused on the dramatic or outgoing class members, make sure to give personal attention and encouragement to quiet children without making them the center of attention. Look for ways to include them such as handing out markers or keeping score.

When minor calamities arise, help a child feel that it isn't the end of the world. **Uh-oh. The juice spilled. That's OK. Here is a sponge, Thomas. You can wipe it up.** When the job is complete say, **Wow! Thomas, you did a good job of cleaning up the juice. Thank you!** This may seem trivial to you but it's a real expression of love to Thomas when you are calm, accepting and confident in his ability.

To help children build relationships among themselves, acknowledge the joy they get from being together ("You boys have such fun together!"), the positive ways they treat each other ("You were kind to give Jake the glue stick") and the skills they have gained ("You and Rosa have learned how to share very well!").

Plan ways to spend time with your children outside the classroom. This will strengthen your relationships with them. Planning an outing to which siblings and parents are also invited or visiting in their homes helps you understand each one better and shows a child you care!

If a child seems uncomfortable entering the classroom, invite him or her to choose one of the quieter activities available. Children who seem to be irritable or over-stimulated will also profit from quiet activities that help restore a sense of self-control. Your calm, friendly manner will also help children relax!

Vary the process by which you form small groups or teams during a session. Allow children to group themselves into teams and after a round of play announce, **If you are wearing (red), move to another team.** Then play another round and let people wearing another color move. This gives children a chance to play on the same team with a variety of others.

When giving instructions to a child, be sure to put yourself at eye level and use the child's name. Say the most important words first. **Jon, please pick up the papers.** Be specific. Instead of "Clean up that mess!" (so general that it confuses most kids) say, **Shea, please put the glue bottles away. Linsey, please put the markers in the basket.** Thank each child by name. **Thank you, Linsey. You are doing what God's Word says to do. God says to help each other!**

Participate in games with children, rather than merely giving directions. This not only builds relationship with the children but also gives you a chance to show children God's love by your actions, especially when the unexpected happens! **Oh dear! I stepped on your foot. I am sorry, Jill. I hope you're OK.** Real-life reactions teach more than carefully planned speeches!

Show children the same respect that you would show to adults.

Your helpful actions, your gentle voice and your friendly smile can say "I love you."

Model for children

the kind of behavior

you want them to show.

KEEPING ORDER AMONG YOUNG DISCIPLES

The word "discipline" comes from the root "disciple" which means "student." Jesus' disciples were His students who learned from His words and actions. Maintaining discipline in the classroom should have the goal that each student is able to learn without distraction. Many behavior problems can be avoided with preventive methods that remove distractions. When problems do arise, behaviors can be viewed as learning opportunities in which the teacher can help a child understand how God's Word can make a difference in even difficult situations.

Preventive Measures

Love and pray for each child. Be a teacher who has a love for God and a love for children, remembering that when a child is the most difficult is the time the child most needs your understanding and love! Look for specific words and actions that will help each child feel loved and wanted. A child may come from a troubled family life or an overcrowded school. Church may be the one place he or she feels safe and appreciated! A child who feels accepted and cared for is likely to display positive behavior. When you pray for an individual child, it increases your love and commitment to them.

Plan a full lesson with choices of activities. Bored children are likely to be disruptive! Keep children interested from the first moment they walk through the door. Prepare a variety of things to do: music, stories, puppets, art activities, games, etc. A good curriculum will offer several choices of activities. As you get to know the interests and abilities of your class, choose the activities that will keep the children involved. Keep some basic game and art supplies on hand if the lesson runs short or if a planned activity doesn't work as well as you thought it would.

Keep the class moving. Children cannot sit still for long periods of time. They have short attention spans. Video games and television have geared children to expect a constant flow of entertainment. Give students plenty of activities that let them move and play as well as quiet time. Avoid spending too much time on one activity; keep the energy level high by changing the pace and location of activities (sit on the floor to hear a story or participate in a discussion, complete an art activity seated at a table, etc.). If children display signs of disinterest (talking to each other, wandering away, etc.), be ready to move on to the next activity.

Prepare all needed materials. Children get restless if the teacher has to hunt for markers, find the missing CD or leave the room to make photocopies. Before class, make a list of all necessary lesson items, books, music, game materials, etc. Put all items in the room ahead of time so that they can be quickly retrieved. If the room is in use immediately before your class, place items in order of use in a container or on a movable cart that you can bring in to the classroom at the last minute. When using audiocassettes, CDs, videocassettes or DVDs, cue the material before class so that the music/program can be started immediately (and be sure you've practiced using the player). Make sure there are enough Bibles for children (if they don't bring their own) and some for visitors.

Use age-appropriate activities. The curriculum you use provides activities for the age level you teach. However, you may still need to modify activities to account for varying levels of skills. Offer drawing or writing as a way to respond to a question, or invite children to give oral responses. Especially in the first few weeks of your class, carefully observe students to evaluate their skills so that in the future you can plan activities better suited to their abilities.

Use sufficient staffing. Ideally, each class is led by two teachers with a ratio of one adult for every six to eight children. One teacher leads the activity while the other teacher(s) help guide behavior or assist students in completing activities. If your class is not sufficiently staffed, ask your supervisor for advice or invite parents to each take a turn helping in the class.

Set limits. Problem behavior occurs when children have unclear boundaries. Set several limits and follow them at each session: "When I flick the lights, I need for you to look at me." "We clean up after art projects." "We stay in the room during class time." Phrase your boundaries in positive terms, telling children what you want them to do rather than what you want them to stop doing.

Praise good behavior. Let children know that their helpful actions are appreciated. Children like to please you. Be sure that all children are affirmed.

Learn about the children. Some children have medical difficulties or special abilities that may cause unusual behavior or interfere with their learning. Talk to the parents and find out what can be done to enhance the child's learning experience.

Dealing with Problem Behavior

Even with the best preparation, discipline problems will arise. Real-life, imperfect children will present teachers with a variety of problem behaviors. The goal at that moment is not just to end the disruption but also to help the child learn.

Avoid embarrassment. Whenever possible, talk to a child individually about a problem behavior. An embarrassed child may act up even more to "save face" in front of peers.

Avoid hostility. Teachers need to be levelheaded, mature adults who do not lose their temper. Shouting, berating, humiliating or grabbing a child are not forms of discipline but forms of abuse. When you find a child's behavior or attitude is causing you to get upset, take a deep breath, whisper a prayer and seek to show love, not anger.

Be assertive. State what the child needs to do ("Keep your hands to yourself," "Listen when others speak") with firmness but not anger. If the child whines, argues or makes excuses, repeat the statement. Some children are skilled at manipulating adults with arguments or bargaining, so avoid debating with the child. When the child sees that the adult will not give in to his or her demands, the behavior is likely to cease.

Get the facts. Avoiding asking a child, "Why did you hit Tracy?" This question implies that if the child can come up with a good enough reason, the wrong behavior will be justified! The goal is not to get the child to explain or blame but to honestly confront what he or she did. So ask the child, "What did you do that was a problem?"

Facing the consequences. If a child continues to misbehave after you have tried to redirect the problem behavior, the child may need to forfeit a privilege related to the activity at hand. If the child misuses markers or game supplies, then he or she cannot participate in activities using those materials until more responsibility is demonstrated. Try saying, "I know you will have a good time playing this game, but until you can wait to take your turn with the beanbags, you'll need to stand here by me." Help children understand that the class will be more enjoyable for everyone when each child cooperates.

While it is preferable for discipline challenges to be handled in the classroom by the teacher, with the help of a supervisor if needed, there may be times when it is necessary to talk with parents about their child's behavior. Communicate positively with parents, asking them for advice on how to help their child participate more enjoyably and effectively.

GOALS AND METHODS FOR GUIDING YOUNG CHILDREN

Definition and Goal

It's common to hear an adult say in exasperation, "What that child needs is some discipline!" It's true that a young child's behavior might frustrate us. It's also true that every adult, parent and teacher has expectations of how a child should act. But it is very important that we understand first what discipline is.

One meaning of "discipline" is "training that corrects, molds and makes complete or perfect." Let's look to Jesus for a definition of "discipline." What did Jesus do to correct and mold adults (who often did not live up to His expectations) and bring them to a place of maturity? Jesus chose *disciples* who would be *disciplined,* or trained, by Him. His goal for their training was for them to become mature in Him, ready to take His Word all over the world. How did He train them? By giving out punishment? By making rules? No. He did it by living with them! Jesus gave them a walking, talking, breathing, listening example of what He wanted them to become. He taught more often by action and attitude than even by word. Most of the disciples' time with Jesus was spent observing and then doing.

What is our goal, then, for the discipline of our children? Good discipline is not what we do to a child but what we do with and for him or her. We guide a child to help him or her grow toward self-control in knowing and doing what is good. We give loving guidance to establish a positive atmosphere for learning!

Methods

"Love me and accept me as I am." Such love gives a child what he or she needs to grow and develop. Children long to feel that someone cares about them and that they are people of worth and value. When a child enters the room, put yourself at his or her eye level. Listen attentively to what a child has to tell. When a child's behavior is out of bounds, kindly redirect the child. Phrase your directions positively: tell the child what he or she *may* do, instead of what he or she may *not* do. Rather than scold or shame a child, focus on the child's behavior. "Chris, we keep the dough on the table. You may pick up what is on the floor. Then you may choose what kind of animal you'd like to make. I see Kelly is making a snake."

Telling Chris he is a bad boy or giving him a list of reasons why we don't throw dough will not help him refocus and choose ways to change. Kindness, clear directions and choices within limits will help any child learn good discipline!

"If you do it, I will do it, too." Children watch constantly. If they hear you talk about how important it is to pick up trash but see you drop paper on the ground, expect that they will drop paper, too. The actions you do, teach far more than the words you say.

"Let me know what is coming next." Young children thrive on the security that comes from knowing the routine. "After we clean up the blocks, we will have our story." Keeping the same order during every class session helps make young children feel calm and secure. Variety is the spice of life, but it is best used sparingly with young children. One surprise a day is plenty!

"I need choices to make." Provide a variety of interesting things for children to do. When children have a choice of activities, they are much more likely to be interested in the activity and are far less likely to create discipline problems; too many choices can have the same detrimental effect. "Tawny, you may make a picture, build with blocks or dress up in the drama corner."

"I need a place to work." If you expect children to work and move without bumping into each other, be sure your room provides enough space to work. Can the room be rearranged so that children can move more easily? What can be cleaned up or discarded so that the room has adequate space for each child?

Responses to Unacceptable Behaviors

With all of our best work and most loving intentions, there will still be those moments when a child misbehaves in a way that requires immediate verbal intervention. For young children, we have only about 10 seconds to correct the behavior in any way that will have meaning for them.

Hitting or Kicking: "Rina, kicking hurts. I cannot let you hurt Dylan. Use words to tell Dylan what you want." Separate the children. Comfort Dylan briefly, and then help Rina move to another activity if need be. Stay with her until she is involved.

Biting: Biting may be motivated by curiosity with very young preschoolers or by frustration and anger as children get older. (Most children know biting is not OK by the time they are around three.) "Biting hurts. We don't hurt other people. We use our teeth for chewing food." Comfort the one bitten and let an adult helper clean the wound and fill out a report. Separate the children. NEVER encourage the one bitten to bite back. It won't help the biter and will create many more problems!

Using Offensive Words: "In our class, we use kind words. That is not a kind word. Alex is building a good tower. You're building a good tower, too." When you say kind words to the verbal offender, you let that child know that you care about him or her regardless of the behavior. That teaches kindness very effectively!

Having a Tantrum: If there is no response to words, hold the child firmly but gently until he or she calms down. Holding the child offers protection as well as control. If other children are frightened by the tantrum, let an adult helper gently take the tantrum-thrower to another room while you briefly explain what is happening. "Kerry is having a hard time. She will be OK soon."

Distracting Others: We all like attention. Most of what human beings do is designed to get attention from another person! When a child is distracting others who are trying to listen, ask a helper to sit beside the child. Sometimes just a touch or an arm around the shoulders will refocus the child. Always make behavior the child's choice. "Tim, if you want to stay in the circle by Jon, you will need to stop kicking your feet. You can sit pretzel style or sit with your legs in front of you." Now there is a choice to be made. The decision is up to Tim. Give a child time to adjust. If Tim continues to kick, say, "Tim, I see you are still kicking. You need to move away from Jon now. You need to sit by Miss Emily." Signal your helper to move the child next to her. When you have simply and positively stated what needs to happen, follow through with the consequences you stated if the child doesn't change behavior.

If more than one child is showing signs of restlessness, recognize that it is time for a change of pace! Stand up, stretch, do a quick finger-fun activity or sing a song. Young children's muscles quickly grow tired in one position. Everyone will be better able to sit still if sitting times are not too long!

When we remember the goals of discipline, the methods of discipline and the power of our own example, discipline becomes the positive tool it is designed to be.

What Can Children Learn About Sharing?

We allow our expectations for each child to vary according to our understanding of his or her unique developmental pace. But when it comes to sharing, grown-ups may hold expectations that are less realistic! To adults, taking turns, or sharing, means cooperation and equal participation. But it has a far different meaning to a child. To young children, taking turns means one child has to give up something, with the possibility of being left with nothing in its place. To the child, it doesn't seem fair! Yet sharing is important and necessary for children to learn as they grow and mature.

Characteristics

Expect that younger preschoolers will not understand much of what it means to share or ways to share. Two-year-olds are discovering the boundaries between themselves and others. "NO!" and "MINE!" help describe those boundaries—and others' rights are not yet understood! Since twos are often involved in parallel play (alongside others but not with them), conflicts may be fierce but less common. Three-year-olds are more likely to interact in play with others and "M-I-I-INE!" is still a familiar cry. When conflict arises with younger preschoolers, it's usually more effective to distract them than to talk too much. For instance, as Mia grabs Joe's ball, describe what you see: "Mia, I see you want the blue ball." Describe a solution: "It is Joe's turn with the blue ball. Here is another ball for you to play with." If you promise a turn with the blue ball later, be sure to keep your word!

Four- and five-year-olds are growing in social awareness. They also have more of a desire to please others and have grown both in their ability to wait and in their understanding that taking a turn means you get to keep it—but only for a while. Acknowledge and encourage children's actions of sharing. "Darla, you shared the block with Brandon. Thank you! That is a way to be kind, as our Bible says to do."

Ideas into Actions

Because taking turns, being kind and sharing are not concrete ideas, they are not grasped in a single class session or through a single lecture.

First, sharing must be demonstrated—by us. Describe ways to share as you demonstrate them. "Liam, I am cutting the apple into slices so that we can all share. Here is one slice for you and one slice for Ethan." When we model kindness and sharing, children see it as well as hear it. They learn far more than when we use words alone! For real learning to take place, examples and experiences must be repeated. Describe these experiences aloud to give children more ways to gain understanding.

To some children, taking turns will still feel like losing out. Because of a child's natural self-centeredness and short memory, it may seem to them that their turn never comes! When you intervene in a dispute, point out times when you have seen a child receive kind actions of others. "Nicki, Meg gave you first turn with the doll. She shared with you. You are sharing with her now. It is her turn. There will still be time for you to have another turn." After Meg has finished with the doll, say, "Nicki, Meg had her turn. Now it is your turn."

As you watch children peacefully involved in an activity together, don't assume that you are not needed! Watch carefully and give suggestions to help children think of ways to share.

"Bill, Heidi needs a truck. You have lots of trucks. What could you do to help Heidi?" Keep comments and suggestions brief; children's attention spans are short!

In an art activity, provide two or three of items such as scissors and glue bottles to be shared by four to six children. Large-scale art activities such as murals and collages help children learn to work side by side. While each child's contribution will be unique, the child will enjoy feeling part of a group effort.

Block and dramatic play activities also provide children with opportunities to practice sharing. Children will enjoy taking turns to stack blocks for a tower. The shared task of building a road will also help children learn to make decisions about how they will work together. In dramatic play, encourage activities such as cleaning house or preparing a pretend meal. Such tasks enable children to have fun while learning ways to help each other.

Expect that a child's willingness to share will vary from week to week. This is a normal part of development. Solve problems in a matter-of-fact manner. "Mara, it's time to give Leia a turn. Maybe next week it will be easier for you to share. Giving a turn is a way to share, like our Bible tells us to do." Simply state the Bible principle; don't force the child.

DISCIPLINE AND PRETEENS

Whether you are a leader of teachers, an experienced teacher yourself, or a novice just getting into preteen ministry, you will need to be ready for some unique behavior challenges that arise in groups of early adolescents. Here are some creative ways to prevent discipline problems before they happen and ways to consistently help students understand and assume the responsibility for their own choices.

▶ **"I'm unique."** Each early adolescent is completely unique and is maturing socially, physically, emotionally, mentally and spiritually at his or her own rate. This means that we have the challenging task of treating each child individually as we determine what we can rightfully expect of him or her and what guidance would be most beneficial to the student and the situation.

There are few cut-and-dried methods that apply for disciplining kids at these ages. While a boy in your class may be into puppies and frogs, the girl sitting next to him may be thinking about makeup, boys and the latest teen idol. We are dealing with kids all across the developmental spectrum. Our discipline methods, whatever they may be, must recognize each child's uniqueness.

▶ **"I'm misunderstood!"** Early adolescents truly believe that they are so different from anyone else in the world that no one could possibly understand their problems, the reasons they do what they do and their feelings. Subsequently they easily fall into a whining and complaining mode concerning home, school and church. Though adults may think the appropriate response is to fix these things, they must realize these named externals are not the true battle. The battle is actually within the early adolescent.

As teachers, we need to realize that we should listen to kids through a filter. For most of our kids, their parents, siblings, teachers, homework load, chores and the rest of life could not possibly be as bad as they would have us believe! The wise leader will listen intently, realizing that the child is sharing an important, emotional message with us, however inaccurate or exaggerated it may be. The leaders should focus on helping the student learn to deal with disappointments and frustrations and to handle their problems in a Christlike manner. The currently popular "WWJD" (What Would Jesus Do?) bracelets offer a great tool for early adolescents to use to work through their episodes of self-pity.

▶ **"I'm changing."** Early adolescence is a period of change; so on any given Sunday, the student you thought you had all figured out last week could suddenly show up as a completely different kid. What the child likes one week, the adolescent will not put up with the next. Emotional roller coasters are a normal part of the preteen's life. And peer pressure and constantly changing fads will further complicate things.

▶ **"I'm tired."** Preteens are experiencing so many physical changes that they are often truly fatigued. They need more rest than they have needed for years. Overly tired kids have a very difficult time controlling their emotions and therefore their behavior.

Be ready to cut your kids some slack on big holiday weekends when you know they will have stayed up too late. When you're involved in activities, make sure to plan in some downtime to let kids rest. They probably will not admit that they are tired if they are doing something fun, but you need to insist on rest. It's the adult who must make decisions about schedules in order to avoid overtiring kids and creating attitude and discipline problems.

▶ **"I'm fragile."** A preteen will do almost anything to avoid being trapped in an embarrassing situation. The trapped student may become a clown or an angry aggressor to protect him- or herself from a perceived threat. When a student behaves in an unusual manner, stop to evaluate whether he or she is feeling insecure about something going on in your classroom.

One place this behavior may show up is when you are dividing kids into teams, small groups, or vehicles. At this age level, we want to stretch kids to meet others and to learn to be social with the opposite gender. However, we must not force them into a social setting that they do not have the skills to handle.

Try to group kids so that each student has at least one friend with him or her. Be sure to have at least two kids of the same gender in each group. A boy or girl who feels alone in a group will get little out of the discussion or activity and may become a discipline challenge.

Early adolescents are vulnerable emotionally, so they need protection from others. The wise teacher will not allow students to inflict pain on one another. Nor will the teacher engage in put-downs, sarcasm or other hurtful remarks disguised as humor.

▶ **"I'm supercharged."** Preteens are full of energy that needs to be channeled. Girls will be particularly susceptible to the effects of hormones as exhibited by mood swings. Boys will be especially rowdy and physical.

It is normal for kids to have a lot of energy. The physical changes that result in these characteristics are part of God's design for their growing bodies.

Physical energy needs to be channeled into movement within lessons and activities. Let the kids get up and change seats, move to a different part of the room, form groups of various sizes and play games or be involved in activities that help illustrate the point of the lesson.

Emotional energy needs to be expressed in the context of relationships. Learn to listen to kids. Help your kids learn to listen to each other. Create an environment that says it's okay to share emotions. One practical tool is to reflect to the student what he or she has shared without showing any approval or disapproval, just acceptance of the reality of the emotions.

When students do get emotional or physical, our best response is to remain calm and even-tempered. This self-discipline models for the students the behavior we desire (appropriate self-control) and it keeps us from further escalating the behavior. Challenging or punishing kids who are being "hormonal" will only lead to more severe discipline problems.

▶ **"I'm angry and afraid. I need to be loved and forgiven."** Two common emotions that can both result in behavior problems are anger and fear. These are dual emotions. When the preteen is fearful, he or she often reacts in anger to protect him- or herself. Fatigue, feelings of inadequacy and fear of rejection are all common elements of the preteen's life and all can lead to "acting out" behaviors.

If you minister to the preteen's needs, you can help prevent behavior problems. Affirm your student's sense of personal worth by praising the student personally and frequently. Make the preteen feel secure in your classroom by using his or her name, giving nonverbal acceptance such as smiles, eye contact and appropriate touch. Make unconditional love the basis of your relationship with each child. Even when they do act out, make sure that you express your forgiveness, acceptance and understanding (none of which requires you to approve of their behavior).

▶ **"I'm bored."** Rest assured. Preteens are supposed to say this. It's in their contract with God! Early adolescents are supposed to go around saying, "I'm bored." Many leaders lose their confidence when their kids start spouting that age-old complaint. After all, we kill ourselves to entertain these kids and they still say, "This is boring!"

Many preteens can't wait to get to the youth program, often encouraged by older siblings or parents to act older than they really are, and they end up missing out on the fun that they should be having in the programs actually designed for their age level. Symptoms of this malady include ditching programs and complaining of boredom or that everything is too babyish.

Don't lose your confidence. Just smile. Listen to them. Don't react to them. Just keep on doing what you know is right for them. There's no use trying to get them to violate their contract with God!

▶ **"I'm too cool."** The preteen is saying to him- or herself, *Everyone is looking at me.* So the logical conclusion is for the preteen to do what he or she thinks all these other people want him or her to do, to be what they want him or her to be. The preteen's perception of his or her peers will greatly influence the preteen's behavior. The preteen's insecurity with his or her own identity and the desire to be accepted by peers will make it important for the preteen to follow the behavior of others. Rather than addressing the symptoms, make sure that what you are doing *is* cool:

▶ Your activities and classroom need to be fun and what kids think is cool.

▶ Make sure that you are perceived by the students as being a fun person. Don't be uptight.

▶ Have both male and female leaders in your room. Boys, especially, have a need to see male role models who prove that it's possible to be a cool adult, male Christian.

▶ Build strong relationships with your students—especially the kids who you see as leaders. They will lead others into accepting your activities.

▶ Have fun yourself, and get involved in your own activities to set the example. Kids will follow the lead of an adult to whom they are able to relate.

▶ **"I don't want to."** This is another common attitude problem that you will eventually experience in preteen ministry. If you give an early adolescent enough time to think about it, he or she will come up with a reason not to do *whatever* you have planned—no matter how wonderful it may be.

So rarely tell preteens what is coming next, at least not everything. Don't announce all the details of your program in advance. Just tell the kids the basics of what they need to know, such as where to meet and what to bring, and then let them be surprised! (This also gives you an "out" in case you have to switch gears midstream.)

▶ **"I'm learning to think for myself."** Don't be shocked, angry or defeated when your students question the existence of God or the truth of the Bible. They may even temporarily claim to not believe at all. More commonly, preteens will question morality and value choices. They'll want to know:

▶ Is it really wrong to steal?

▶ What's so terrible about cheating?

▶ Is it OK to lie? (Especially if you can get away with it?)

Some of these questions may be an attempt to shock you. But others are a necessary part of the child's search to internalize values that were once automatically accepted from parents and other authorities.

These questions are not meant as challenges to your beliefs and are not meant to put you on the spot. Students this age are simply challenging their own beliefs as they rethink what they have learned from their parents and other adults. Embrace this process, because it is a necessary step that the child must take in order to move toward independence and adult faith.

Always welcome and honor the student's faith and morality questions. Enthusiastically receive them and respond to them respectfully. Let them know that asking questions is good. The more unconditional love students feel while they are searching, the more likely they are to come through the process spiritually healthy on the other side.

Intellectually, preteens are transitioning from concrete thinking to abstract thinking. Like most of the changes in early adolescents, these modes of thinking will advance at irregular and individual paces. Be prepared for a variety of cognitive levels and answers that reflect them.

Use open-ended questions to help all of your learners be involved. Encourage the questioning inherent with the maturing thought processes of preteens as they rethink their faith. Stretch them to think more and to ask more questions. Walk closely with preteens through this time of internalizing faith and values.

▶ **"I want to sit with my friends."** Friendships are important to preteens and fitting into the group becomes a high priority. Kids will do whatever it takes to make friends and keep them. They are far more interested in their social standing than in your lesson, so allowing kids to sit with a friend removes one obstacle to creating a good environment for learning.

As an early adolescent rethinks his or her beliefs, the influence of peers will weigh more heavily on decisions than ever before. And though the preteen's parents will influence him or her less, the parent still has a profound influence on the child. For these reasons, don't fight the preteen's desire to be with friends at church, even though these friendships may at times appear to create discipline problems.

The way you group boys and girls at this age can either create or prevent behavior problems. Give kids a chance to be with one or two friends during any small group, class or activity. Occasionally being with a friend causes problems, but this privilege can also be used as an incentive to motivate the kids toward good behavior. Explain that if sitting with a friend causes a disruption, the friends will be separated. The desire to be with friends is so powerful that most students will be strongly motivated to behave!

If you are wondering if boys and girls are compatible in the same group, you're not alone! As adolescence approaches, girls tend to mature more rapidly than boys. So a group with both fifth and sixth graders is likely to have noticeable differences in maturity levels between older girls and younger boys. Some leaders choose the path of least resistance and completely separate girls and boys. However, if both girls and boys are involved in an interesting activity, they are unlikely to create a disturbance over who happens to be working alongside.

▶ **"I want to talk and talk and talk!"** If you are trying to use a lecture style of teaching and do not adequately account for the social needs of your students, you create an atmosphere ripe for discipline problems. Be sure to plan in regular neighbor nudges and small-group discussion in which all of your students have the opportunity to talk. They will talk anyway, so plan for this time to be profitable by telling them when they can do it and what they will discuss.

PREVENT DISCIPLINE PROBLEMS WITH PRETEENS

Filling Your Students' Emotional Tanks

The first job of a preteen teacher is to do whatever he or she can do to fill early adolescents' emotional tanks. There are many ways to do this:

► Listen carefully and sensitively to them when they want to share.

► Encourage them to be their best.

► Encourage them when they feel their worst.

► Accept them just the way they are.

► Phone them during the week.

► Remember their birthdays.

► Write notes to them "just because."

► Honor special achievements.

► Spend time together doing things kids like to do.

► Attend special functions, such as games, concerts and award ceremonies.

► Pray for their special needs.

Your second job is to avoid draining the emotional tanks of your preteen students. With preteens there is a fine line between having a sense of humor and putting kids down. Keep your smile, but never embarrass these fragile egos.

Making Your Boundaries Clear

► **Kids want and need boundaries.** If a child never pushes against the boundaries, the child never gains the security he or she needs. Expect kids to test you. Sometimes when kids are pushing the limits and complaining about rules, they are truly asking you to show them love by *not* giving into their requests or demands. In their attempt to relate to the cool early adolescents, some leaders mistakenly think that they must remove all or almost all of the boundaries. This is simply not true. Removing boundaries causes insecurity that leads to further acting out as the preteen desperately searches for some boundary further away from normal behavior.

Part of our role in the classroom is to be the solid rock that kids can test, push away, and then come back to when they need to be loved and filled up again. When we do not consistently enforce limits, we lose our ability to be the secure foundation that kids want and need.

► **Expect the best.** As mentors and disciplers of preteens, we need to have the highest of expectations for the early adolescents we lead. These kids desperately want to know how to live and they want to know how to please us. Our expectations will subtly show through in all we do. The students pick up on these expectations and consciously or subconsciously attempt to live up to them. Therefore, if we believe the best and hope the best, we're more likely to get the best!

▶ **Tell the kids what you want.** Some discipline problems exist not because there are no boundaries but simply because we have never made clear to the kids what those boundaries are. We must remember that our kids have different adults with different expectations in every sphere of life: school, home, Mom's house, Dad's house, the babysitter, coaches and even Sunday School and midweek programs.

Talk with your co-teachers to agree on what the behavioral expectations will be for your kids. These expectations must then be clearly spelled out from time to time so that your students will be aware of what the game plan is at our church. Key times to review the expectations are at the start of a new year, at the beginning of a new program, after a major break or holiday and whenever kids seem to be forgetting what you want them to do.

Loving Kids Unconditionally

Much of our discipline of preteens is discipleship with lots of loving patience. Just as Jesus patiently loved His disciples (and us) through their failures and shortcomings, we must do the same with our students. We are loving them to maturity in their Christian faith and walk. When leading preteens, look at every discipline challenge as an opportunity to be Jesus in their lives. Every problem is in reality an opportunity to help our students see where they must become more like Christ and how to do so.

In order to do this, we must be focused on the kids and what is of benefit to them. We must be selfless in our leadership and ministry. We cannot serve preteens with the focus still on ourselves. These kids will know instantly if we are more concerned about ourselves or about them. They are so focused on themselves already that they can tell if we aren't! We must be ready to have tough skin, to receive little thanks and to grin and bear some rudeness from time to time.

When we feel loved by someone, it is much easier for us to obey that person and to cooperate with him or her. This is true, to a lesser degree, even with people that we just like. As adults, we experience this on a regular basis. When our boss treats us well, it's no big deal to do him or her a favor or to work a little harder to meet a deadline. When a good friend asks us to go out of our way for him or her, it doesn't seem like such an imposition.

The same is true of preteen kids. If our students have really experienced our love, even when they know they are being unlovable, they will find it much easier to behave appropriately in our programs.

This means that some of the hardest to love and hardest to discipline kids may be the ones who are not experiencing unconditional love at home. (Not experiencing unconditional love does not necessarily mean that it is not present. Some children have loving parents but for one reason or another just don't receive their love.) These kids need some extra love and acceptance from us.

TIPS FOR CORRECTING PROBLEM BEHAVIORS

No matter how much work you do preventing discipline problems, you will undoubtedly experience a few challenges that will require your appropriate and timely response. Here are some quick dos and don'ts for disciplining early adolescents:

▶ Do smile and take a deep breath.

▶ Don't lose your temper, yell, scream, or belittle the child.

▶ Do speak directly to the student.

▶ Don't embarrass him or her in front of his or her peers.

▶ Do have the student verbalize what the inappropriate behavior was.

▶ Don't ask why he or she did it.

▶ Do help the preteen understand why the behavior was inappropriate.

▶ Don't threaten consequences that you are unwilling to carry out.

▶ Do maintain a sense of humor.

▶ Don't think that it's the end of the world.

▶ Do talk with the student after you discipline him or her to make sure that the student knows you still care about him or her.

▶ Don't be inconsistent in applying the rules.

▶ Do ignore inappropriate behavior when it seems the child is just looking for attention.

▶ Don't ignore behaviors that disrupt the class or might hurt someone or something.

Get Preteens to Take Responsibility for Their Behavior and Choices

▶ **Early adolescents need to understand the impact their behaviors have on other people.** Empathy is a quality that we must continually teach early adolescents. As they move from concrete thinking to abstract thinking, they are able to think beyond punishment to consequences and impact on others. We teach empathy by identifying it, talking about it and modeling it whenever possible.

▶ **Early adolescents need to experience real consequences that appropriately help them take responsibility for their decisions.** An important part of our discipline and discipleship of preteens is to help them learn that their behavior has consequences. Kids must learn to take responsibility for their decisions, contrary to what they are being taught in our society and in the media. We must treat them as responsible agents, not victims, so that they learn to own their mistakes and enjoy their successes.

Consequences must never diminish the child's self-worth or damage the relationship between the adult and the child, but they must be painful enough (such as loss of privileges or extra chores) to help the child understand the seriousness of his or her actions and choices.

Discipline Tips

We often assume that punishment and discipline are the same: They are not! Punishment focuses on controlling a child's behavior. Discipline focuses on loving the child, helping the child to do the right thing. It teaches and encourages, as well as corrects. When we try to understand a child instead of merely control him or her, when we let a child know we're on his or her side and want to help the child know what to do, we give true discipline, based on love and respect.

Even when we don't approve of a child's behavior, we always accept that child as a person valuable in God's eyes. Acceptance means recognizing the child's worth and feelings without judging or condemning. It's based on the fact that God loves and accepts each of us. It does not mean we permit that child to engage in destructive behavior. Rather, it means we care about the child enough to help her find ways to overcome troublesome behavior and the reasons behind it.

Make the rules in your classroom few, fair and enforceable. This way, children are able to remember the rules. Consistent enforcement means children will know that the rules always apply! Don't rattle off the rules in a list. State a rule only in a situation where it applies. **Chantel, we are kind here. Our rule is to take turns with the bunny. I will count to 5. Then it will be Neal's turn.**

When a teacher focuses on a child's shortcomings, the child feels hurt, rebellious, humiliated or rejected. Rather than make negative remarks about what a child is not doing correctly, focus on the positive actions you see. **Robert, thank you for picking up those crayons. Leah, you moved over to make room for Dan. That's a great way to show kindness!** You will soon find that many other children are doing positive actions on which you can then comment!

While children find security in the limits you set, they also need to be able to make choices within these limits. Choosing a color of paper, an activity center or a toy with which to play often heads off discipline problems before they begin. Always offer a choice in which either alternative is OK with you so that you are never pressure a child to choose your favored option.

In a class session, take the time early on to recognize the efforts and positive behavior or individual children. Notice what each child is doing and comment. **You're really good at this, Marcus** or **I appreciate the way you shared that, Leah.** This will likely stop disruption in its tracks. When children already know they are seen and appreciated, they will display more positive behavior! Giving attention for good behavior causes disruptive behavior to drop off (it no longer has any value!).

Never focus on a child's shortcomings or mistakes. The child equates criticism of work with criticism of person. Remarks such as, "You glued this wrong" or "Let me do that for you" imply that the child is incompetent. Instead offer help if the child seems interested. Remember that even for older elementary children, the *process* of doing the activity is far more important than the finished *product*.

Discipline Tips

Never allow a child to make fun of another child or criticize another's work. And do not embarrass the one who said the hurtful words, for that behavior was learned from someone else! Instead, state the rule positively. **We are kind with our words.** Then help both kids focus on the abilities God has given them. **Ron, each one of us colors differently. Everyone makes good art. It's fun to see how many ways we color! Your picture has lots of red. Errol's has lots of blue. God made you both able to do good coloring!**

When a child disrupts others, first observe for a moment: Is the child bored? Is the disruption a bid for attention? Are you expecting an unrealistic attention span? Is the child is overtired? Over-stimulated? Try changing the pace of your activity or invite that child to participate in a specific way (keep score, etc.).

Children are in the process of learning to listen. They are often unaware that words an adult is speaking over their heads have anything to do with them! If a child seems reluctant to obey, consider that he or she may not have heard what you said. Get at the child's eye level, look at the child eye-to-eye and then give the direction.

The way a child behaves is often tied to what he or she thinks you expect! When you consistently show that you have confidence in a child to be kind, patient and friendly, the child's self-confidence grows and his or her behavior reflects the confidence you expressed

You may have a child in your class who is aggressive toward others. As with any other child, accept the aggressive child as he or she is: don't expect or require that the child change in order to earn your affection! Remember that this child learned the behavior from someone else. If the aggressive child frightens or hurts another child, be firm but friendly. Remove the aggressive child from the situation and clearly explain what needs to happen in order to return to the group. When the child returns, notice and affirm every positive behavior. Tell and show the child you appreciate his or her efforts.

If a child's activity is dangerous or too rowdy for the space, invite the child to a quieter activity to see if that will calm the child. **Rosa, you may rock the doll.** If this doesn't work, go to the child and quietly give him or her a choice of other activities. **Rosa, you may read a book or you may jump while standing next to me. But the blocks are not a safe place to jump.**

When children have a brief struggle over the glue or the truck, wait to see if the children can settle the problem themselves before stepping in. When children do arrive at an acceptable solution, acknowledge their success. **Alex and Diego both wanted the glue. They decided to take turns. Thank you, Alex. Thank you, Diego. You obeyed the Bible!** This helps the children observing as well as the ones involved to understand that they can find workable solutions.

Discipline Tips

With any child, try redirecting behavior in a quiet, loving way before a problem starts. Often, children simply need a change of state provided by a different activity. If misbehavior persists, don't scold or shame the child. Rather, let the child know that you are glad to have him or her in the class but that you cannot allow the behavior.

If you have persistent problems with children's behavior, take time to consider whether the space you are using is too small or not useful for the activities you plan. Sometimes a room that is too small, too hot or too cold, has uncomfortable furniture or is too dark or light is a cause for children's misbehavior.

While you are with a child, focus on positive behavior. Teachers sometimes feel it necessary to point out to children the things they do wrong. Instead, point out only the things they do right. Catch them in the act of doing good, be alert to children's positive behavior and then specifically acknowledge their efforts. **Jamal, you helped Kevin with that chair. Thank you!** Saying, "Jamal, you're a good kid!" is so vague that Jamal likely will not connect his action with your comment and won't know what behavior to repeat!

Always express an instruction or a rule in positive terms. Instead of saying, "No hitting!" say, **We use kind words and kind actions. We use words instead of hitting.** After stating the rule, always tell a child what he or she can do instead of what not to do.

If a child in your class is a show-off, acknowledge him or her, laugh along with the child and then move on. Don't be afraid to laugh; often a teacher afraid of losing control of the situation will put down the child and in the process become an adversary. However, laughing along with the child builds rapport as you bring the situation under control. Give that child positive attention early in the session, if possible, and be sure to name his or her contributions in front of the group.

Some children expect you to solve all the problems they encounter. Encourage those children to find ways to solve their own problems. Give them words. **How do you feel when Mark cuts in line? What can you say to Mark? What is a way to solve your problem? Tell Mark what you told me. Tell him it makes you angry when he cuts in line.** Watch the result. Quietly thank both parties. **I'm glad to see the way you solved your problem. Thank you.**

Good discipline is what you do with and for a child, not what you do to a child.

139

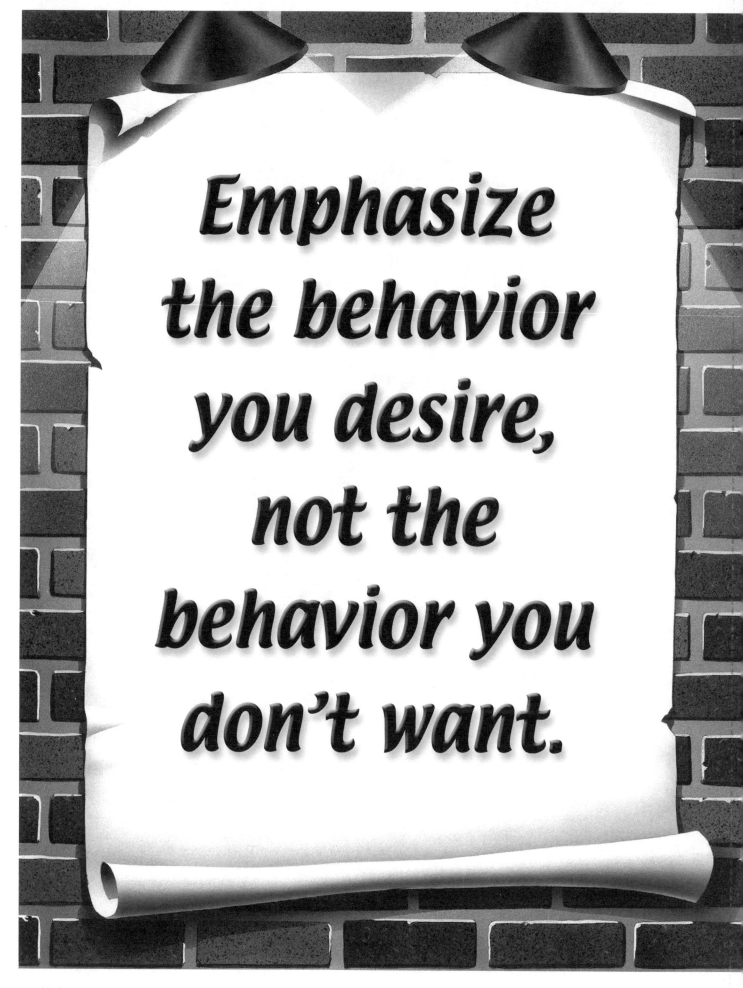

Emphasize the behavior you desire, not the behavior you don't want.

Give each child individual attention before negative behavior occurs.

Establish a few basic rules phrased in positive words.

HELP CHILDREN TO DO RIGHT, NOT JUST TO STOP DOING WRONG.

How Do We Learn?

For the busy teacher at church, it's tempting to approach limited lesson preparation time with the notion of "one size fits all." That is, every child will get maximum learning out of every activity. However, as each person has different facial features, each person learns in different ways. Some children are more receptive to certain teaching techniques than others. Children use different senses to gather information. The challenge is to provide for a variety of learning styles to reach each child. Although most of the children in a classroom may be most comfortable with one learning style, the teacher must also be prepared to engage children who have other styles of learning.

Learning Styles

Learning styles describe the way people use their senses to process information as they learn. Educators have classified three types of learning styles. Most people will fit somewhat into more than one category. Few people are completely of one style to the exclusion of others. Most children cannot describe how they learn best but do know which activities they like. Discovering the learning styles of children can help in lesson planning and in finding the most meaningful activities.

Auditory learners. These children best gather information with their ears. They prefer to hear oral instructions instead of following written directions. They like to hear a story read aloud rather than reading it silently on their own. They listen carefully during discussions and hear nuances in voice pitch, volume and tone. Working with music, using tape recorders and reading aloud from the Bible or a script will help these children learn effectively.

Visual learners. These children use their eyes to learn. They follow written instructions more easily than hearing a teacher give directions. They like lots of visual stimulation, such as posters, pictures, multimedia, graphs, maps and charts. They like to fill in worksheets and research written information from a book or the Internet. They like to sit close to you and near to visual aids, so they can see clearly. In a discussion they watch the speaker's face and hand gestures.

Tactile learners. These are hands-on, active, mobile learners. They prefer using their hands and bodies rather than their ears or eyes. They love games, art activities, motions, pantomime and any activity that gets them moving. These children delight in building models, making repairs and working with mechanical objects. They love to make discoveries and find things.

Multiple Intelligences

Another view of the way in which people learn most effectively is called multiple intelligences. Seven types of intelligences have been identified by educator and author Howard Gardner. (Note: While additional types of intelligences have been identified, the first seven are the most commonly accepted by teachers.) These categories or types of intelligences identify talents and skills, and have nothing to do with I.Q. testing or whether or not a person is intelligent. Knowing a child's type of intelligence can help you identify and utilize a child's gifts. No one intelligence is better than the others, and every learner possesses a mixture of these categories. Each type possesses its own unique gifts and strengths. All skills are needed for the building of God's kingdom on earth.

Visual intelligence. These children think in pictures. They like reading, writing, working puzzles, drawing, painting, watching videos, looking at pictures or creating a graph. Visual children do well with art activities and decorating the room.

Verbal intelligence. These children are excellent speakers and prefer working with words instead of pictures. Their skills are speaking, listening, storytelling, writing and humor. Count on these children for leading a discussion, skits and public speaking.

Logical intelligence. These children are the so-called "computer whizzes" and "math brains." They excel with logic and numbers, and they love doing experiments. Such children enjoy learning for its own sake and ask many questions. These children are fascinated by nature and enjoy working with shapes and complicated puzzles.

Bodily intelligence. These children are great in sports and active games. They possess above-average physical coordination, strength and balance. They work well with their hands and like to keep active.

Musical intelligence. Obviously, these children are the singers, musicians and composers. Their minds process rhythm and sound better than verbal or visual information. They may prefer to memorize facts and Bible verses by singing the words instead of saying them. Get their attention with hand-clap patterns or a musical tone. Older children may be able to write a song for the class to sing.

Interpersonal intelligence. The person with interpersonal intelligence has great empathy and enjoys working with people. This person can understand other points of view and sense the moods and feelings of others. Such people like to bring about reconciliation and build bridges. These traits may not be well developed yet in children, who may not be aware of such gifts. However, these children understand people well enough to be manipulators to get what they want. They can be bossy because they are good group organizers. They may be the ones who automatically divide up the teams and give orders when it's time for games. These children are peacemakers and may be the ones who try to stop a classroom brawl. They're the group leaders for small-group activities.

Intrapersonal intelligence. This type is more abstract and mental than the others. These are the dreamers and philosophers who are self-aware and reflective. They analyze their feelings and relationships with others. It's possible that the great saints, visionaries and philosophers of Church history were this type. Young children do not think in abstract ways, but such tendencies can be seen in a child who perpetually daydreams or frequently asks why things are the way they are. Such children may be supercritical of themselves, since they spend much effort in self-analysis and evaluation without guidance. They may need a teacher to give them assurance and encouragement that they're OK.

The Value of Learning Styles

God made each of us unique and He loves our uniqueness! Even in the way we learn new information, each of us is different. Consider the learning styles and strengths of the children in your group and then make sure to provide a variety of learning experiences so that each child is included and will have opportunity to explore God's Word in different ways.

THE EIGHT WAYS PEOPLE LEARN

LEARNING STYLE	TYPES OF ACTIVITIES THAT HELP LEARNER	TIPS FOR CONNECTING WITH LEARNER
LINGUISTIC	The linguistic learner learns best when involved in ▶ Reading and writing activities, using words creatively ▶ Talking, discussing and storytelling	Use discussion and creative storytelling. Challenge these kids to memorize.
LOGICAL	The logical (or mathematical) learner learns best when involved in ▶ Experiments, analyzing topics ▶ Problem solving, answering tough questions	Help students challenge and defend the faith. Stretch their thinking by asking open-ended questions.
VISUAL	The visual (or spatial) learner learns best when involved in ▶ Drawing, building things, art projects, mapping ▶ Visualizing and then creating things or doodling ideas	Provide activities in which students create visual representations of what they've learned.
MUSICAL	The musical learner learns best when involved in ▶ An environment with musical mood setters ▶ Singing and listening to Bible words set to music	Have your students help supply popular Christian CDs from which you can choose appropriate mood music for before and after class. Play and sing along with CDs of Bible passages set to music.
KINESTHETIC	The kinesthetic (bodily) learner learns best when involved in ▶ A variety of short learning activities ▶ Moving, touching, playing, acting, running	Minimize furniture in your room so that you may quickly, easily and frequently shift the activity from one part of the room to another. Have kids role-play Bible stories and applications of lessons.
INTERPERSONAL	The interpersonal learner learns best when involved in ▶ Leading, building friendships, talking ▶ Small groups, teams, social settings, projects	Make cooperative learning a regular part of your learning environment (including pair shares and small groups). Allow get-acquainted times each session.
INTROSPECTIVE	The introspective (or intrapersonal) learner learns best when involved in ▶ Meditation, reflection, prayer ▶ Self-study projects, one-on-one times with teachers and other students	Allow for some quiet reflection in each class and don't assume quiet kids are shy.
NATURALIST	The naturalist learner learns best when involved in ▶ Outdoor activities in God's creation and natural surroundings ▶ Activities utilizing plants, animals, nature items	Take your class outdoors or plan outings, camps and retreats. Have windows in your rooms.

ACTING OUT EVERYDAY LIFE

The dramatic play area provides a place where young children can pretend to be anyone they want to be! Children can go from simply experimenting with costumes and props to fully re-creating their world in any way they can imagine it! It enables children to practice the social roles and activities they see around them.

Teachable Moments

When children are playing out everyday situations, there are many opportunities to act out kindness, forgiveness and patience. Don't assume you are not needed in this setting. Your role is vitally important. And it's simple! Get to know each child. Ask open-ended questions ("What do you think will happen if . . .?" "How do you think we can solve . . .?") as children play. Your simple suggestions can help them see solutions to problems, help them understand ways to be kind or share and can help them see how the day's Bible verse applies to real life. If children's play seems to stall, ask a question or two to help give them new ideas.

Always be alert for those moments when you can make a brief comment on how a child's action reflects the day's lesson focus or Bible verse. Acknowledge and encourage positive actions you see as children play! "Stephanie, I see you are sharing the cooking pots with Mara. That's a way to share and be kind, like our Bible tells us to do! Thank you!"

Acting out Bible story events (even before the story is formally told) is an ideal way for young children to learn Bible truths! It involves children's bodies as well as minds. Stories told informally this way have great impact. And since young children love repetition, hearing and acting out the Bible story more than once delights them as it reinforces Bible truth.

Characteristics of Play

Social Interaction: Two or more children within the group talk about what they will play. They take on roles and then interact in that context. They may often transform an object into another use (a spatula becomes a microphone) or do an imaginary action (moving hands in ways to symbolize eating).

Verbal Communication: Children talk naturally as part of the pretending. The teacher stays alert nearby, watching for times when he or she can make a comment that helps to extend thinking, make predictions, try new ideas or relate children's actions to the Bible words or focus of the day's lesson.

Levels of Play

A child's interest and activity in dramatic play reflect his or her level of development. Most children under three are likely to simply rock a baby, pretend to *be* the baby or play alongside other children, rarely involving anyone else in their activities. Since their ability to use words is limited, they often use play as a way to express ideas. As children grow through their third, fourth and fifth years, imaginative play becomes more and more complex. As children mature, they learn to interact with other children and often adopt the roles of family members. They spend longer periods of time in imaginative play and enjoy using costumes and props such as household items, adult clothing and accessories. They also enjoy playing out the roles of community helpers: mail carriers, firefighters, doctors, etc.

Basic Materials

The basic supplies needed for dramatic play activity are fairly simple: toy dishes (plates, bowls, cups and utensils), tablecloth, several washable dolls, easy-to-manage doll clothes and dress-up clothes (women's and men's). For classes of mostly young children, do not provide utensils or toy baby bottles as they will likely try to put them in their mouths. Other items to add might be toy food, doll bed, telephone, plastic jewelry, wallets, discarded camera, lunch box, briefcase, ties and scarves.

Costume and Prop Boxes

Children may not especially enjoy it when adults dress them up, but they do love to dress up when they are provided with a variety of interesting clothing items and props! While basic dress-up items and props should be available in the dramatic play area all the time, rotate other items to keep dramatic play interesting.

To effectively rotate extra props and clothing, organize them by themes such as Bible times, grocery store, mail carrier, gardening, mechanic, restaurant, baby care, etc. Gather costumes and props for each theme into clear plastic boxes or large boxes with lids (office paper boxes work well). Label boxes. Regularly launder and clean all props and clothing.

BLOCKS ARE MORE THAN PLAY!

If there is a spot in an early childhood classroom that is a perpetual favorite with some children, it is the block area! When young children play with blocks, they experiment with the physical properties of solid objects. They solve engineering problems, learn to make decisions and practice cooperation and sharing. Blocks also provide a place for children to have the physical release of large-muscle movement and the freedom of imaginative play. Never dismiss the block area as unimportant!

During block play, look for opportunities to relate children's actions to the Bible truth. Conversation with young builders can give them *mental* building blocks of ways to know and do what God's Word says. "You built a bridge, Ron! I also saw you give Joe a turn with the long blocks you were using. You shared with Joe. Thank you. Our Bible verse tells us to do good and share." Block-building provides firsthand experiences in practicing concepts such as sharing, helping, taking turns and exercising self-control.

Sometimes children will begin to build items of their own choosing (airports, towers, roads, houses, etc.), even when you have stated "Today we're going to build a big block boat and talk about a time Jesus traveled on a boat." It's OK for children to build their own structures. However, it is important that you stay involved with the block-building. Look for ways you can connect the child's activity with the Bible story or verse. "Bradley, you're building an airplane. When have you been on an airplane? When Jesus lived on Earth, there were no airplanes. One day Jesus traveled on a boat."

Block-Play Stages

Young children go through very distinctive stages of block play.

Stage One: Blocks are carried and put into or taken from containers.

Stage Two: Blocks are stacked, built into small piles or laid next to each other. (Twos and threes are often working side by side at this point in parallel play.)

Stage Three: A space is enclosed and bridged. (This is an important step in developing problem-solving skills.)

Stage Four: Patterns of blocks are arranged to make a structure. These patterns are often symmetrical and sometimes built with others.

Stage Five: Structures that are built are named and used for dramatic play in the block area.

Stage Six: A construction is cooperatively planned and built with others ("Let's make an airport!"); the structure is named before it is built, and other items are used to enhance the imaginary play.

By the time children are four or five years old, they have usually moved into the last stages of block-play development. However, some children will use block play area as a place to relax through using the large-muscle activity or the chance to work alone. There is no right or wrong way to play with blocks as long as they are being used safely.

Teacher's Role

Just because children are absorbed and busy in block play does not mean it is time to take a break! Instead, look for ways to help children enrich their play, resolve conflicts or think

through situations. "Here is a little horse. Would you like to put it in your barn, Joycelyn?" "Karen, you and Mandy both want the same block. What is a way you can solve your problem?" "Kevin, is your road as long as your arm? How could you find out?"

Don't intervene every minute, but when you see frustration surfacing, ask a question that will help a child recognize the next step in solving the problem. "What do you think will help your tower stand up better? How can you make the bottom of your building wider, Jayce?" If a block becomes a weapon, simply repeat the rule: "Blocks are only for building. What would you like to build now, Zach? We could build a zoo."

Basic Materials

Provide many different sizes, shapes and colors of wooden, cardboard or plastic blocks. Blocks for children under three years of age should be lightweight and easy to manipulate. Provide enough blocks so that several children can build at the same time. Four- and five-year-olds need a larger number and variety of blocks. Wooden unit blocks are the preferred basic set. (Note: In a set of unit blocks, each block is a unit of a larger block; two of the smallest blocks equal one of the larger size, etc.)

Sturdy toy cars and trucks should be a part of every block area. Other accessory toys include toy people, toy animals and toy trees. Four- and five-year-olds enjoy using signs (traffic signs, building signs, etc.) in their block play. Even simple recyclable items like clean oatmeal boxes and film canisters provide children with materials to expand their creativity. Manipulative building toys, such as Legos or Lincoln Logs, integrate easily into block play.

Block Storage

Blocks and accessory toys should be stored on low open shelves to make it easy for children to see and help themselves. Avoid piling blocks into bins if possible. Instead, trace around each block shape onto colorful contact paper. Place the shape on the front of the shelf where that shape of block belongs. The sorting and matching needed to put away blocks in their places becomes a learning process in itself. If you have no shelves, gather some sturdy cardboard boxes, fold flaps inside and lay boxes on their sides for shelves.

To keep a space for children to move back and forth to the block shelves, lay a masking-tape line several feet away from the fronts of the shelves. Tell children to always build on the other side of this line, so others have room to remove and return blocks without knocking down anyone else's work.

Providing adequate space and high-quality blocks is a valuable gift to your children! Young builders can know and do what God's Word says.

Block Rules

Only a few clear rules need to apply in the block area:

► Stack blocks no higher than your chin.

► Keep blocks in the block area.

► Use blocks only for building.

► Knock down only your own towers and only when no one is in the way.

CREATIVE ART FOR YOUNG CHILDREN

Art activities are among the most used—and most misunderstood—experiences offered to young children. Young children have no sense whatsoever of what adults expect them to produce when art materials are offered. They are small scientists: for them, art materials are not a means to make a pretty product by adult standards but the means to discover what happens when, for instance, random paper scraps are stacked together and glued into a pile!

Process, Not Product

For young children, using art materials is about the experience of creating and the process of discovering. Remember that for young children it is the *process*, not the *product*, that matters. Encourage children to explore materials freely. Relax and recognize that sometimes it is a greater learning experience to swirl the glue with fingers than it is to create what the teacher had in mind! Art gives children the chance to express their feelings and thoughts and to release tension as well. Give them freedom to experiment creatively.

Teachable Opportunities

As a child and teacher use art materials together in a relaxed and creative way, natural opportunities arise for conversation. Such teachable moments often provide the perfect times to help a child understand vital Bible truths! "I see lots of blue in your picture, James. What other things did God make that are blue?" "God gave you hands that can draw lots of little circles, Josie. Let's thank Him!" Include God in your conversation through word, prayer or song to positively reinforce how much God values that child!

As children work, relate the Bible verse to what you see children doing. "Lee, I see you gave Michael a turn with the blue crayon. Thank you. Our Bible says to share with other people. You are doing what God's Word says to do!" "Lena, Weston doesn't have enough room. What could you do to help him? Thank you for moving over, Lena. You are being kind. God's Word tells us to be kind."

Helping, Not Hindering

When a child shows you his or her work, invite the child into conversation about the art. NEVER ask, "What is it?" The comment to make is, "Emily, tell me about your picture!" or "I see many squiggly lines, Kyle—tell me about those lines." And NEVER attempt to fix or finish what you think needs to be changed in any child's art.

If a child says, "Draw it for me," suggest, "Let's see how much you can do by yourself first." Encourage the child and help him or her feel assured that no one will judge his or her work.

A child may comment, "Leo's picture is ugly!" or "He copied me. That's not fair!" Deal gently with both the critic and the criticized. "Mason, Leo made his picture the way he wanted it." You may also say, "If Leo's picture is like your picture, that's OK. Leo must have really liked your picture." Don't put down the child who voiced the criticism; instead, help the child see that each person's work is valued.

Basic Materials

Make sure you have plenty of the following supplies on hand: newspaper or plastic tablecloths (to protect surfaces), scissors, glue bottles and glue sticks, markers, crayons, chalk, tape, play dough, discarded magazines and catalogs, collage materials (yarn, ribbon, cotton balls, chenille wire), colored and white construction paper, stapler and staples, paint smocks (old men's short-sleeved shirts from a thrift shop serve well) and butcher paper.

Preparation

For children to enjoy an art project, they need to hear as few warnings as possible. They need to feel successful. As you get to know the personalities and capabilities of each child, you can tailor the activity to the group's needs. And a little preparation will go a long way in keeping a small mess from becoming a big one!

Cover tabletops and floors with newspaper or plastic tablecloths. Secure on all sides with masking tape.

Keep a supply of premoistened towelettes, no-rinse hand-wiping solution or paper towels handy for messy fingers and small spills. Set a trash can where children can clean up easily.

Activities that use potentially messy materials (glue, paint, etc.) may be difficult if your teacher/child ratio is too large or if you do not have adequate space or furniture. In such cases, you may need to substitute easier materials (crayons, etc.) to deal with.

EXPLORING GOD'S WORLD

A young child's plea "Let me see!" means "Let me touch, feel, shake, taste and smell it!" Nature Bible learning activities use the senses to heighten a child's ability to learn. Firsthand experiences are the core of learning for young children. Exploring God's world helps a child begin to sense the extent of God's love, care and wisdom. Hands-on exploring gives children many opportunities to learn about God and themselves. Whether taking a nature walk, touching items inside a bag or sniffing and comparing a series of scent containers, children are eager to explore their own abilities and the wonders of God's creation. Some nature Bible learning activities involve direct examination of natural items (bark, rocks, shells, leaves, etc.). Others involve the creation of scenes using natural materials such as sand, rocks and sticks, the collection and display of natural items or the discovery of the child's own wonderfully made characteristics.

Nature Bible learning activities may also incorporate those simple demonstrations of natural law that you may take for granted as an adult. Exploring the way magnets work or the way light makes a rainbow through a prism calls us back to sense the wonder of God's astounding plan and care. As we express our own wonder and appreciation, we truly and effectively communicate a great deal about God's character, love and power. A child will then sense that Bible truths are not separate from life but are a real part of it. Young children are natural learners full of curiosity and eager questions. Linking the truths of God's Word to the wonders of God's creation is delightfully easy!

Guided Conversation

An essential part of the teacher's role in a nature Bible learning activity is to provide words for a child, helping him or her identify the experience and relate God to it. Once this relationship is made, the child is able to think about the Bible story or Bible verse in terms of a firsthand experience. Without such guidance, nature learning activities become just so many interesting experiences.

Some of the nature Bible learning activities will help familiarize children with a concept they will hear about in the Bible story. For example, pouring water through nail holes punched in an aluminum pie pan to simulate a rainstorm helps a child understand the big rainstorm in the story of Noah. Other nature Bible learning activities will encourage children to demonstrate obedience to a Bible verse as they experiment with items of God's wonderful creation.

Basic Materials

Having some basic materials on hand will enhance the experiences of the children and make it easy for you to lead children in hands-on examination of God's world. Include these items in your supplies: several magnifying glasses, a variety of nature items (rocks, shells, living plants, sticks, etc.), large tubs for water and/or shallow pans or boxes for sand play, fabrics in a variety of textures and newspaper or plastic tablecloths (to protect tabletops).

Because they involve every part of the curious child, nature Bible learning activities will more than likely be a class favorite!

MEMORABLE MUSIC FOR YOUNG CHILDREN

In today's world, music is often thought of as something to listen to, instead of something to make! Many adults claim they cannot sing, but especially in an early childhood classroom, every adult has absolute permission to cut loose and sing! Your singing teaches children that music is God's gift, that it brings joy and that it includes everyone. Beyond that, music is one of the most powerful teaching tools we have because of the combined impact of melody, rhythm and rhyme.

More Than a Time Filler

A song can fill in time gaps, regain children's attention or give them a chance to move. These are all good reasons to sing! However, avoid asking "What do you want to sing?" It takes some time for a child to make you understand what song he or she wants to sing, and the songs a child chooses are unlikely to relate to the lesson of the day.

Be sure to choose songs that reinforce the Bible truth for the day and contain biblical concepts that are clear to young children! Your curriculum should provide songs developed specifically to teach young children about God and to help them memorize Scripture in an age-appropriate way.

Some teachers may want to sing the old favorites. Too often, we adults have an emotional tie to a childhood song; however, our favorite childhood Sunday School songs may confuse young children! Consider first whether an old favorite will help children understand God's Word at their own level. Other teachers may feel most comfortable singing songs that they are used to singing in adult worship services. However, in most cases these songs use vocabulary and concepts that are abstract and symbolic in nature and, as a result, they are not understood by young children.

When you choose a song that reinforces the day's biblical truth, you are making the best use of every moment of teaching time. Give children as many chances as possible to learn biblical principles and Scripture while they sing, clap and have lots of fun!

More Than a Solo Act

Sometimes a teacher is intimidated when a group of small children stare glassy-eyed while he or she sings a solo! Remember that children who have experienced music only as something to listen to will participate first by simply watching and listening. (The younger the child, the more listening and less singing he or she will do.) If a song doesn't include motions or clapping, add them. Clap on the rhythm or invent finger motions to go with it. When you do the motions, children can be involved as they imitate you, whether or not they are singing. One goal of music is to involve every child, so each one learns Scripture and biblical concepts in a fun and memorable way.

If you are deeply uncomfortable singing a song, repeat the words of the song as a poem or invite another member of your teaching team to lead the music. You may also play the music on a CD to help both you and children enjoy the music.

Remember, you are not performing or providing entertainment. You are using a song to guide children in learning. Your musical perfection is unimportant. However, your enthusiasm and interest are vital! Be willing to make mistakes. If you forget the tune, keep going with the words. Children will be delighted that you, too, are learning. Relax and enjoy the children's response to the songs. When you truly sing from a heart of love for the Lord, children are quick to catch your feeling of joy.

More Than Voices

There are more ways to participate in music than simply singing! Besides involving every child through clapping and other motions, consider making some simple rhythm instruments. They will spice up any musical experience! Using rhythm instruments also develops a child's mind and coordination as well as being another way for a child to participate.

To Make Instruments

It doesn't require much money to make sturdy homemade rhythm instruments.

▶ Tie small bells together with sturdy string or ribbon for children to shake.

▶ Unsharpened pencils make excellent rhythm sticks or drumsticks.

▶ Drums come ready-made from empty coffee cans with plastic lids. Cover the can with colorful Con-Tact paper.

▶ A thrift-store pan lid makes a wonderful cymbal when struck with the eraser end of an unsharpened pencil.

▶ Shakers are easily made from plastic jars, small water bottles or salt boxes. Simply insert small stones, popcorn kernels, macaroni, beans or rice (each makes a different sound!); glue lid or opening securely closed. Children can then guess what item is inside making the sound. Shakers can be covered with colorful Con-Tact paper or decorated with puff paint or glitter.

To Use Instruments

Here are a few ideas of how to use the rhythm instruments in your class:

▶ Have a praise parade. Play a selected song from a children's cassette or CD while children march around the room, playing the instruments. Children may also simply play without a recording as they march.

▶ Play a freeze game. Play recorded music while children play instruments and walk in a circle. Stop the recorded music as a signal for children to freeze in place. After children freeze, they trade instruments with others and then continue again at your signal.

▶ Allow children to explore. At times, leave several instruments out with which children may experiment. You may wish to add a cassette player with a children's music tape already inserted. Children play the cassette and use the instruments to practice keeping time to the music.

Less of a Problem

Children may find ways to use the instruments that we adults haven't imagined! If a child uses an instrument as a weapon, simply take it and show the child the correct way to use it. Then invite the child to repeat your actions. "Aidan, would you please show me how to use the sticks like I showed you?" Most children will need no further instruction.

Children may have difficulty sharing rhythm instruments. Be alert to reinforce their positive behavior. "Seth, I know you like the red shaker best. Thank you for giving Jake a turn with it, even when it's hard to do!"

Never tell a child to stop singing or to sing more quietly. When the noise level is too high, simply repeat the song in a whispery voice. "That was great! This time, let's sing the song in a whisper."

Enjoy children's freedom to make music with all they have. Singing with them can help you rediscover joy in your own voice!

PLAY GAMES AND LEARN

Games for young children are not the same kinds of games that older children or adults play. For young children, games are more like organized guided play. They may involve exploring, combining and manipulating materials. Other games may involve movement, simple responses or recalling information while enjoying activity and feeling included.

For young children, games need to be involving (that means very little time spent waiting for a turn!). Games need to be easygoing and noncompetitive. They should not involve a long list of rules. A young child may follow rules for a while, but as excitement builds, the rules often slip away! The focus of a game for young children is on the fun of doing, not on winning. Such games need no winners or losers, for the excitement of meeting the challenge in the game is enough.

Guided Conversation

Using guided conversation turns a game activity into discovery learning! Make use of the conversation suggestions provided in your curriculum. These conversation starters will help you relate the child's activity to the lesson. Keep in mind the lesson focus and Bible verse for each lesson. Then your natural conversation can tie children's activities to the lesson's Bible truths. Some games may connect directly to Bible story action. Briefly telling parts of the Bible story can help make the connection.

Age-Level Characteristics

Two- and three-year-olds enjoy the challenge of matching colors, shapes or sizes of items and pictures. Movement games for younger ones include rolling a ball, dropping clothespins into a container, tossing a beanbag into a bucket, playing Follow the Leader or Simon Says (without anyone ever being out). Such games are easily adapted to the children's developmental level. Playing the game in more than one way helps develop thinking skills and heightens interest.

Four- and five-year-olds are able to play simple board games and concentration games with a limited number of game pieces. Increase the challenge in skill games such as tossing a beanbag by moving the target or inviting children to toss the beanbag in a different way (with both hands, under a leg, etc.). Use lightweight balls to play simple toss-and-catch games. Bowl to knock over plastic two-liter bottles. Push lightweight balls along the floor with plastic baseball bats or brooms.

With young children, expect to play a game over and over again. Young children love repetition because repeating an activity helps them gain experience and skill. Feeling successful and competent should be one goal of any game!

The Playing Area

Plan what you will need to do to create a playing area within your classroom. You may need to move unneeded furniture or rearrange chairs or tables. If necessary for certain games, mark boundaries with yarn, masking tape or painter's tape. (Be sure to remove masking tape from floor after each session.) If you have little space in your classroom in which to play games, consider alternatives: outdoor areas, a hallway or a gymnasium.

Basic Materials

Some games require no materials at all. Other games require items that can be found in most classrooms or homes. The following supplies can be used in many games: beanbags, several soft balls in various sizes, butcher paper, markers, masking tape (or painter's tape) and yarn, colored construction paper and scissors.

ALL THE CLASSROOM IS A STAGE

Drama activities provide children with stimulating ways to make Bible stories come alive and biblical concepts real. Children of all ages love to play act and pretend. Their natural creativity and lack of inhibitions make them natural actors.

Drama activities may sound complicated and hard to prepare, but with an emphasis on process instead of product, drama activities are easy to teach and do not require extensive rehearsal. The goal is for children to apply the concepts to their lives, not to give an award-winning performance. Thus, children of all acting abilities can participate. Here are a variety of methods to keep children acting!

Types of Drama Learning Activities

Act out the Bible story. After hearing or reading the Bible story, children act out the roles using their own words. (Younger children, or children unfamiliar with impromptu speaking, may simply pantomime the Bible story action as a narrator either tells the story or reads it from the Bible.) Costumes are not needed, although Bible-times costumes can be used if there are several on hand. Children may also enjoy resetting the story in modern times. Brainstorm possible situations and actions with children before inviting them to act out the contemporary version. Ask questions such as What kind of problems do kids your age have that are like the problem in the story? If Jesus walked into our (town) today, would anything happen that would be like our story?

Use puppets. Many children who would not feel comfortable acting out parts themselves feel confident when using puppets. Collect a variety of puppets to keep on hand in your classroom. Puppets can be inexpensive and simple, made from socks, small paper bags, gloves, stuffed animals, dolls or plastic foam "heads" decorated and put on long sticks. The "stage" can be as simple as a table turned on its side. For classes that plan to spend a lot of time with puppets, craft a more permanent stage by hanging cloth from a plastic (PVC) pipe frame. Puppets can be bought from educational or church supply stores, by mail order or over the Internet. Children enjoy using puppets to lip-sync along with prerecorded music.

Dress up in costumes. Keep a container on hand with old clothes and props. Many such items can be donated by church members or purchased inexpensively from thrift stores. Older children may want to make their own Bible-times costumes out of discarded fabric.

Role-play situations. In this type of drama activity, children act out a situation without a script. Children, grouped in pairs or trios, are either assigned or choose a topic, problem or question related to the Bible truth of the lesson. The children discuss possible situations together, plan a course of action and present the story to the audience with improvised dialogue. Role-play can be used to demonstrate examples of Christian living (confronting bullies, being caught in a lie, peer pressure, etc.) and helps children to see how biblical concepts can be lived out in everyday life.

Use "what if" questions. This method is similar to role-play except that each child pretends to be someone else—often a character in a Bible story. Drama activities like these help children develop understanding of a character's actions and explore other perspectives. Sample "what if" questions include What if you were David and God had asked you to fight Goliath? What if you were Moses and God had given you the Ten Commandments? What if you were a leper begging by the gate and you saw Jesus coming? "What if" questions can also be used to help children apply Bible truth to contemporary situations (What if you were a new immigrant to America and couldn't speak English?)

Pantomime stories. This is wordless storytelling, using pantomime movement and gestures. In pantomimes, encourage children to use exaggerated facial expressions and motions. As in the game of Charades, children enjoy pantomiming a story for others to guess.

Read skits. Older children enjoy reading and acting from scripts. Your curriculum may provide skit scripts or you can purchase books of plays. Costumes and sets can be as simple or elaborate as the children want to make them. Scripts are helpful for children who have difficulty thinking up their own stories and dialogue.

Tips on Using Drama Activities

Although a stage is not necessary for classroom drama, open space is often needed so that children do not bump into furniture. If the classroom is too small to allow free movement, move the class outdoors or into a large unused room. Some churches have a stage in the fellowship hall that might be available during class time.

Some children feel uncomfortable speaking in front of others. Alleviate shyness by using puppets or pantomime. Another alternative is to let these children do the backstage jobs, such as gathering costumes and props or setting up the stage area.

Since the emphasis is on process and not product, it is not essential for children to give great acting performances or to repeat scripted lines perfectly. However, some children may want to clown around and act silly. Give the children a few minutes to play with the props and "get the sillies out." Then stop and talk about the story again to get the children in a focused frame of mind before they start again. Praise all of the children for their participation. Children with dramatic talent may want to show off their skill. Let children use their gifts but also encourage other children to participate in starring roles as well.

If you are using scripts, provide highlighters for children to mark their parts. Explain any unfamiliar vocabulary ahead of time and help them practice pronouncing unusual words or names. If your group has more members than the script has parts, divide major roles between two or more "actors."

As with most learning activities, children benefit from repetition. Your children will be able to add expression and other dramatic effects each time they repeat a dramatic presentation. The more you use drama activities, the better your children will be able to act and the more fun (and learning!) all of you will have.

MUSIC REACHES KIDS!

A powerful way to implant in children God's Word and its principles is to sing with them. Songs learned early in life retain significance and can plant truth deeply in children's lives. The songs in your curriculum communicate God's love and His work in children's lives in words they understand.

The thought of presenting music in the classroom, however, can be scary for teachers who don't feel musically inclined. Some may feel they sing off pitch, can't remember lyrics or can't sing as well as a professional recording artist. However, remember that you are singing in front of a room of children, not music critics. Children will not judge a less-than-perfect singer because they, too, are developing their own musical abilities. Children love music and movement, so don't hesitate to integrate these elements into your class for effective learning.

Ways to Use Music in Class

Transition times. A transition "theme song" signals the class that it is time to move on to another activity. Depending on the age of your class, consider using songs during transitions as children arrive and depart, move to and from large group times, and clean up supplies. When the children hear and/or sing the song, they can prepare themselves for the next activity. Choose a favorite upbeat children's song from the curriculum you use or an instrumental recording of a lively classical song to use as a transition signal.

Mood. Using a variety of songs in group singing is a good way to offer a change of pace in your lesson. Some songs are more lively and will encourage participation. Other slower-paced songs can help to settle students and prepare them for prayer or a Bible story.

Movement. Children like activity and love fast, bouncy tunes. Use hand gestures or other motions (clapping hands, stomping feet, etc.) while singing to illustrate the lyrics. Many songs tell a story, express emotions or describe actions. Let the children act out the words or create motions as they sing. Many children are familiar with American Sign Language and will enjoy signing the words to a song.

Some songs with motions attempt to express highly symbolic concepts that children often misunderstand. Just because a tune is catchy and the motions are fun does not mean children are learning the intended concept.

Instruments. Children can easily learn to play percussion instruments, such as drums, shakers, cymbals, triangles, chimes and bells. Older children may be skilled at piano or guitar. Find and use the talent in the class. However, avoid pressuring a child to be a regular class accompanist.

Music as ministry. Children can practice and sing songs during worship or for nursing home residents, homebound church members or church events.

Art and music. Let children create their own songbooks of favorite songs by writing out the words, decorating the pages and attaching the pages with brads or ribbons. Children will also enjoy drawing pictures for some of the lyrics. Invite children to contribute to worship services by providing materials for them to design and create banners that illustrate a phrase or two from a favorite song.

Teaching Music

A teacher need not be a musical expert to lead singing and teach new songs. The main key is preparation, not talent.

Knowledge of the song. When introducing new music, memorize the words and tune so that you can give attention to the children, not to looking at the sheet music. Practice singing at home to feel comfortable with the song.

Use of prerecorded music. Many children's audiocassettes, CDs and music videos are available with your curriculum and/or from church supply stores and music stores. Learn a new song by playing the CD several times and then play the CD in class to introduce the song to the children. Sing along with the CD and invite your students to sing along with you until the song is learned. Some music is available in karaoke version—only the instrumental track. If prerecorded music can't be found, have a musical friend sing or play the song into an audiocassette recorder, or invite your friend (or a choir member) to teach the song in person.

Learning new lyrics. Write the words to a new song on a large poster, chalkboard, white board or overhead transparency so that children can easily see them. Displaying words in this method helps children look up, so they can sing louder than if their faces are buried in song sheets. Another advantage of displaying words on a poster, board or overhead transparency is that children are not flipping through songbooks as they sing. For young children still learning to read, use pictures instead of words when appropriate.

Discussion. Talk with children about the songs you sing together. Ask questions such as What does this song help us learn about God? What does this song remind us to do? When would be a good time to remember and sing the words of this song? Explain any unfamiliar words. For effective learning and reinforcement of your lesson aims, use the songs that are provided with your curriculum and/or select songs that fit with the lesson's Bible truth and not simply because they sound nice or are useful as time filler. To be understood by children, songs should not use abstract words that express little specific action or feelings. Make sure it's clear what the words in the song are teaching children.

Repetition. When children like something, they want to experience it over and over. They may want to sing a song they like several times in one session. Repetition also helps the children memorize the lyrics. When teaching a new song, sing it for several classes in a row.

Making a Joyful Noise

So what if a student (or you) sings sharp or flat? God sees the heart more than He hears the voice. Even shy children can be encouraged to participate in group singing as you model your enthusiasm and the purpose of your singing: to give praise and worship to God.

PLAY GAMES WITH A PURPOSE

Incorporate a variety of games into your lesson plans to help motivate children's enthusiasm. Avoid the temptation, however, to use games just to fill time or to work off childhood energy. Instead, choose games that help you reinforce the lesson. Children may not be aware of the direct learning value of a game, but they will learn as they participate enthusiastically just because they enjoy the game.

Bible games are best played to develop cooperation within teams, not competition between individuals. With teams, as each person shares his or her talents, students learn to cooperate and build up the community of Christ. The emphasis is on the group's goal, not individual accomplishment. Students are given the opportunity of learning to be fair, to be honest and to take turns. Providing both active and quiet Bible games ensures that children of varying learning styles will be able to participate in games that appeal to them.

Active Games

Active games require an open space free of obstacles so that children can move and run. These games help provide a change of pace when students have been sitting for a while, or during special events such as Vacation Bible School, retreats or camps. Active games can be played outdoors on a level grassy playground area or indoors in a church gym or fellowship hall. Some active games can be played in classrooms if space is cleared by moving tables and chairs to the side of the room.

Think of these games as "play with a purpose." The object of these games is not to build muscle or stamina but to encourage teamwork and reinforce biblical truths. Popular active games are finding hidden objects, relays and tossing games.

Quiet Games

Quiet games can be done with students sitting at a table or on the floor. These games often require the use of a worksheet or activity page and are often more knowledge-oriented than active games. Quiet games may include mazes, codes, ordering words of a Bible verse and jigsaw and crossword puzzles. They can be played individually or in teams, with each student answering a question or getting help from teammates.

Tips on Effective Game Leadership

▶ Alternate active and quiet games to keep student interest high. Children who are not skilled in active games may feel more comfortable participating in quiet games.

▶ Avoid using strenuous active games when children are dressed in clothing that parents do not want to have soiled. If needed, provide smocks or large shirts for children to wear if children will get wet or dirty during the game.

▶ Always think of safety first. Make sure there are no sharp edges or points on game items. Never let students run with scissors, sticks, spoons or hard objects. Only use soft foam balls indoors and never allow balls to be thrown at someone's face. (Keep adhesive bandages on hand for an accidental cut or scrape.)

▶ Practice the game before class to be sure that it will work and it is not beyond the students' skill level. Make sure the jigsaw pieces fit, the clues are accurate, and the maze can be solved.

► Keep the game simple. Especially with younger children, the concept of working as a team to accomplish a task may be difficult. Games such as relays or games based on familiar children's games are easy for teachers to explain and for children to understand. Most of the game time should be spent playing the game, not explaining complicated rules. Demonstrate exactly what the children are to do. Give students a practice round or a warm-up try so that they don't feel anxious or frustrated in playing the game.

► Alternate the ways teams are selected so that children have opportunities to interact with a variety of classmates. Avoid letting children select their own teammates so that no one will feel left out. Teams can be formed by children wearing the same color of clothes, children with birthdays in the same month, children who have the same type of pet, the same number of letters in their name, initials of their first name, hair color or drawing names from a hat.

► Make games as noncompetitive as possible. If prizes are given, be sure each child receives a token for participating. No one should feel left out or as if he or she lost out. Consider using terminology such as "first winners" and "second winners" to help all children feel valued and still encourage healthy competition.

TEACHING THE "WRITE" WAY

In providing Bible learning activities that meet the varying needs and interests of children, one of the most useful and enjoyable activities is creative writing! If interesting activities are introduced with enthusiasm, even beginning writers will be motivated to join in. Every session doesn't have to produce a great art project or provide an active game—a pencil and paper can also be effective and fun teaching tools. For example, very often children will give more thought to writing answers than they will to giving quick oral responses.

Keep in mind that creative writing does not require a lot of training to use. Any child who can write can write creatively. Any adult who can write can guide students. Writing does not require a lot of materials, as do craft projects, or a large amount of space, as do some games. Writing can be an ongoing activity that can be stopped, stored on a shelf or in a drawer and restarted later. Writing activities can be completed as a group or by individuals. Writing helps the lesson move from head knowledge into heart knowledge as the child restates the Bible truth in a way that is personally meaningful.

In planning writing activities, two decisions need to be made:

1. Will others see the writing or is it only for the child's eyes? Some writing, such as personal feelings, is best kept private. Tell children in advance if this writing will be for sharing with the class or parents.

2. Will students write alone or with others? Some students may struggle with their writing skills and may be more comfortable working in a group. If children are not used to creative writing experiences or if their writing skills are just developing, they may feel more confident by participating in a group writing activity.

Give some simple but interesting suggestions to get young minds working. Begin telling a Bible story, then stop and let children write out an ending. Or give them a question to answer, such as How would you feel if Jesus washed your feet? or a sentence starter to complete, such as One way I can show I love God is by . . .

Ways to Use Writing

► Write a letter to a Bible story character (or write a letter from the character).

► Write a letter or make a greeting card for a senior citizen, hospital patient, missionary family or absent classmate.

► Write a Bible story as a newspaper article. "Flash! Big Flood Covers World!" "Soldiers Puzzled by Empty Grave!"

► Write a cooperative free-style (nonrhyming) poem. Select a topic, such as "God's Power in Nature." Each student contributes one sentence. After class, arrange the sentences in order and write or type the poem. Reproduce the poem on colored paper and distribute copies to the class.

► Write an "advice column." Give the students a question to answer, such as How can brothers and sisters in a family get along? or What should a kid do when his or her friend lies a lot?

► Keep a prayer journal. In class, let students decorate construction-paper covers and attach blank sheets of paper. During the week, students write or illustrate prayer requests,

Bible verses they have read, how they have helped others and their thoughts about God. Remind students that their journals are confidential!

▶ Draw a Bible story as a comic page. This assignment is good for older students who love video games and graphic novels. Students who don't want to draw can write the captions and dialogue.

▶ Use a computer. Many children are computer literate. If the church has a computer lab, let children type and print out their thoughts. They can e-mail messages to their home computers from church as reminders to pray or read the Bible during the week!

Special Tips

Use colorful pens and paper. Children need not be restricted to regular lined white paper and blue or black pens. Use colored paper or parchment. Add stickers or let children decorate the margins of paper. Try recreating an illuminated manuscript similar to medieval times by letting students draw illustrations and fancy capital letters. Pens and markers come in many ink colors. Be sure each pen's tip is thin enough for easy writing. Older children may use pens with special calligraphy tips and ink cartridges. Avoid using tips that must be dipped in ink, as these tips could be messy.

Have a dictionary handy. While this is not a composition class, a child may want to use an unfamiliar word or just have difficulty with writing. A child may want to do better if the writing will be shown to parents. Help children find spelling and grammar helps as needed. Write Bible names and place names on a chalkboard or white board so that children can spell them.

Suggest alternatives to writing. Quite a few children may not feel comfortable doing a lot of writing. Children can speak their ideas into an audiocassette recorder so that their words can be transcribed after class. An ESL child can write in his or her native tongue and explain to the class the meaning in English. A child can dictate thoughts for the teacher to write down and then illustrate the words.

USING ART TO TEACH THE BIBLE

Children love to make things with their hands! As infants, they mold their baby food into lumps and then progress to sand castles, mud pies and twig figures. Creative art activities engage many of a child's senses, but the goal of art activities is not simply to make pretty objects to take home and show to parents. The end result of an art-based Bible learning activity is to provide a stimulating, multisensory way for children to learn and apply Bible truths to their lives.

Process Versus Product

Art activities may sometimes have a "product" orientation: to create an attractive object for display by following directions accurately to reproduce a standard item. But in the classroom, focus on a "process" in which the doing of the art is more significant than the end result.

The advantage to focusing on "process" is that in creating individual pieces of art, children are not judged by their artistic abilities. A child may be hesitant to participate in an art experience if he or she feels that his or her ability is lacking. No child should be judged by the ability to accurately draw objects or by who is the neatest in using scissors. All artwork has value!

At times, it is useful to create craft items, but the primary goal of art activities should be to allow self-expression. Simply putting together an object only demonstrates that the child can follow directions. Giving children the freedom to create their own art encourages self-expression, thinking skills, creativity and greater satisfaction in the final product. As children work, the observant teacher can gain insights into the child's interests and understanding. Also, as children are allowed to express their own thoughts and feelings, they come to feel accepted and valued.

There are two reasons for using art activities in teaching:

1. Allows children to be active, rather than passive, participants in learning;

2. Puts abstract concepts in concrete terms that children can comprehend.

Tips for Leading Art Activities

Make the art relevant to the Bible lesson. There is a temptation to use art activities only as time fillers. It's easy to hand out pages from a Bible coloring book when the lesson runs short. However, even a simple creative art activity that invites a child to express his or her understanding of a Bible story or verse will expand the impact of a lesson on a child's life. Take advantage of the tested and proven ideas presented in your curriculum rather than spending precious time developing your own creative ideas each week. If, however, you need additional art ideas, consider these:

► Illustrate scenes of a Bible story to make a book.

► Cooperate with other students on a mural depicting Bible story scenes or contemporary situations in which children are obeying Bible truths.

► Use paint or decorative markers and scissors to make praise banners, identifying reasons to thank and praise God.

► Decorate the cover of a prayer journal to be used in class or at home.

► Create puppets to use in acting out ways to demonstrate love for God and others.

As a child works on an art activity, ask questions to help the child apply the Bible truth: "What happened just before the scene you are making? Which person in this scene do you think is a good example to follow? Why? What could you do this week that would show kindness like the good Samaritan did? What are you doing in this picture that is the same as what Ruth did in our story? How would it help the person in your picture if (she) remembered our Bible verse today?"

Be prepared. Experiment with the materials and the activity before class to be certain that the activity can be finished in the time allowed and that it is not too difficult. Note tips for success that can be shared with the children. If needed, briefly show a sample of your finished creation when introducing the activity, but then put away the sample to allow children to create in their own way.

Reduce cleanup. Avoid messy cleanup by providing glue and glitter that come in easy-to-control squeeze pens or tubes. Use erasable colored pencils instead of permanent markers. Cover tables with newspapers or plastic tablecloths. Keep plenty of wastebaskets, paper towels and cleaning rags on hand. Have children wear paint smocks or large washable shirts over their clothes. Give children plenty of time to assist with cleanup. Cooperating together on cleaning up the art materials can be a teaching time for children. Establish a consistent place in your classroom where art projects are placed to dry. As much as possible, avoid art projects that need more than 5 to 10 minutes to dry so that students don't carry wet objects home. (It's best not to make art projects that need to be left at church to dry, because some children may not be back the following week for pickup.)

Praise the art and the effort. Consider children's art to be their gift to God. Even the simplest attempt is worthy of acceptance. Praise children for their effort, use of color, creativity or the joy they show while making the art. Children appreciate that their effort is honored.

Learning Styles Tips

Variety is not only the spice of life but also the key to capturing interest and stimulating learning! The best activity will soon become stale if used too often. (This applies more to older learners than younger ones; preschoolers have a much greater need for repetition than do older children.) To address the different learning styles of children in a class, you will need varied approaches. While the goal is always to promote Bible learning and life application, there is almost no limit to the variety of ways in which that goal can be reached!

Visual learners sometimes become overly anxious about how a project "looks" to them or to others. The best way to help this child relax and enjoy is to first provide not a "craft" that must be made to certain specifications, but an open-ended activity. As the child watches others, he or she will gain confidence. Remind children, **There is no certain way to decorate your bag. You may use the shapes or make a picture. You may use the markers or the glitter glue. Whatever you want to do with your bag is OK.**

For some visual learners, planning ahead helps to prevent them from feeling frustrated as they begin to draw or do some other visual art project. Encourage children who are interested to sketch an outline or to lay pieces in several ways before plunging into a project.

A child may say, "I can't draw" or "Do this for me." The child may be saying that he or she is not feeling confident trying a new experience. Your best help is likely to be through words such as these: **It's hard to try something new. I understand. Make a start and then see how it goes. You can try again if you want. This doesn't have to be perfect.** Avoid platitudes such as **Just do your best!** Or **It's easy.** Acknowledge the child's feelings and be sure the child knows you're on his or her side.

Auditory learners enjoy not listening so much as talking! Those children who "think out loud" and who are perhaps the most likely to blurt out an answer are probably auditory learners. The act of talking and hearing themselves talk, listening to music, singing, chanting or speaking in rhythm, all have great interest for these learners. (This is a great blessing for teachers who want their children to memorize Bible verses. A verse set to music seems to immediately be well-remembered by an auditory learner!)

Kinesthetic learners (and perhaps nearly all children are kinesthetic learners in some ways) are people who need to move. They need to fiddle with things, keep their hands busy. All the while, they are learning both from the thing they are fiddling with and also from what they are hearing. The fiddling seems to increase their ability to listen!

Learning Styles Tips

Games are the best way to help kinesthetic learners to apply Bible truth. So instead of avoiding physically active games, use them! They will ultimately help you keep the classroom situation in hand because they provide a much-needed change of state. For a child (especially a kinesthetic learner), sitting still can by uncomfortable to the point of pain! To keep games from getting out of hand, be sure your rules are few and simple and keep the rounds of play fairly short.

A Bible-times costume box is a good addition to any children's classroom. Even older elementary students may find themselves enthusiastic about playing out a Bible story when there are fun and interesting costume pieces to wear! It's not necessary to make or buy elaborate costumes: visit thrift shops or garage sales for items such as bathrobes, sandals, men's neckties and costume jewelry (the Bible is full of kings and queens!). For very little money, you'll soon have an impressive collection! For headdresses, try lengths of fabric and scarves that are washable, just to avoid the possibility of head lice.

To appeal to more than one learning style, invite children to respond in more than one way to a question: by writing or drawing an answer, by saying an answer in a different voice or by recording an answer and then playing it back; by acting out an answer or modeling something in clay that is a clue to the answer.

To help kinesthetic learners who need to sit still during a Bible story, provide paper on which to draw out a scene from the story you are telling or provide dough with which to model a story object. Those busy hands will ensure greater attention!

Dramatic play is a way to involve kinesthetic, auditory and visual learners: children move, talk and listen, all while exploring the visual delights of dressing up in costume! The benefit of the experience lies in the learning that takes place, not the quality of the performance. Bible stories come alive when children pretend to be the characters!

Auditory/verbal learners might enjoy creating their own dialogue of a Bible story; however, visual learners might prefer to have a script to read aloud. Give silent parts to those who don't wish to speak but want to be involved. Never force a child to participate; a drama always needs an audience!

Planning learning activities that do not follow your own style of learning may not appeal to you. But there is great value in planning a wide variety so that each child really connects effectively with Bible truth! Try taking a learning-style test to discover your own learning styles— such tests are available on the Internet for free. Once you know your own learning styles, you'll be more aware of the styles of the children you teach and can then plan activities that best suit them.

Give tasks that let children succeed.

Communicate with Busy Parents

To be truly effective, a child's learning includes parental involvement. Children will attend regularly and be happy students when their parents actively support their classes at church. Developing good parental relationships, however, requires good communications.

Never assume that children will tell their parents necessary information. A child may forget or may pass on incorrect information. That's why it's important for you to get information directly to the parents. Also parents have positive feelings toward church when they establish a personal relationship with you and feel that you care enough to keep them informed.

Getting the Word Out

What do parents need to know? Parents are busy, and church news may be lost among the other information with which they deal. Clearly labeled parent letters and flyers need to be brief and to the point so that parents quickly see what they need to know.

Let parents know the topics and Scripture verses taught in class so that they can do follow-up learning at home. (Note: Your curriculum may provide take-home papers or handouts. Ask your supervisor or age-level coordinator for any handouts your church might provide.) Parents want to know about class projects, trips away from the church and their child's participation in church activities. Parents need to be told if their child became sick during class. If a child is continually disruptive in class, ask parents for suggestions to help the child get along better with others. Discipline and illness issues need to be kept confidential, told only to the parents involved.

Personal contact. Whenever possible, greet parents when they drop off and pick up their child. Relationships are built through continual contact and friendly greeting. However, this is not the time or place to talk about confidential information. If you have an issue to discuss or need further information from a parent, arrange an appointment for later in the week.

Just the facts. Prepare written information to distribute to children and their parents. Mail the information to the home, or create a "talk box." Set up a box by the classroom door with a hanging folder for each child. Written material is filed under the child's name. Parents are encouraged to check the folder when they pick up the child. If the folder is empty, then you will know that the parents received the information. If parents do not pick up their children from your classroom or do not attend for several weeks, mail or e-mail time-sensitive information.

Mass communication. Use the post office, e-mail and telephone to contact parents. Each method has its own advantages and drawbacks. Postage for letters can be expensive. E-mail is fast, but won't reach parents who don't have computer access. The phone can be time-consuming if a large number of parents need to be called. Telephone trees are faster but can break down easily. Decide which method is most effective for your class.

Dealing with Parents

Get information. When parents bring a child to the class for the first time, make sure that you or other greeters get as much information as possible: address, phone numbers (including cell phones and pagers), names of siblings, the child's school and hobbies. It's important to know if parents are divorced and sharing custody. It's critical to know if the child has food allergies or health needs or is on prescribed medication. If the child is disabled, ask about the child's abilities. The more you know, the better the child's needs can be met.

Get the parents involved. The best way to keep parents excited about church classes is to involve the parents as active participants. They can provide snacks or art supplies. Parents can take turns helping as classroom assistants or event chaperones. Parents with special talents can share their skills with the class.

However, be conscious of possible burnout. Parents don't want to spend huge sums or feel that they are being overworked. Spread out the tasks so that no one person is providing all the supplies or doing all the work.

Inviting parents to participate. Offer the task as a ministry opportunity, not an obligation. When recruiting parents to teach, assure them that materials and training will be provided. When recruiting chaperones, tell the parents exactly what's expected of them (cleanup, transportation, etc.). When they come to help, don't expect the parents to do something other than what they were told.

Difficult parents. Occasionally, some parents present a challenge. They may feel their child is not getting enough attention or refuse to believe that their child has discipline problems. Always listen to a parent's comments and consider ways to make sure their needs and the needs of their child are addressed. If parents have ongoing complaints, ask your supervisor to set up a meeting with you and the parents. Let the parents describe their feelings. Make listening your main job. Some people feel better when they know someone has heard them. Sometimes the complaint is only a symptom of a larger problem out of your control. Stay calm and respond in a nondefensive manner. Try to work out a win-win solution for everyone, although occasionally individual parent requests cannot be met without negatively affecting the whole class.

CONNECTING WITH FAMILIES

"Family" means something different in every household! One family might eat home-cooked meals together daily, play games and read books together, seldom watching television. However, another family might eat together only at restaurants, rarely play games or read at all, regularly watching selections from their vast video library! The values expressed by each of these styles may be quite different, but the fact is, each family's values and style are unique. While we each hold our own set of unspoken expectations about how families should be, what are practical ways we can best connect with and support the diverse kinds of families our children represent?

Awareness

Once, the family unit likely to be walking into a local church was two parents and two children. Today, the likely family unit may be one parent and three children, two grandparents and a grandchild, or two parents and one child. Family configurations have changed. However, the changes and challenges faced by families also create great opportunities! As we pray for each child, we can ask God to make us aware of the best ways to connect with that family and become agents of His grace to them. (The goal is not to interfere but to become a loving and supportive friend to every child and family, whatever the situation.)

Empathy

Where divorce or separation is part of the family situation, children are often under stresses that they themselves don't recognize. Always remember that the child had no choice in the situation. Your extra patience, nonjudgmental words and kindness are crucial! Build a bond of understanding with the child. "I hope you have fun with your mom next weekend, Rita. We'll miss you! But we'll see you on the next weekend." Your words help the child know you are on his or her side.

These children are also likely to be shuttled between parents, resulting in irregular attendance. If it's possible, record both parents' names, addresses and phone numbers (even if only one parent brings the child to class). When information needs to go home, be sure a copy is mailed to each parent. When a child misses the class, mail copies of his or her activity pages and take-home papers to the proper address. This will help the child feel connected with the class and will keep information flowing to both parents.

Sensitivity

As you talk about families, avoid assumptions about family life. Include references—without sounding negative—to children whose families are composed of other than traditional members. Be sensitive to children who live in a blended family or in shared custody situations. Help each child feel valued and loved. "Noah and his mom are a family. Amy and her brothers and her mom and dad are a family. Justin and his grandma and grandpa are a family. Sheena has two families. She lives with her dad and brother sometimes and lives with her sister and mom sometimes." As you explain and show acceptance, children will feel more positive and comfortable about their own families.

You may see a child's parents only when they drop off or pick up their child. It's important that you let them know you support their efforts to parent their children and teach them about God. Assign one friendly welcoming teacher or helper to the important task of greeting parents and briefly showing their child's work. For some parents, this contact may be the only conversation they have while they are at church! As you see parents' interest rise, invite them to observe the class (without pressuring them to volunteer as helpers!).

Support

Teaching young children need not end when they run out the door. No matter how busy we are, teachers of young children have unique opportunities to help young families. Our support can be something as simple as a conversation at the door that sparks an interest in an article on parenting in a take-home paper, or it can be something as involved as planning a play-date event for children and parents. Young parents may be more eager to connect with each other than you expect! Mutual support and fellowship is something they need and sometimes don't have time or money to do on their own. Creating a safe place for grown-ups as well as their children is one more way you can support and love young children and their parents.

GET THE SUPPORT OF PARENTS

Modern life makes many demands on families. A two-day weekend may not provide enough time to shop, visit friends and relatives, do homework, take family trips, participate in sporting events, celebrate family events, finish household tasks and relax. When Sunday morning rolls around, parents may feel too tired or too busy for church. Because most children are brought by their parents, it's important to recruit parents as your allies in helping their children establish good attendance habits.

Enlisting Parental Support

Educate parents. As you have opportunity through phone calls, personal conversation, class open house, newsletters and e-mail, help parents understand the importance of bringing their children to church regularly. A child who attends regularly is likely to continue church participation as an adult—not only because the habit is established, but also because the child has built solid friendships through regular attendance.

Classmates at church may be from different schools or areas of town and may only see each other once a week. A student who attends infrequently does not have the opportunity to cultivate these significant relationships. As a result, the child may feel lonely or isolated at church and so becomes less interested in attending. Even if a child complains about activities or teachers at church, he or she often will remain eager to come to church to see his or her friends. Especially as children move into their teen years, it may be difficult to begin new friendships at church, so it is important for friendships to be established at an early age.

Communicate with parents. Maintain regular contact with parents as best you can. Look for opportunities at church events to introduce yourself and talk to parents. Ask parents for e-mail addresses so that you can keep them informed of lesson plans, Bible memory verses, needed supplies and special events. Always communicate with parents in a positive manner. Be ready to share an activity the child particularly enjoyed. Parents will be interested in their child's class at church when they know what's going on. If a child is new to your class, be sure to find out if the child has food allergies, medications or special needs.

Host an open house. A good way to acquaint parents with your class is to invite parents to meet you and observe in the classroom. Provide refreshments and let parents participate in the lesson activities. If your classroom isn't big enough for all parents to attend at once, invite a different group of parents each week for several weeks in a row.

Dealing with Sunday Morning Conflicts

Some of the children in your class (and their parents) may face the difficult choice of choosing between church and sports activities on Sunday morning. What used to be exclusively church time can now be crowded with children's sports functions. There are no easy solutions to this situation. Children may feel resentful toward church if they must give up all sports activities to attend Sunday services.

In addition to helping parents understand the impact of regular attendance at church, here are some tips for what to do if a parent tells you that the child will be missing your class for a sports activity.

► If you have multiple services, suggest that families attend each week, even if they must attend a different service time.

▶ Encourage the parent to involve the child in a church activity that meets at another time (weekday, Saturday evening, etc.).

▶ Invite the child to attend class dressed in their sports clothes, so they can come directly before or after the sports activity.

▶ Make plans to send lesson materials to the child each week (take-home papers and/or student worksheets provided by the curriculum, etc.). Encourage the parent to read and talk about the materials with the child.

▶ Look for ways to continue your relationship with the child: Send an e-mail each week, schedule a class event (picnic at the park, pizza party, etc.) at a nonconflicting time. Send birthday or we-missed-you cards from yourself (or schedule a time during class for students to make these cards).

Parent Tips

Keep a pen and a pad of sticky notes with you as you engage children in conversation about projects they are working on. As children talk, write down some of what they say. Attach the child's words on the sticky note to their paper. (If you choose to write directly on the child's paper, show respect to the child by asking permission first.) This added information will give parents an insight into their child's thoughts and a personal connection to what happened in class.

Establish a location near your classroom door where children regularly place all take-home materials. Remind parents often to check this table or shelf each time they pick up their children.

Whenever you see a parent of a child in your class, don't forget to mention something the child did or enjoyed in a recent class session. This is a simple but effective way to build positive relationships!

Create an interactive environment with parents through an e-mail newsletter or a website. Do parents know your e-mail address? Do you have theirs? Does your church website have a page or link where parents of the children in your class can go to get more information about your class or department? Parents will likely be more responsive to the needs of the class, prepared for events that are coming up and possibly even more eager to help if they have a place to go for updated information!

Keep note cards, birthday cards and stamps at hand for your own use and for your students as well. Not only is it important that you remember birthdays and send notes when a child is absent, but children also enjoy sending a card to absent classmates or those who have had a birthday. It's a small investment that will pay huge relational dividends!

Some classes expect the parent of each class member to take a turn as a helper in the class (usually not more often than once every two months). Have a sign-up sheet at the door. This cooperative process not only solves the problem of having enough volunteers but also gives parents a window into what their child is learning and a sense of ownership in the class. Send out e-mail or voicemail reminders a week and a day or two ahead of time.

Consider inviting a parent or two to share information about his or her work if it can be related to the week's Bible story or aims: a landscaper could bring in plants to explore; a parent who enjoys cooking could provide a Bible-times or holiday snack; a musician could bring in one or more musical instruments to help your class praise the Lord!

There are many family configurations among the children in your class. Some may have a two-parent nuclear family. Others may live with one parent, with grandparents or other relatives, with foster parents or in a group home. When you talk about families, be sure that no child feels his or her situation is unacceptable. We live in lots of different kinds of families. **God gave us people to love us and care for us and that is good!**

Parent Tips

When a child says, "Danny doesn't have a dad," or another comment that may embarrass a child, simply state facts: Not every child lives with his or her parents. Fathers and mothers don't have to live with their children to show love to them. Riki's daddy is in the Army. He writes her letters. Dylan's mom calls him every week. His grandparents take good care of him. God gives us many people to love and care for us. Model a loving attitude: No matter the situation a child is in, the child did not choose that situation. No child comes from a "broken" home; we are all broken in some way. And God loves to heal every one!

Organize a family event for your class and their families. Depending on the ages of your students and their siblings, you may want to have a summer swim time, a fall harvest party or a Christmas caroling event. Whatever you choose, keep it simple to allow lots of time for families to interact with other families and with you. Such relaxed, get-acquainted kinds of times will go far in building strong relationships among the families and the children you teach.

With parental permission, prepare a roster of class member's names and phone numbers and email addresses so that parents and children may be in touch with the others in their class.

Keep a clipboard or a white board (with attached pen) near the doorway of your classroom. Use it to write reminders or positive comments. A clipboard with a page for parents to write notes to you or ask questions is also helpful.

Perhaps it sounds old-fashioned, but there is nothing like visiting a child from your class in his or her home! A visit strengthens your relationship with the child, shows you how the child lives and can be a real encouragement to parents. Make this a positive time, getting to know the family and affirming the ways they are blessing and helping the child. If a home visit isn't possible, consider inviting that family to your home for a simple meal or to a park for a picnic.

Poll parents for parenting topics of interest to them and then organize a potluck once or twice a year. Provide child care and a speaker on a topic of interest to your parents: Save dessert for a time after the speaker finishes so that parents have plenty of time to discuss the ideas that have been put forth. Or, have a question-and-answer feature on your website or a send round robin email to gather ideas from other parents in answer to a parent's question. Providing learning for parents will positively impact the children you teach!

If you hear from a parent that his or her child doesn't like to come to class, take some time to find out why. Discover that child's particular interests and skills. Perhaps you could plan an activity to capitalize on that child's interests. When children know they matter to you, they become enthusiastic about coming to class!

Always communicate with parents in a positive manner.

EDUCATE PARENTS OFTEN ABOUT UPCOMING EVENTS AND VOLUNTEER OPPORTUNITIES.

HELP PARENTS UNDERSTAND THE IMPORTANCE OF THEIR CHILD'S ATTENDANCE

HELLO, GOD, IT'S ME!

One of the most awesome responsibilities of the teacher at church is to give children the tools of prayer. Even young children can approach their heavenly Father with the confidence that He hears their prayers. It's never to soon for children to establish a habit of daily prayer.

What to Teach About Prayer

God listens. Children may feel that they are too young or insignificant for God's attention, or that God is only interested in grown-ups. Assure children that God cares and wants to hear from them at any time (see Matthew 7:7-8).

Some children may feel that when they pray, they must feel or express deep emotions. Let your children know that God hears, even if they don't feel like anything happened!

God provides. God is the source of everything on Earth. Children can give prayers of thanksgiving for food, shelter, clothing, friends, family and safety (see Psalm 103:1-5).

God is not a magician or Santa Claus. Prayer is often seen as something magical that grants instant requests. A child may feel sad or angry when a prayer did not "come true" right away. Sometimes prayers are answered after a long time. For example, a chemistry set is a great birthday present, but a very young child would not be able to use it. The child would need to get older and learn more before using it. Sometimes God waits for children (or adults) to mature before answering a prayer.

People commonly pray when they want something. Children often pray to get certain gifts for Christmas or that their team will win the championship. Sometimes God answers prayer not by giving us what we want but by giving the strength and wisdom to work for it. A child who works hard to earn an allowance can save money for a bike. A team can win a championship with practice and good sportsmanship.

Reassure children that God wants them to pray about all their needs and concerns, and that they can depend on God to always love and care for them (see Philippians 4:6).

God likes to hear prayers for others. Besides praying for their own needs, encourage children to think about and then pray for the needs of others. Children can pray for their parents (especially absent or divorced parents), siblings, friends, schoolmates, teachers and pets (see Matthew 5:44; Ephesians 6:18; James 5:16).

Why didn't God answer my prayer? In an imperfect world, bad things happen. A child can be caught in an ugly custody battle during a divorce. A child may be the victim of abuse or a criminal act. Natural disasters and accidents can destroy a family home. A family member or favorite pet dies. Children may wonder why a caring God would allow things to happen that they consider tragic.

Reassure children that God understands how they feel and that God can make something good come out of a bad situation (see Romans 8:28). For example, when a disaster happens, people in a church or community often help each other. God is still present and working through these people to see that needs are met.

How to Pray

Keep it simple. Children may feel that they need poetic language and "thees and thous" to pray. Children can talk to God in ordinary language.

Keep it honest. Children may feel that God will punish them if they are angry, upset or doubtful. It's okay to talk to God about unhappy feelings. God wants to hear how we feel.

Keep it short. Prayers don't need to be long or cover every subject. Young children can begin with short sentence prayers as they learn to pray.

Be a role model. Children will become comfortable with prayer when they see adults praying in ways that are appropriate and appealing. Make prayer a regular part of your class. Talk about personal answers to prayer during class.

Use a simple format. ACTS is a common acronym you can use to teach children how to pray.

Adoration: Praise and thank God for His love and power.

Confession: Admit actions and attitudes that do not show love for God and others, and say "I'm sorry" for sins.

Thanksgiving: Thank God for the good things He gives us.

Supplication: Ask God for things you need.

Keep a prayer journal. Older children can write down their petitions, thanksgivings and answers to prayer. They can record biblical prayers that they use in class. Lead children to make prayer journals by decorating a notebook or attaching sheets of paper together with a ribbon and cardboard cover. Prayer journals may be kept as personal, not to be read by other students.

Pray for the Children You Teach

Why Pray?

You may teach toddlers, preteens or wiggly second graders; you may enjoy teaching or may feel it's a duty. Ministry to kids may seem as natural to you as breathing or it may burn you out. It might even terrify you! But whatever your current attitudes and feelings about your role as a teacher or helper, there is a simple and easy way to move from duty to delight, from burnout to enduring flame, from your current level of ministry to an even higher level. It may sound too simple to believe, but praying for your students during the week will transform your ministry!

If you're willing to take the plunge and make a consistent effort, you will discover that praying for the kids you teach will change your class from the inside out: you'll gain new perspective, discover creative solutions to problems and gain God-given insights into the lives of even the most difficult children you meet. This prepares you to be the channel for God to use in transforming the kids in your class—even the one you are thinking of right now, wondering whether or not you even want to pray for *that* child!

Let's begin with looking at the way Jesus Himself prayed (remember, He was the teacher of a "small group" of 12!): According to statistical analysts, Jesus' recorded prayers consist of 40 percent giving of thanks, 40 percent declaration (of who God is and what He does) and only 20 percent petitions or "other." Let that model settle into your mind: Nearly half of Jesus' time spent in prayer was spent not asking, but thanking, God!

What might happen if we spent 40 percent of our prayer time for the kids we teach by thanking God for each child and for what God is doing in each one of their lives? (Perhaps it would bring an attitude adjustment for some of us!) When we thank God, our own words focus our hearts and minds upon who He is and what He is able to do instead on focusing on the problems. If we were to spend another 40 percent of our prayer time declaring what we know about God and applying it to the situations related to the kids we teach, imagine how that would change the kinds of prayers we pray!

Taking the model of Jesus' prayers as a kind of baseline, try these practical ideas to increase prayer focus on the kids you teach:

Place a copy of your class roster on your refrigerator, next to your computer or in another place where you often see it. When your eye catches a name, take a moment to thank God for that child and pray for his or her needs.

Write each child's name onto an individual sticky note. Add at least one positive characteristic you have noticed about him or her ("great smile," "likes to help," etc.). Post notes where you will often see them (near a computer, on a dashboard, etc.). Whenever you see a note, thank God for the ways He is working in that child's life. Pray for a need that child has expressed.

To be sure you have the chance to pray for each child, add their names on sticky notes to pages of your day timer or squares of a calendar.

Pray especially for the children for whom you have the least natural affection. If you have a co-teacher or helper, spend time in prayer together, whether in person, by phone, e-mail or text message, thank God together for that child and for His solutions to the problems.

When you have difficulty with a child, write that child's name at the top of a piece of paper. Below the name, brainstorm several ways God might use that child in the future (hyperactive=great energy for God's kingdom, verbal=future pastor, evangelist!). Post the paper where only you will see it occasionally. Whenever you see the paper, thank God for that child's characteristics and for the ways He will use that child in the future!

Use the power of praying God's Word! Pray the week's Scripture passage or Bible memory verse over the children in your class as you prepare. Ask God to make you creative and clear in teaching and them able to understand and put into practice what they hear.

Every child comes from a family: Don't forget to pray for the parents! (Remember that a child's disruptive actions often relate to what goes on at home.) Thank God for each family member, for what He is doing in each family, and invite Him to show you ways you can help with the family's spiritual growth.

I don't get it.

Why is it so important to spend time thanking God and declaring His character and His power?

We may have learned by example that prayer is verbally listing for God what things are wrong (in our opinion) and how God should correct the problem. Besides the reality that the creator of the universe does not need our advice (however wise it may be), this kind of prayer easily slides into worship of the problem itself instead of the God who solves the problem! By making thanksgiving and declaration the primary parts of prayer, we avoid repeating to ourselves and to others the great difficulty of the problem and our perception of the impossibility of finding the solution: such words take us dangerously close to slandering the power of the One who said, "Is there anything too hard for me?" or the good intentions of God toward us, as Israel did in the desert ("He left us out here to die!"). As we focus our thoughts and words on God's ability and His love (even for those we cannot love), we worship the One who answers prayer and solves problems, finding it ever easier to pray in every situation (see Ephesians 6, 1 Thessalonians 5:16-18)!

Praying with the Children in Your Class

All too often, parents are already at the door when we call out, "Any prayer requests?" That's not likely to result in much focused prayer time. Here are a few ideas for sparking an increase in prayer among the kids you teach.

For Younger Children

As a group, thank God for items in categories (things that have fur, things that we eat, things that make a sound, things that begin with the letter *A*, etc.). Volunteers may take turns to say,

"Thank You, God, for...". Younger children may simply add the word they thought of to your spoken prayer.

Invite children to draw a picture of something for which to thank God and then to hold up that picture while saying a prayer of thanks. Younger or less verbal children may simply hold up the picture as a prayer.

Invite children to complete a sentence starter ("God is good to give me ..."). Older children will enjoy adding on to the responses of other children: "God is good to give a cat to Anna, grapes to Jake and pizza to me."

For Elementary Children

Preprint cards or slips of paper with the words, "How may we pray for you this week?" Have these in the same place every week or make a time during each class to fill out the cards. These cards will give you great insight into the concerns and needs of the kids in your class.

Prepare a prayer box where children may leave requests at any time. When children know that they may write or draw a prayer request anytime, they are more likely to do so when they remember a request.

If your class seems reticent to speak or write prayer requests, give them a specific category under which to think of a request: one friend at school, two family member, chores, homework, scary situations, etc.

A class prayer journal can be an exciting way to build prayer into your class. Write and date each request; invite children to make notes so that they can pray for each other during the week. Leave space so you're able to write down the answers! Ask for reports on answers and add them as they are reported.

Several times a year, go back through your class prayer journal as a group; review the ways God answered prayers and thank God for His answers.

Invite kids to write a request on a sticky note and then exchange that note with another class member. If your class seems interested, invite them to add their phone numbers so that members who exchanged notes may call each other to hear the result of their prayer.

Helping Young Children Talk to God

Prayer can be a meaningful part of worship for young children. However, it is sometimes done in ways that make it seem strange, boring and unrelated to a child's life. What are some ways we can help young children grow in their desire and ability to express themselves to God?

Understanding in Words

As much of a mystery as prayer is to some of us adults, what can young children understand about prayer?

▶ God wants us to talk to Him. He wants to hear what we have to say!

▶ We can pray anytime—not only in Sunday School or church but in the car, at the store, anywhere!

▶ We can pray by saying words out loud or by saying words to ourselves. We can sing prayers, too.

▶ We close our eyes because it helps us think about what we are talking to God about, instead of what we see around us.

Understanding in Action

The way you pray teaches far more about prayer than any words you say! When you pray, it shows children that prayer is important to you. Your attitude of reverence and trust is keenly felt by a child. When you pray, you show children what prayer is. If your prayers are short and specific and if they make sense to a young child, you are also teaching that prayer is simple, genuine and deals with things that matter to young children.

If you think that prayer is mainly for grown-ups or that young children aren't yet able to pray, your prayers will reflect it. Because young children so easily absorb unspoken adult attitudes, they will soon conclude that they can't pray. Instead, take this opportunity to consider what Jesus said about our need to become like little children! Prayer is not a performance for God or for anyone else. Enjoy learning how to pray simply, honestly and directly. It will change your prayer life and will effectively teach prayer to children.

Throughout a class session, provide opportunities for short, simple prayers during activities. "Look at the way your hands can draw those little circles, Josh! Let's thank God for your hands. Dear God, thank You for Josh's hands. They can draw little circles! In Jesus' name, amen." "Jenna, you shared the crayons with Eliot. That's a way to obey God's Word. Thank You, God, that Jenna knows how to share. In Jesus' name, amen." These occasional and natural prayers teach a child that God cares about every part of life.

If a child is reluctant to pray or unfamiliar with praying aloud, involve the child in prayer in other ways. For example, ask a question. "What is something you like to eat?" Then include the child's answer in a thank-you prayer. "What is one way to obey God by being kind?" After the child answers, ask God's help in being kind, mentioning the specific way suggested by the child.

To help children know prayers need not always be spoken, sing songs that are prayers with the children. Comment, "The words of the song are meant to be sung to God. It is a prayer." Children may wish to close their eyes as they sing, to help them remember that the song is a prayer.

Understanding Bible Prayers

Adults may feel that young children should memorize Scripture prayers such as the Lord's Prayer or a prayer from the Psalms. While it is true that young children have a facility for memorization and that words memorized in early childhood are well-remembered, these Scriptural phrases are long and many of the words are beyond a young child's understanding. When a child is older, memorizing these significant passages will be a more meaningful experience than during early childhood.

Remember, the most meaningful and trustworthy way to teach children about prayer is your prayers. Ask God to work by His Spirit to use your example—and trust Him to do so, in childlike faith!

Prayer Tips

Prayer is a part of life that might be expected to be taught by memorized words ("Now I lay me down to sleep ..."). However effective that may be for giving children words to begin with, there is just as much real power in the prayer of a child as there is in the prayer of a theology professor—for the power lies not in the one who prays but in the One to whom he or she prays! God values the prayers of little ones. Be sure to let children know that you, too, value the prayers they pray.

Prayer is best learned through doing. Provide plenty of opportunities to pray to God. Most young children will need for you to supply some words. Make prayer a successful experience for every child. Be sure that children know God understands what they mean, even if they cannot say the word they wish to say.

As you participate in activities with children, pray aloud often. **Our game was fun! Thank You, God, for helping us play that game.** This not only models words they may use but also helps them to realize that indeed, we can talk to God anytime, without bowed heads or folded hands. Children need to see that we can communicate with God in any situation!

It's easy to love and accept happy, cooperative children. However, to love and accept each child "as is" is the mandate Scripture gives us! The whirlwind of a boy who upsets all your best-laid plans, the little girl for whom drama seems to be the only way to communicate—it's easy to sigh over them and then forget them for another week. But God says that His kingdom is about relationships, not our plans or our ideas! Loving such children must begin with prayer. Take time to target one or two children in your class every day. Thank God for each child, for his or her abilities and potential; imagine how God might use that child in the future. The more "unlovable" a child is, the more the child needs love! Your genuine love and acceptance may be the only place that child begins to understand God's love.

Older children will enjoy writing prayers. They may find it a novel idea that one may write, sing or paint a prayer. As you lead children in prayer activities, explain that prayer is simply talking to God; as you pray, use simple words and short sentences. Giving a model they can understand is far better than a long prayer that makes prayer seem boring or something only for adults.

As you see abilities children display, pray aloud during activity time: **Dear God, Thank You that Alisa knows how to take turns. Thank You that Carlos can stack the blocks so high. Amen.** This helps children realize that God is the source of their abilities and that He is interested in what they do!

Prayer Tips

To help children realize that God is interested in things of interest to them, draw or write out prayers (younger children may draw and dictate words). As children work, talk with them about their work and then pray aloud with the child. **Dear God, Gino is worried about his sick cat. Thank You for loving his cat. Thank You for loving Gino. In Jesus' name, amen.**

Take a praise walk with children. Begin by praising God in sentence prayers for the things you see on your walk. As children get the idea, invite them to pray sentence prayers of thanks aloud or silently, eyes open, as they walk.

For prayer to be meaningful to children, avoid symbolism. Don't use terms such as "cover them in the blood of the Lamb" or "use them in the foreign fields." Can you imagine what images come to the minds of literal thinkers? Instead, use words that children will understand; keep the scope of the prayer within the child's level of experience.

When a child volunteers information that a family member or pet is sick, stop the action and take a moment to pray aloud. This helps everyone remember that God is here, now, ready to listen and able to help!

As you eat a snack together, take the opportunity to first thank God for the food or invite a child to pray. This is sometimes overlooked but can be a powerful teaching time! During snack time, invite children to tell about times they pray at home. If a child does not respond, don't press; many children never hear a prayer at home. You can say to children: **Some people pray long prayers. Some people pray short prayers. God hears us no matter what way we pray to Him. Our Bible promises God will hear us when we pray.**

During prayer times, never let a child become embarrassed. If he or she cannot think of words, calmly supply them with an idea and then be sure the child knows that God hears and understands what is in our hearts. As you make prayer a successful experience, they will grow confident that God hears them.

Your attitude of reverence and trust will be keenly felt by children. The most meaningful and trustworthy method of teaching children to pray, is to pray—with them, for them, in as many ways and times as possible!

Short specific prayers teach that prayer deals with things of interest to the child.

EMOTIONAL AND SPIRITUAL SAFETY

How can we best make our church a safe place for children to grow spiritually?

Emotional and spiritual safety is important. Meeting a standard for children's physical safety is not only a good thing, but it is also required by law! Safety in the emotional and spiritual realm is equally important. But it may be overlooked or minimized, even at church. However, it should be a priority, for it is an integral part of helping kids know Christ and grow in Christ!

Emotional and spiritual safety sends a message. Every child who participates in our children's ministries deserves and needs to know that he or she is valued, loved and protected. Everything we say or do as leaders and teachers should communicate that message. Our goal is not only that children gain "book knowledge" (know the Ten Commandments or the books of the Bible, etc.) but also that their lives be transformed through knowing God's Word, understanding what it says and then learning how to apply it daily. Because we have the world's highest goal, we must be sure that children receive the world's highest message by our behavior—a biblical message of love and care.

Emotional and spiritual safety creates an environment for growth. Children's lives can be hurried, complicated and confusing. They may come to our programs carrying far larger burdens than we imagine! The church should be a place where it is emotionally safe for children to talk about what is going on in their lives and where it is spiritually safe for them to ask hard questions and be heard, acknowledged and answered. When we are committed to children's emotional and spiritual safety, we nurture their growth into wholehearted followers of Christ.

Core beliefs are the basis for providing safety. When adults hold the following core beliefs, they are ready to foster emotional and spiritual safety for children:

Servanthood. Believing that we are all here to love and help each other.

Value. Believing that each child is valuable as a person, both to God and to us. Children will know they matter to God only when they see they matter to us.

Faith. Believing that every child can have a bright future in God's family. Children need for us to see their spiritual potential.

Trustworthiness. Believing that a child's trust is a delicate gift that must be treated with care.

Honor. Believing that when we honor a child, we honor Jesus.

Some actions that nurture emotional and spiritual safety:

▶ Placing oneself at a child's eye level.

▶ Listening with interest to what a child has to say.

▶ Giving frequent and genuine smiles and safe touches.

▶ Using a child's name lovingly and often.

► Telling a child the truth and making truth understandable to him or her.

► Being honest when you don't know an answer by saying you don't know.

► Finding an answer and reporting it to the child.

► Giving a child a choice in activities.

► Phrasing directions positively so that a child knows what he or she can do.

► Helping a child take responsibility to change problem behavior.

► Helping the child find ways to change negative behavior rather than making negative comments about the child's character.

► Making sure no child ever feels he or she is a burden or a problem.

► Making sure no child receives a negative label but does receive words of love and blessing.

These actions flow from the beliefs above. Beyond being professional, Christian teachers are called to live in ways that genuinely display Christlike character.

PHYSICAL SAFETY

Creating a safe environment for children to learn God's Word should be placed with high importance in any church setting. When we create a secure atmosphere for children, we tell them that we care about their learning experience at church. Not only should we protect children from the physical abuse of others (bullying, mistreatment of children by adults), but every children's ministry should adopt preventive methods to ensure that children are unable to cause harm to themselves. In response, children will feel comfortable enough to interact with their teachers and peers in learning spiritual matters.

Keeping in line with standard ministry procedures such as making sure parents sign each child in and out of children's services, ensures that each child is physically accounted for and will be picked up by the correct person. Additionally, having parents complete a registration form for their children also plays a vital role in gaining information about how to keep the child safe. The registration form should include questions like Does your child have any allergies to food or non-consumable materials (glue, crayons, markers, etc.)? With this information, you will know not to involve the child in any activities that can be harmful to the child's well being. Instead, offer the child an alternative activity that meets the needs of the day's lesson topic.

What to Do When I'm Sick

If you're not feeling well, do not attempt to teach your class. It is far too risky to be around children when you are ill. Many contagious illnesses can passed along to children this way. Do stay home and contact your supervisor or a substitute and inform him or her of your absence.

What to Do When a Child Arrives Sick

When a parent arrives with a child who has visible symptoms of an illness (coughing, sneezing, runny nose) or if symptoms develop during class time, talk to the parent and politely explain the safety policy. If the parent has a difficult time understanding, positively inform the parent that it would be better to have the child stay home. You might say, "I'll really miss having Devin in class today, but it's better for him and the other children if he goes home."

What to Do in an Emergency

Every class should have a plan of action to follow in the event of an emergency. This plan should be well developed and practiced often in order to maintain the safety of each individual. Here are some helpful steps to take in planning emergency procedures.

Be aware of emergency exits.

Have a designated meeting place for your class.

Be aware of natural hazards that are common to your area (earthquakes, tornadoes, etc.) and know the effective safety conduct methods (stop, drop and roll; duck and cover methods, etc.) for each possible hazard.

Post emergency procedures and an evacuation map in your classroom.

Inform parents and your supervisor about your emergency plan.

What to Do If Someone Is Injured

If you haven't already participated in adult and child CPR and First Aid training, it is highly encouraged. This training provides valuable knowledge that could save a precious life. If you have participated in this type of training and someone is severely injured, administer the proper aid and contact the authorities (calling 911 in most cases) for help. In addition, it helps to know where phones are located in the building and if you have one, use your cell phone when you can't get to a landline phone.

Make sure to report any injury that occurs whether small or large. Documentation of minor accidental injuries can help parents feel secure in knowing their children aren't being abused. When an injury occurs, swiftly document the incident and notify your supervisor and the parents.

Pay Attention to Your Surroundings

Being alert in children's ministry is key in taking a preventive approach to the physical safety of children. These are simple steps that you can take in examining your church facility to keep a safe environment for children.

Identify the Location of Smoke Alarms, Fire Extinguishers and First Aid Kits. Knowing the location of these items can help you quickly identify and resolve what could become a dangerous situation.

Secure All Exposed Wires with a Security Cover. With younger children, cover all exposed electrical outlets with outlet covers. Younger children tend to stick things into uncovered outlets.

Conduct Visual Checks of Play Areas. Most church play areas are accessible to the public. Conduct a thorough visual check of possible dangers to children (broken glass, cigarette butts, empty beverage cans, etc.).

Identify and Use Appropriate Storing Areas for Supplies. Store cleaning supplies and craft supplies (scissors, glue, etc.) out of the reach of children.

Safety Tips

Hand washing is often missed at church because there are no nearby washing facilities. Before a snack or after playing with a messy item such as dough, provide wipes with which to thoroughly clean hands and make it a game: You wipe your hands and children imitate you. Describe your actions: **I'm wiping between my fingers. There, my thumb is clean!** This ensures that hands are clean and everyone has fun doing a complete job.

For very young children who still put things into their mouths, be aware of the rapid spread of germs. Set up a system to keep classroom toys clean and germ-free. Teachers or parents may take turns to bring toys home for sterilizing or keep germicidal wipes at hand.

When you have planned a game, take a moment before children arrive to scope out possible hazards in the playing area. Be sure there are no loose rugs, slick floors or items to trip over. Clear away potential obstacles and try the game action yourself to see how it will work best.

Emotional safety may be one of the more overlooked areas of our safety-conscious society. Make it a rule in your classroom that "We don't say, 'You can't play.' " When children know they are expected to be kind, they are likely to live up to your expectation!

Block-building is one of the best ways for younger children to learn a variety of skills. Here are few rules for keeping block activities safe: One person may not knock down another person's building; a construction may be no higher than a child's chin; blocks are used only in the block area; blocks are never thrown.

Lay a line of masking tape (or make some other visual boundary) several feet away from the block shelf. Make it a rule that block-building must take place on the far side of that boundary so that others may have access to the blocks.

If a block, a tube, or other toy becomes a gun, simply state the proper use of the item and then offer the child a choice of a proper way to use the item. **Kyle, we are using the tubes to build a house. Where would you like to put that tube?**

Be mindful that there may be a child in your group who finds it difficult to trust others because of an abusive situation in his or her life. Let the child know that you will listen to what he or she has to say without judging. Make your class a safe place emotionally for every child.

If a child indicates that an abusive situation exists at home, report your conversation to your supervisor. In many states, the church may be required to report allegations of abuse. If your church does not have clearly defined procedures for awareness and prevention of abuse, purchase appropriate resources from your local Christian bookstore and set up a reporting system.

Make your class a safe place emotionally and physically for every child.

LEADING A CHILD TO CHRIST

Many adult Christians look back to their elementary years as the time when they accepted Christ as Savior. Not only are children able to understand the difference between right and wrong and their own personal need of forgiveness, but they are also growing in their ability to understand Jesus' death and resurrection as the means by which God provides salvation. In addition, elementary children are capable of growing in their faith through prayer, Bible reading, worship and service.

However, children (particularly those in early elementary grades) can still be limited in their understanding and may be immature in following through on their intentions and commitments. They need thoughtful, patient guidance in coming to know Christ personally and continuing to grow in Him.

1. Pray.

Ask God to prepare the children in your class to receive the good news about Jesus and prepare you to effectively communicate with them.

2. Present the good news.

Use words and phrases that children understand. Avoid symbolism that will confuse these literal-minded thinkers. *Discuss these points slowly* enough to allow time for thinking and comprehending.

a. "God wants you to become His child. Do you know why God wants you in His family?" (See 1 John 3:1.)

b. "You and all the people in the world have done wrong things. The Bible word for doing wrong is 'sin.' What do you think the Bible says should happen to us when we sin?" (See Romans 6:23.)

c. "God loves you so much, He sent His Son to die on the cross for your sin. Because Jesus never sinned, He is the only one who can take the punishment for your sin." (See 1 Corinthians 15:3; 1 John 4:14.) On the third day after Jesus died, God brought Him back to life.

d. "Are you sorry for your sin? Tell God that you are. Do you believe Jesus died to take the punishment for your sin and that He is alive today? If you tell God you are sorry for your sin and tell Him you do believe and accept Jesus' death to take away your sin—God forgives all your sin." (See 1 John 1:9.)

e. "The Bible says that when you believe in Jesus, God's Son, you receive God's gift of eternal life. This gift makes you a child of God. (See John 3:16.) This means God is with you now and forever."

As you give children many opportunities to think about what it means to be a Christian, expose them to a variety of lessons and descriptions of the meaning of salvation to aid their understanding.

3. Talk personally with the child.

Talking about salvation one-on-one creates opportunity to ask and answer questions. Ask questions that move the child beyond simple yes or no answers or recitation of memorized information. Ask what-do-you-think kinds of questions such as:

"Why do you think it's important to . . . ?"

"What are some things you really like about Jesus?"

"Why do you think that Jesus had to die because of wrong things you and I have done?"

"What difference do you think it makes for a person to be forgiven?"

Answers to these open-ended questions will help you discern how much the child does or does not understand.

4. Offer opportunities without pressure.

Children are vulnerable to being manipulated by adults. A good way to guard against coercing a child's response is to simply pause periodically and ask, "Would you like to hear more about this now or at another time?" Lovingly accepting the child, even when he or she is not fully interested in pursuing the matter, is crucial in building and main-taining relationship that will yield more opportunities to talk about becoming part of God's family.

5. Give time to think and pray.

There is great value in encouraging a child to think and pray about what you have said before making a response. Also allow moments for quiet thinking about questions you ask.

6. Respect the child's response.

Whether or not a child declares faith in Jesus Christ, adults need to accept the child's action. There is also a need to realize that a child's initial responses to Jesus are just the beginning of a lifelong process of growing in the faith.

7. Guide the child in further growth.

Here are three important parts in the nurturing process:

a. *Talk regularly about your relationship with God.* As you talk about your relation-ship, the child will begin to feel that it's OK to talk about such things. Then you can com-fortably ask the child to share his or her thoughts and feelings, and encourage the child to ask questions of you.

b. *Prepare the child to deal with doubts.* Emphasize that certainty about salvation is not dependent on our feelings or doing enough good deeds. Show the child verses in God's Word that clearly declare that salvation comes by grace through faith (i.e., John 1:12; Ephesians 2:8-9; Hebrews 11:6; 1 John 5:11).

c. *Teach the child to confess all sin.* "Confess" means "to admit" or "to agree." Confessing sins means agreeing with God that we really have sinned. Assure the child that confession always results in forgiveness (see 1 John 1:9).

GUIDING THE YOUNG CHILD TOWARD JESUS

Each of us moves through the spiritual development of life in as much of an individual rate and way as we do in any other area. God knows each person intimately; therefore, He works differently in every life. Whatever one's rate of growth or plan of development, God is tirelessly at work to bring us into closer relationship with Himself! Acknowledging this helps us rest in His good plan and look for His hand in the experiences that cause us and our children to develop spiritually.

When we present Jesus consistently by both our actions and our words, we lay a foundation for a child to receive Christ as Savior. When is a child ready to receive Christ? Remembering God's ceaseless work, we need to be sensitive facilitators of that process. God's Holy Spirit calls a child into relationship in His time, not ours. We should never put up walls, but we also should never push or manipulate children. We need to give children time and opportunity to ask questions, think through ideas and respond at their own pace. While some children at this age level (especially from Christian homes) may indeed pray to become members of God's family, accepting Jesus as their Savior, expect wide variation in children's readiness for this important step.

▶ To help a child give words to thoughts and feelings about Jesus, ask many open-ended what-do-you-think and tell-me-more questions. "Tell me what you like best about Jesus" will help you gain insight into what a child does or doesn't understand. This will also help you to give a child the information he or she needs, instead of an answer that doesn't apply! Kindergartners especially want to know more about many aspects of God. Every question we answer creates an opportunity to help the child understand more about a personal relationship with Jesus.

▶ Talk individually with children. Something as important as a child's personal relationship with Jesus Christ can be handled more effectively alone than in a group.

▶ Talk simply. Phrases such as "born again" or "Jesus in my heart" are symbolic and far beyond a young child's understanding. Focus on how God makes people a part of His family:

God loves us, but we have done wrong things (sinned).

God says sin must be punished.

God sent Jesus to take the punishment for the wrong things we have done.

We can tell God that we have done wrong and tell Him we are sorry for our sin. We can ask Jesus to be our Savior.

Then God forgives us and we become a part of God's family.

Consistently share this information whenever a child seems interested but only for as long as the interest lasts. Lay a good foundation for a lifetime of solid spiritual growth!

Salvation Tips

Telling the good news about Jesus is more than words alone. The telling, for a child, is mainly done through your demonstrations of Jesus' love. Every child should feel secure and loved in the church family. For the child whose home situation has not fostered feelings of love, you need to make special efforts to notice and encourage that child's actions. Use the child's name often as you chat. Be interested in what he or she has to say. Listen attentively. These actions all build loving relationships. And loving relationships are what God's family is all about! Show the love of Jesus in a way that a child can see and understand.

Most young children can understand that Jesus is always their friend and helper. The plan of salvation in Jesus Christ is simple and clear enough that some young children can understand it and respond to it at their level of child-like faith (particularly those who receive Christian nurture at home). Keep in mind, however, that spiritual birth, like physical birth, is part of a process. A baby must develop in the womb before birth. Jesus compared the preparation of the heart to the planting of seed which bears fruit at the proper time.

Every time you are with children, not only when you are talking about Jesus' death and resurrection, you are building a foundation of spiritual understanding for each one. As you model the love of Jesus in every situation, seeds are being planted. You may be the first person in a child's life to explain the spiritual truth, that Jesus is God's Son and that He died to take the punishment for our sins. But without the loving actions that have shown that love, the words have little meaning. Pray for the Holy Spirit's guidance as you nurture the spiritual understanding of the children in your class.

It is important that children get a growing understanding of who Jesus is and what God has done to make it possible for us to become part of His family. Whenever it is appropriate, talk with children about God's gift of salvation. **What did Jesus do so our wrong actions could be forgiven?** If a child indicates interest in talking with you about joining God's family, arrange to talk with the child after class or during the week. It is best to do this individually rather than in a group so that a child's thoughts and ideas are his or her own.

Are you praying regularly for each child in your class? One of the greatest privileges of serving in children's ministry is to help children become members of God's family. Ask God to prepare the children in your class to receive the good news and to prepare you to communicate the good news in an effective way.

Talk individually with children who indicate an interest in joining God's family. Something as important as a child's personal relationship with Christ is handled more effectively one-on-one than in a group. A child needs to respond individually to the call of God's love with a genuine response—not because the child wants to please peers, parents or the teacher. Take time to become familiar with age-appropriate words that explain the gospel and understand the steps to help a child become a member of God's family.

It is effective to talk with children about the family to which they already belong—even if that family is a group or foster home. This provides a mental "hook" on which to hang new ideas about becoming part of God's family. With the idea that each of us is cared for by someone, belongs to a human family, we can then encourage children with the truth that God wants them to be a part of His family.

When talking with a child about salvation, avoid symbolic words such as "born again" or "ask Jesus into your heart." These phrases are beyond the understanding of children. Using the idea of joining God's family gives children a familiar basis from which to think about salvation.

Get to know each child's spiritual background and maturity level. The age at which a child grasps the meaning of personal salvation can vary greatly, depending on his or her background and training. Pray that the Holy Spirit will keep you sensitive to every child's spiritual need.

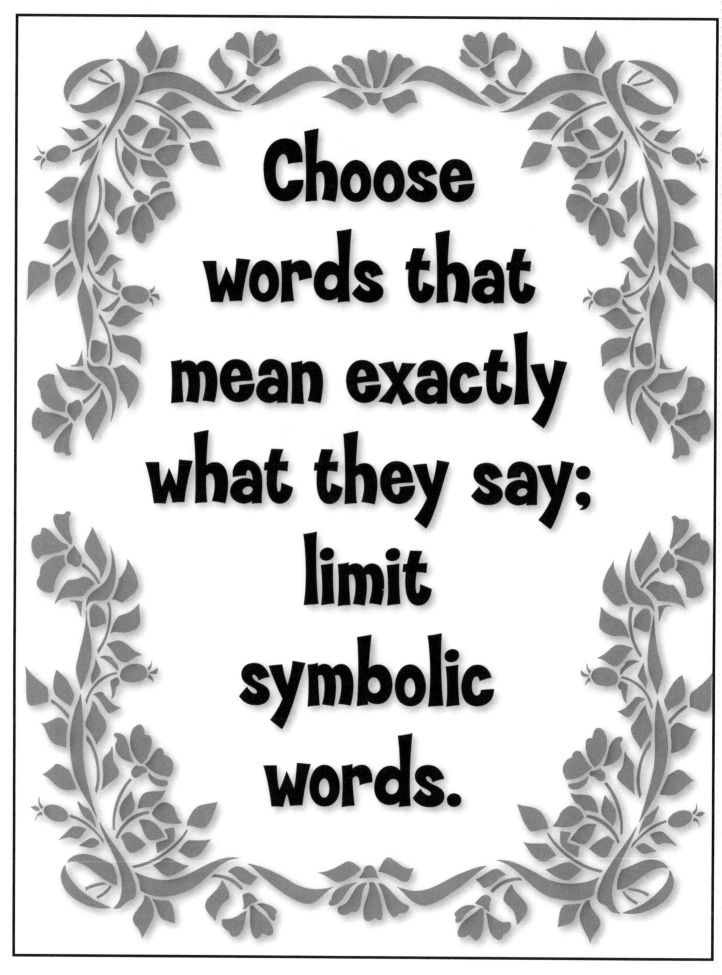

Choose words that mean exactly what they say; limit symbolic words.

Children absorb attitudes more quickly than they do words.

ACTIVITY PAGES HELP CHILDREN TELL THE STORY

Purpose

Some days, a class of overexcited, rowdy preschoolers can tempt us to plunk down an activity page in front of each one and gratefully take a break. But this resource has great potential for learning if we stay actively involved!

The student activity page has a twofold purpose: first, to provide each child with a personalized visual aid to use in reviewing the Bible story; second, to help children think and talk about what the Bible truth means in their daily lives. Not a craft or an art activity, it is an interactive way to reinforce that day's Bible truth.

Plan

Every Quarter

At the beginning of the quarter, separate and store each lesson's pages and stickers in a labeled envelope or clear resealable bag. (A paper cutter can make cutting pages and sticker strips easier.) Many churches have senior citizens or older children involved with weekday club programs who can do an excellent job of preparing activity page materials.

Every Week

Before each class, take out that lesson's page and a set of stickers. Become familiar with how the page works. Prepare children's pages if needed by prefolding and then unfolding. When a page requires cutting, depending on the skill level of your class, precut some or all of the cuts.

During class before handing out the pages, talk with the children about the pictures on the page, so they understand its purpose. Use your page and stickers to demonstrate how to complete the page (cutting, folding, etc.). Seeing your demonstration will provide a visual guide for children.

During this demonstration and while children complete their own pages, provide opportunities for children to talk about the scene or action on the page. Ask simple specific questions to help children recall the action the page illustrates. For example, begin the story and then ask, "What happened next?" Let a volunteer tell. Involve as many children as possible. In classes where children are just beginning to use words to communicate, suggest a child answer your question by pointing to the appropriate figure on the activity page.

Participation Tips

Repetition and Review

Young children enjoy the color, the stickers and the action of the activity pages. More than that, young children learn best through repetition! The activity page provides a fresh way to illustrate and repeat the Bible story, both in class and then at home with family. And with hands and minds busy, children often respond freely and listen eagerly as you guide the conversation. Be sure to use the questions and comments provided in your curriculum to help children think about and talk about the page.

Assistance

Try to assist only when a child cannot complete a task. As you get to know the children in your class, you will know which children may need extra help.

If an older child is not interested in doing the activity page, say, "It's OK if you don't want to work on your page right now. But all of us need to sit at the table together." Often, after a few moments, the child will decide that the page is an acceptable activity after all! You may also provide a quiet alternate task, such as drawing on blank paper or looking at books. Send the uncompleted activity page home and suggest that parents may invite the child to work on the page when interest is shown.

Some children may make a few marks on the page and announce, "I'm done." While children should never be forced to complete an activity, there are often questions that can be asked to encourage further participation. "Everyone gets to color the flowers a different color. What color are you going to choose?" "Which picture on your page shows the beginning of the story? The end?" Engage the child about the scene or action on the page or invite him or her to retell the Bible story.

Folding and Cutting

To help a child fold his or her own page, hold the page in the proper position. Then tell the child to press and rub where he or she wants the fold.

When a child does his or her own cutting, hold the page taut for him or her.

Stickers, Taping and Gluing

For very young children, peel the backing from around a set of stickers to make them easy for small fingers to remove.

To simplify tape use, pull off and stick pieces of tape on the edge of the table, rather than handing a child a roll of tape.

Some lessons suggest optional touch-and-feel materials to add to the activity page. Gluing is done most easily with glue sticks. However, small glue bottles also work well if you tell children to use tiny dots of glue. Try seeing who can make the smallest dots!

CLEANING UP FOR FUN!

Taking care of materials and equipment is a basic part of life learning. When you have a positive attitude toward cleanup, you can make it interesting, giving clear expectations and generous encouragement and appreciation. When children enter a room that is reasonably neat and clean, children are more likely to respond to your guidance in keeping the room neat. Point out how there is room to play a game when the toys are put away, or comment on how everyone can easily find something to build with when the blocks are stacked on shelves. Take delight in pointing out the ways children are helping, showing love and obeying!

Cleaning Up Takes Time

Be sure to give cleaning up enough time. It should not be an afterthought. Plan this time into your schedule to help children understand that cleaning up is a valuable activity. Five to ten minutes before cleanup time, move to each activity area to give the children advance notice. "We'll be cleaning up soon."

When children are not ready to transition into cleaning up, let them work a little longer and tell them it is fine to do so. But if they have no choice, be clear! Don't ask, "Would you like to clean up?" Say, "It's time to clean up now. We need to put away the blocks. The puzzles need to go back into the racks." If a child has a hard time making the transition, acknowledge his or her feelings. "I see you were having a lot of fun. It's time to put the puzzles away now. But we'll be sure to put them out again the next time we are together." (Be sure to keep your word!)

Remember that to most young children the concept of cleaning up may not be any more clear than the concept of paying bills or flying to Atlanta. They may have some experience of it but not much genuine understanding! They need the tasks broken into manageable portions. Directions need to tell them what they can do, not what to avoid. Instead of saying, "Don't start playing with the blocks again!" try "Liam, you and Sean need to finish putting the blocks on the shelves. Would you like to stack the long blocks first or the short blocks?"

► Give plenty of advance notice.

► Make your expectations clear.

► State your directions positively.

► Give a choice to refocus resistant helpers.

Cleaning Up Can Be Fun

Make cleaning up an interesting experience and a way to have some fun!

Games

► Play I Spy. As children clean up, simply say, "I spy something orange on the floor." The challenge is to spot and put away the item you described. Acknowledge the child who puts away the item. "Robert, you spied the orange toy. You put it away. Thank you! You know your colors!"

► Play Freeze Cleanup. Play music while children work with the goal of the game to finish cleaning up by the time the music stops. To increase interest, stop and start the music periodically. Children freeze when the music stops. (Note: The faster the music, the more quickly children will move. However, if putting things in their proper places neatly is your goal, play music that is bright and energetic but not too fast. (Vivaldi's *Four Seasons* might be a good choice.)

▶ Challenge children to move in a different way as they clean up. "Let's all walk on tiptoe (or stomp or slide or march) today while we clean up!" "Clap your hands every time you put a toy away!"

▶ Challenge children to find and count five things that need to be put away. For older children, repeat the challenge increasing the number by one or two each time.

Songs

Singing a simple song effectively signals cleanup time and acknowledges children as they work.

▶ Sing these words to the tune of "The Farmer in the Dell": "It's time to clean our room, it's time to clean our room. Hi-ho, the derry-oh, it's time to clean our room." Then as you see children work, sing: "Dayna's picking up, Dayna's picking up. She's picking up the blocks and cars; Dayna's picking up." Or sing: "I see Eli work, I see Eli work. He's cleaning up our living room; I see Eli work." A song that includes a child's name and how he or she is helping works wonders!

▶ Sing these words to the tune of "Mary Had a Little Lamb": "Now we're going to clean our room, clean our room, clean our room. Now we're going to clean our room and then it's time for (snack, naps, lunch, the yard, etc.)!" Acknowledge a child's actions by singing "Shelby's helping clean our room, clean our room, clean our room. Shelby's helping clean our room and then she'll have a snack!" This tells children what comes next and helps them see cleaning up as part of getting ready for the next activity.

▶ Sing the same song as a cleanup signal every time. This auditory cue helps children transition. When adequate time is scheduled, children need not hurry, running madly to throw things into boxes. Rather, they can move slowly enough to stop and appreciate the neat results of what they are doing!

Cleaning Up Needs Storage

When a room has low shelves for storage of toys, games, puzzles and blocks, children's eyes are drawn to the shapes and colors of equipment. Choosing a shape of block or finding a particular toy is less frustrating.

▶ Use bins only for small toys. Have a separate bin for each kind of small toy, so children can sort toys as they put them into the bins. Mark the side of the bin with a picture of what belongs inside to help children sort items. (Cut pictures from the boxes the items came in!)

▶ When children remove blocks from block shelves, it's best to keep free floor space, so others have access to blocks. Lay a masking-tape line about three feet from the block shelves. Instruct children to build only on the side away from the shelves.

▶ Puzzle racks are available at most school-supply stores. Encourage any child who uses a puzzle to put all the pieces back in place and set the puzzle back on the rack. (Mark the back of each puzzle piece with the same number or symbol or draw outlines of puzzle pieces on the puzzle boards, so you can quickly put puzzle pieces together if needed.)

Cleaning up is worth the time, worth the effort of making it fun and worth having appropriate places in which to store items. This makes cleaning up an enjoyable part of the routine, instead of a reason to whine. (This does not guarantee a neat bedroom when a child grows into a teenager, however!)

GETTING FROM ONE ACTIVITY TO THE NEXT

Transition times are those times when children arrive, leave or move from one activity to another. Quite often, transitions happen when an adult announces, "It is time for..." The activity level in the room may increase. Some children become aggressive, some withdraw, and some wander about the room, unsure of what to do next. Teachers may then respond with more directions, louder voices and greater frustration!

Planning for Transition

Transition times need not be chaotic catch-all times. It is unfair to expect children to wait in line for everyone or to sit quietly until the next part of the session gets underway. When we plan transition times as well as we plan the rest of the session, tensions are lowered and learning can take place, even while children are moving through the transition. During transition times, it should be our goal to help children grow in self-control and self-direction.

If transition times are a problem, take time to consider what is causing the problem. Are the times too long? Too short? Is there no activity ready for children who have made the transition quickly? Are there times when teachers seem to disappear? Once you have analyzed your situation, select the signaling techniques below that will best help your children prepare for and enjoy these times. Think of them as "happy breaks," instead of "dreaded chaos"!

Prepare children for what is coming next. Near the end of any activity time, it's important to quietly tell them, "It will soon be time (to clean up, to listen to a story, to have a snack)." Avoid making a general announcement across the room. This tends to create a stampede mentality!

Plan adequate time for children to make the transition (pick up toys, wash hands, etc.), so they do not feel rushed. Once the transition has begun, another teacher should be waiting to begin the next part of the session for the children who are ready first. Children should not be punished by having to wait! Beginning another activity also encourages others to finish, so they can join in.

Signaling Transition Times

Finger Play

As young children move from one part of the session to the next, finger-play activities can help them make those transitions smoothly. An alert teacher prepared with a simple activity can draw the group together, help them focus on what is coming next and give them the physical and mental break they need.

Consider repeating the same finger-play activity for a series of sessions to signal a particular transition (such as the beginning of circle time). Children love to know what is coming next and they enjoy knowing a finger-play activity well enough to repeat it easily. If and when interest seems to lag, introduce a new activity.

Songs

Signal the beginning of a transition time such as cleanup with a song or chant, so everyone can join in as they work together. Songs that include a child's name and tell what he or she is doing will increase children's interest and participation!

Common Transition Times

Entering the Room

When children enter the room, there will be a better (and shorter) transition time if teachers are prepared. One teacher or helper should be available near the door to greet parents and children. Several learning activities should be prepared from which the child may choose. Once a child has been greeted and talked with briefly, he or she need not wait for others to arrive but may go directly into a learning activity.

Using the Restroom

When children need to use the restroom, they should be able to do so whenever they need to. Young children do not have the control to wait! However, if restrooms are not located where children may use them at will, asking children individually if they need to use the restroom during learning activity times or transition times can lower the number of mass exoduses to the bathroom. (Follow your church's guidelines for taking children to the restroom.)

During Group Times

Group times should not be sitting torture for young bodies that need to move! Use finger play and songs to create short transition moments. When children fidget or fight, they are telling you that they need a mental and physical break.

Ending the Session

When the session is over, remember that happy endings help children feel loved and affirmed and eager to return. Use a finger activity or a song that says good-bye and reminds children of God's love and care. This gives dismissal a joyful tone. Give each child a special sticker or stamp children's hands for celebratory feel and simple recognition. One or two teachers should always be available to continue activities that will enrich and reinforce the day's learning (finger play, books, songs, simple games). One or two teachers should be available for the sole task of greeting parents, checking children out and having children's materials ready to go home. (Note: If some or all children will attend another session, carefully plan with other teachers and leaders what children will do during the time of transition, how new arrivals will be integrated into the group and who will lead children in continuing activities.)

Avoiding Problems

► Lines should be avoided wherever possible. It is simply not worth the energy to get children to stand or walk in a line! If children must stand in a line, invite them to imitate the way you are walking (tiptoe, march, slide, walk like a duck or an elephant, etc.).

► Signs can help to minimize interruptions and make for smooth transitions at the door. When there is information all parents need to know, post a sign by the door, rather than trying to tell everyone the same message.

LEADING CHILDREN IN A LARGE GROUP

When we consider that many children now watch 35 to 40 hours per week of visual media (TV, videos, computer games), it's easy to wonder if a simple group time can keep a child's interest. Thankfully, the answer is yes! When all children in the classroom sing together, play a game together or listen to a story together, the live interaction is better than any interactive media experience. It's also a powerful place to demonstrate the love of God and connect His Word to children's daily lives!

Be Prepared

Because these large-group experiences can have great value, use a few preparation strategies to maximize the time. Nothing loses the interest of a group of children faster than a teacher rummaging around, trying to find or prepare something!

Before the class session, place the materials you will need for group time at the group-time area. If you are able to store items in your room from week to week, consider keeping a small rolling cart of stackable bins or baskets to hold group-time materials: flannel figures, story items, puppets and nature objects can all be organized neatly, ready for use. If you choose to have large-group time in a different area, your materials are portable. And children are usually fascinated to see what will come out of the baskets next!

During the class session, while one teacher is leading the large group, the other teachers and helpers in the room sit among the children. These teachers and helpers are then able to model appropriate behavior as well as be available to redirect the attention of a wandering child.

Be Flexible

Limit the total number of children in your classroom to 20 to 24 children. Keeping the group this size allows for children to see the visuals easily and gives each child opportunity to interact with you and others in the group. Some churches prefer to have even smaller groups for Bible story time so that personal attention is given to each child.

Consider the length of the activities or story and customize the length of any activity to meet the needs of your group. Keep in mind that the length of a Bible story should be approximately one minute for each year of the child's age. If an activity is working well, be prepared to expand it! If an activity is not working, have other activities ready as alternatives. Always be alert for that restless inattention that tells you it is time to change activities. If you are working with other helpers, the helper may provide another quiet activity for a child who is too young or too restless to stay with the group.

Be Inviting

Set a tone for group time that will make children eager to participate! As soon as one or two children are ready, begin with a fun interactive activity that will draw children into group time. Sing a song in which children's names are sung or spoken as they arrive to help even the most reluctant one get to the circle before the song is over, so he or she can be recognized. Instead of a song, you may play a game that allows each child to participate. When you begin group time with a song or an activity that looks and sounds like fun, each child feels welcomed and important.

Be Visible

If there's one consistent complaint voiced during a group time, it's "I can't SEE!" Instead of seating children in a semicircle, try staggering carpet squares or other markers in two or three theater-style rows, so each child has a clear view of you and the visuals you use.

Hold a visual aid up next to your face or set it on a nearby low chair so that you can maintain good eye contact and so that children can see your expressions as they hear you tell the story. If children's attention wanders, put the visual facedown in your lap and say, "I'm going to show this picture when you are looking quietly at me."

The younger the children are who you teach, the more likely it will be that they will want to get up and handle the visual aids. Gently redirect them to a sitting position. "As soon as you sit on the floor, I'll show each one of you the picture." Then show the picture to each individual child.

Be Observant

It's easy for one child's inattention to completely distract the whole group and the teacher besides! If you observe that a child is having difficulty keeping his or her attention focused during the group activities, try one of these options:

▶ Invite the child by name to participate in some way. "Jon, can you hold up your hands like the man in the story did?"

▶ Begin a song or finger fun to refocus everyone's attention.

▶ Thank children who are participating and paying attention. "Teresa, thank you for watching me while I told the story."

Make Your Class Schedule Work

For maximum learning in early childhood classes, a schedule creates a few firm points that allow for a great deal of flexibility in between!

Preparation

We are far more successful in every aspect of teaching if we are well prepared. The teacher's early arrival allows time to lay out materials, plan for a variety of factors unique to that day and pray with other teachers or helpers.

Schedule

Step 1
Bible Learning Activities • 20-30 minutes

Purpose: To help children talk about and practice Bible truths while participating in one or more learning activities.

Step 2
Bible Story Time • 10-15 minutes

Purpose: To provide children with informal worship opportunities and to help children hear and respond to a Bible story and Bible verse.

Step 3
Bible Sharing Time • 15 minutes

Purpose: To help children review the Bible story and talk about ways to obey the Bible verse in everyday life.

(Note: If children will be in a session either before or after Sunday School, plan carefully what children will be doing during the transition time between sessions, which staff will be responsible for supervising children and how arrival and departure of children will be handled with a minimum of disruption to the ongoing program.)

Bible Learning Activities

Teaching begins when the first child arrives! Teachers should never be busy with preparation when even the earliest arrival comes to the classroom door. One adult should be ready to greet each child and offer a choice of activities. The teacher's readiness ensures that children are not left to wander about the classroom and that valuable teaching time is not wasted. Greet each child at his or her eye level; listen to what the child has to tell. Help the child become involved in an activity. Teachers and helpers should be ready at each activity to guide conversation that helps children understand the day's lesson focus as well as give children ideas of how to expand an activity.

Why begin with Bible learning activities? Why not begin with an assembly? An organized assembly or circle time is very difficult to begin with the first child's arrival, and each subsequent arrival is distracting. Waiting to begin wastes the best part of the schedule. At the last meeting you attended, when were you most interested and alert? Probably at the beginning! If you had to wait for everyone to arrive so that the meeting could begin, your interest probably lagged. Preschoolers are "here and now" people. While they are fresh and eager to learn, they need immediate involvement in activities that will connect God's Word to their lives. Beginning with an assembly time also often creates greater separation problems. A shy or reluctant child finds it easier to become involved in a fun and inviting learning activity.

Ideally, there should be two or more Bible learning activities ready as children arrive, so children are able to choose which activity they prefer to participate in first. A teacher or helper should be in each area, ready to involve children and engage them in conversation. To effectively involve a child in an activity, begin to do it yourself. As children become involved, remain nearby to observe, engage in conversation and relate the children's activities to the lesson focus and Bible verse for the session.

If one learning activity area overflows with children, teachers in the other areas should invite children to join them. If the overflow persists (some activities are simply a big hit!), rotate children through that activity, so everyone has a turn; use colors of clothing, type of shoe, etc. as simple ways of dividing the group.

Near the end of Bible Learning Activity Time, it's important to let children know what is coming next. Go to each area and tell children it will soon be time to clean up. Signal the beginning of cleanup time with a song or chant, so everyone can join in the song or chant as they begin. One teacher should move to the Bible Story Time area so that the first children who arrive there don't have to wait but can begin an involving activity. This also encourages others to finish cleanup and come to the Bible Story Time area.

Bible Story Time

The second major time segment in the schedule brings all the children and teachers together in a semicircle on the floor. (Children may sit in chairs or on carpet squares if the floor is not carpeted.) Bible Story Time is made up of several components: a gathering activity to help children readily join the large group, a song or two, a prayer, an interactive activity that involves repetition of the Bible verse and the Bible story.

The variety of experiences in Bible Story Time helps children experience a needed change of pace in the session. Children will tire less readily when they are given a balance of active and quiet things to do. This time spent in a large group also helps the teacher call attention to the lesson focus as each activity takes place.

Telling the Bible story is a key component of the large-group time. The objective in telling Bible stories to young children is not primarily for them to remember the details of the events; it is to allow the narrative to reveal God's involvement in everyday life. Introduce the Bible story by asking a question, giving a listening task or showing a story-related household item that will catch children's attention. Use the flannel figures or other visual aids provided to illustrate story action. Conclude the story by linking the action of the main character to the lives of the children.

Some churches prefer to divide the class into groups of four to six children with a teacher telling the story to each small group. In these small groups there is ample opportunity for personal interaction between teacher and children.

At the end of Bible Story Time, briefly give directions for the next time segment. Dismiss children a few at a time (dismiss according to what color children are wearing, first letters of first names, with a song, etc.) to tables to complete their activity pages. This way, there is not a stampede but an orderly movement to the next part of the schedule.

Bible Sharing Time

During Bible Sharing Time, teachers lead children in completing an activity page. The activity page is a personalized visual aid for each child to use in reviewing the Bible story and in sharing together ways the Bible truth can be applied in everyday life. Be ready to use your activity page to demonstrate how to complete the page. Your visual example of the steps needed will do more to help children understand what to do than all your words combined!

As children complete the activity page, talk with them about the Bible story. Use the questions suggested on the page and in your teacher's guide. Invite children to use their completed pages to tell you the story.

Transition

When children have finished their activity pages, be sure to plan what they will do next. Some churches dismiss children to a free time of outdoor or indoor play, providing children with a much needed change of pace. Other churches continue with valuable teaching, making use of the enrichment activities provided in their teacher's guides. Continuing on with enrichment activities help parents get a glimpse of the kind of learning in which children have participated. Activities continue until parents (or the next session's staff) arrive.

Take a moment at the end of every class session to ask yourself and your coworkers, "Did the children accomplish the aims listed in the curriculum? Why or why not?" As you take a few minutes to review, you'll find strategies that work best for your class, successes with which to encourage each other and matters for prayer throughout the week.

A Schedule That Works

What is the most effective way to link God's Word to a child's life?

Some of us confess to being fruitless gardeners: We buy seed with great enthusiasm but then don't have take time to prepare the soil. So we toss seeds willy-nilly over unprepared ground, maybe throwing a little mulch over them and watering once or twice. We don't mark the place where we tossed the seeds, so when weeds grow instead, we aren't inclined to pull them because surely some of our seeds are sprouted among them. Not much fruit results!

Many of us would have to admit we teach children in a similar fashion: Enthusiastic but poorly prepared, we scatter seed over unprepared children, seldom nurturing, cultivating or evaluating what takes place during a class session. Could this be part of the reason we see very little fruit?

An Intentional Plan

Effective Bible teaching requires us to pay attention to the lesson aims, to use class time wisely, to creatively involve students in the Bible learning process and to develop personal relationships with the children. Sound impossible? Such things don't just happen: They develop from an intentional teaching plan.

Here are some likely results of having an intentional teaching plan:

▶ Children will come to class in anticipation, knowing that the schedule and activities are planned with them in mind;

▶ Learning aims or goals will be more easily accomplished because the activities in a session are chosen so that they build on each other;

▶ Activities and teacher-to-student ratios will aid personal interaction, so teachers can share God's love and their faith with children!

Four Goals to Consider

Goal 1: Have specific lesson aims that deal not only with biblical knowledge but also with attitude and behavior. Meaningful aims take into account what children *know*, how they *feel* and what they are going to *do* about it. The more you pay attention to what results you want, the more likely you are to provide activities that achieve those results. Since the ultimate goal is shown by a change in behavior, effective aims are stated in terms of what students will do to show that they have learned. It is important to realize that while some children know and understand Scripture, and even feel good about it, they never *do* anything about it—their lives are not changed by the truth that they learn. Our goal is to teach so hearts and minds are changed; such change is shown through actions and choices! The world is not influenced by Christians whose actions and choices look just like those of unbelievers.

Goal 2: Plan for everything that occurs in the session to work toward accomplishing the aim. Church leaders agree on the value of teaching God's Word. Sunday School, midweek groups and Bible classes all place a high priority on communicating spiritual truths. However, these programs all face two similar obstacles: They only meet one to two hours a week and they often experience hit-or-miss attendance.

Then, in spite of the short time teachers and children spend together, other things (announcements, special music, taking attendance, birthdays, etc.) invade part of the learning time. Classes often start late due to tardiness of students or because teachers are busy with last-minute preparations. Early arrivals are forced to wait until class time "begins" when they could be involved in meaningful activity. The end result is that the valuable time for the real purpose of the class (Bible study, learning activities, relationship building) is cut to a minimum. Class becomes a "sit and listen" situation in which students have no opportunity to discover Bible truths for themselves or to interact with their teachers and with each other because "we've got to get through the material."

The most practical solution is to be sure all of the activities, songs, discussion times, study groups, etc., become avenues used to accomplish a single set of learning aims. Begin with activities that start a child thinking about the Bible truths to be studied. (These activities also allow for students to arrive at varying times.) Structure sessions so that students are involved in studying God's Word for themselves to discover Bible truths, balancing teacher input with child interaction. Challenge children to apply the Bible truths to their lives in ways they understand and take specific steps of action as a result of what God's Word teaches.

Goal 3: Provide a variety of creative learning activities to help students discover Bible truths. The third aspect of an intentional teaching plan is to involve children in a variety of activities, because just as each child is different, so are the ways in which children learn. Each child needs to be motivated and challenged according to his or her unique abilities and interests. This can best be done by providing a variety of learning experiences and offering choices whenever possible. How many learning activities can you think of right now? There are *hundreds*! Yet some teachers stick to their old favorites (usually the way in which they were taught). Lecture, discussion and questions need to be interwoven with other activities that will make Bible study intriguing and help children understand truth in terms that have real meaning for them.

Goal 4: Create a balance of teacher input and student discovery. Strengthen relationships through teacher and student interaction. Two elements are necessary to make learning happen: *time* for teachers to guide learning in a direct fashion (leading a Bible study, telling a Bible story, guiding a discussion) and *initiative* by children to discover and apply Bible truths (reading and commenting on a Scripture passage, participating in a Bible learning game, drawing a picture in response). A key factor in an intentional teaching plan is to discover the right balance between the two.

Grouping elementary students into small groups of six to eight students will encourage personal discovery and application of Bible truth. Within small groups, teachers and students can relate on an individual basis and can ask and answer questions to connect Bible truths to children's lives. Teachers can share experiences from their own lives that relate to a Bible truth and can evaluate and clarify children's understanding of concepts and ideas.

Elementary Session Schedule

The teacher of children in the elementary grades has the awesome responsibility of effectively communicating God's Word to children whose life circumstances are not only quite different from the teacher's but also may be quite different from other children's. A session schedule needs to allow for significant interaction among teachers and students as well as many opportunities to read and understand the Bible. This is foundational to helping children begin and grow in their relationship to Jesus Christ.

The following schedule allows teachers to teach children through meaningful learning experiences, each experience contributing to the session's learning aims.

Schedule at a Glance

Step 1

Discover • 5 to 15 minutes

Purpose: To help build relationships among students and start them thinking about the life focus and/or memory verse of the lesson.

Step 2

Bible Study • 20 to 30 minutes

Purpose: To guide students to read, study and discuss the Bible for themselves.

Step 3

Apply • 20 to 30 minutes

Purpose: To help students explore the relationship between the Bible truth they have been studying and their day-to-day experiences.

Before the Session

Teachers and helpers arrive 10 to 15 minutes early in order to prepare the classroom or to make a smooth transition between staff.

During the Session

Children arrive during the first 10 minutes of the session. A teacher or helper welcomes children at the door and supervises check-in procedures. (In large churches, check-in may take place elsewhere on your facility, but a teacher or helper still needs to be available to greet children as they enter the classroom.) As children enter the room, they are immediately involved in a discovery activity that introduces the life focus or memory verse for the lesson. Teachers and children can also be involved in relationship building as they interact and participate in activities together. Discovery activities accommodate varying arrival times and can be led by teachers with a small group of students or with all students together. Depending on the type of activity, the ratio of students to teachers and the space and materials available, more than one activity may be offered.

These brief activities at the beginning of the session help the child begin thinking about the concepts that will be developed during the session. When possible, offer a choice of activities not only to help meet the varied needs of students but also to allow each child involved to accept personal responsibility for participating and learning.

The second major time segment is Bible study. Students can be grouped in small groups or in one large group, depending on the number of teachers and students. To provide the most learning and interaction among students, it's best to group no more than 12 to 14 students

for Bible study. During this time, the teacher introduces the Bible story, weaving in opportunities for students to find, read and discuss Bible verses. This segment becomes much more than listening to a story as children become active participants. Even beginning readers can find the books in the Bible or locate names of Bible characters. Some churches include worship activities such as songs and prayer, and video or DVD Bible story presentations.

During the third and last part of the session, the teacher guides a small group of children in discovering the relationship between the lesson's Bible truth and their day-to-day experiences by using a creative learning activity that encourages students to identify and discuss specific ways their behavior can be affected by the day's lesson. Over a period of weeks, a variety of learning activities are provided so that each child's interests and needs are met. (In large churches, each teacher may lead a different activity, allowing each child to choose the activity most appropriate to his or her learning style.) A key element of this time is the conversation that takes place between teacher and child. This time segment is a wonderful opportunity for teachers to nurture spiritual growth in children, not only by modeling and sharing their own spiritual growth, but also by guiding children to discover and plan steps of growth. (Note: This time segment may wrap up with one or more brief worship activities (song, prayer, group activity).

At the End of the Session

Depending on your church's schedule and safety policies, children either move into the next session, or they are dismissed or picked up by parents. Teachers briefly communicate with parents about their children and the activities they enjoyed.

After the Session

Teachers and helpers evaluate the session (whether aims were met, what challenges arose, what benefits were seen, etc.), clean up the classroom or work with incoming teaching staff to allow the start of a new program or class with a minimum of disruption.

Additional Sunday Morning Programs

In many churches some or all of the grade-school children may participate in an additional program that takes place either before or after the Sunday School session. Elementary-aged children need a change of pace to vary the program from Sunday School. The additional program needs to include new topics, different activities, a wide variety of learning approaches and a varied time schedule, all used with the intentional plan to accomplish the learning aim chosen for the session.

SHIFTING GEARS IN THE CLASSROOM

Transition times are those moments when one activity ends and the next one begins. It can also be when students move from one room to another, when the class begins and when it ends. Transitions can be noisy and chaotic as children put away items, stand up, sit down, move around and shift from being active to quiet. Because an elementary class has many activities, transition times occur frequently. Your challenge is to smoothly move energetic children out of and into the activities with a minimal amount of noise and disruption.

Know the schedule. Be prepared for what's next on the schedule. If you don't know the next activity, your students will quickly become disruptive. If you begin the wrong activity by mistake, go ahead and finish it. Stopping in the middle and starting something new is even more disruptive.

Plan the schedule well. Children may find it hard to end a fast-moving game to suddenly be still for prayer time. Likewise, after a tiring game they may not have the energy to listen to a long story or do serious thinking. If possible, have a time for a "cool down" activity right after a hectic game to give children time to settle down.

Be prepared. Have all the necessary items (art supplies, Bibles, game equipment, etc.) stored in the classroom where they can be easily found. Be sure that supply cabinets and closets are unlocked or that the teacher has a key on hand. Children can get out of hand if the teacher has to stop and look for supplies or has to leave the room to get something.

Schedule adequate time. Children may not want to stop what they're doing because they haven't finished their art project or they are having too much fun at games. Set aside sufficient time for cleanup. If possible, make a sample art project at home to determine the needed time. If the children are enjoying a game, allow a few extra minutes to play it a second time. It's better to omit one or two activities than to cram in too much. If one activity runs too long, readjust a new activity so that there is sufficient time to finish it.

However, children can get bored if too much time is spent waiting after a project is completed. If the children finish an art project quickly or lose interest in the game, move on to something new. It's better to end an activity while child interest is high.

Make it a game. If the children are slow getting started on the next activity, turn it into a fun challenge. Use a timer to test their speed and give a small reward when the class beats its best time. Mark the times on a chart so that children can see their improvement.

Give warnings. Children may not want to abruptly stop what they're doing. Give advanced notice a few minutes before it's time to move on. Younger children may not comprehend "five more minutes," so give concrete warnings they understand: "You can run the relay one more time." "We'll sing the song one more time."

Make use of signals. Use hand gestures, ring a bell, flick the lights on and off or sing a special song to indicate transition time. Use a different signal for crafts, cleanup, music, storytelling, games, end of class, etc. When the children see or hear the signal, they know what activity is coming up. Have children take turns giving the signal.

Give individual attention. Rather than shouting orders to the entire class, speak to individual students. This reduces the noise and children are more likely to hear and understand the directions.

Have special spaces. Mark off areas of the room for different activities. When it's story time, the children know to move to a certain area, perhaps a rug where they can sit. When it's art time, they walk to the art table. The teacher does not need to spend time with explanations.

Give directions, and then move. Children may have difficulty focusing on your directions when they're moving or walking. Give instructions while children are seated or standing quietly, and then allow them to move after everyone has understood and asked questions.

Plan how to line up. It's good to have an interesting plan for lining up so that students don't push and shove to get in front. Students can line up by age, by height, by the color of their clothes or by the schools they attend. However, vary the plan. Tall children and the oldest don't always want to be at the end of the line. If there's a large group, line up a few at a time by small groups, rows or tables.

Lead quiet treks. At times the class may need to move outside the classroom to the outdoors, the sanctuary or the kitchen. Children may want to talk and giggle while they walk or leave the group. This can disrupt other classes meeting in the building.

To keep children from talking, make it a game as well. "Let's see who can be the most quiet and tiptoe to the next room." Have children pretend they're walking through a jungle and they don't want to disturb the wild animals, or lead children in a game of Follow the Leader to keep their attention while moving from one place to another.

Avoid using punitive methods: "Anyone talking won't get a cookie!" This creates bad feelings and dampens student enthusiasm.

If children need to walk a long way and there is no need to be quiet (such as when walking outdoors or when nobody else is nearby), have the children sing or chant a verse as they walk. Lead children in a rhythmic pattern of clapping and finger snapping to help keep their hands busy and prevent pushing and shoving.

Be ready at the start. It's easier to begin class if students are immediately involved in a discovery activity when they enter the classroom. This puts their minds in learning mode. Create excitement for the class: "See how many of these hidden cards you can find." "Try out these experiments at the table."

Plan a routine ending. During class time, children not only need variety but also like to be part of routines. Have a standard dismissal practice: Sing a song, say a prayer, eat a snack. Use the same pattern each time so that students get a sense of closure. Think of a calm and orderly activity that will enable arriving parents to find their children easily.

Schedule Tips

Does your program time allow for small-group activities? This is a valuable time: children build relationships with other children and with a significant adult, are able to ask questions and to share prayer requests. Don't overlook the value of building small-group experiences into your schedule.

Individual activity time is a child's chance to see if he or she understood the Bible teaching presented and how those Bible principles apply to his or her life. When the schedule allows only for large-group times, a child seldom has the chance to reflect and consolidate the things he or she learned.

Remember that when your class schedule meets the needs of children, there are far fewer discipline problems or crowd-control issues! An effective schedule gives children opportunities for large-group, small-group and individual activities. The activities are planned to meet the varied learning styles of those in the class. And cheerful, cooperative children are the likely result!

Children have short attention spans; schedules should be adjusted accordingly. But when you can see that children are restless, try a simple change-of-state technique that can be quickly dropped into the schedule. Stand to repeat the Bible verse together, using motions as a transition to that next activity. Or simply say, **One, two three, all eyes on me!** and then give children a quick series of physical activities. (Place your hand on your head. Wiggle your fingers. Bend over and touch your toes. Shake a friend's hand. Now sit down.) Then move on to the next activity, with children refreshed by movement.

When you see children wiggling in their seats or beginning to elbow each other on the floor, what does that tell you? This restlessness tells you that it is time for a change of state. Whether you invite children to stand up and stretch, to act out some story actions with you or help you to think of and act out motions for the Bible verse, lay aside preplanned activities if they are not working. Flexibility and creativity are keys to good teaching.

Have you considered changing the space arrangement in your area as you move through the schedule? Invite children to push back tables, to place chairs in a circle, etc., in preparation for the next activity. This not only gives them a physical activity but also involves them in wondering what is coming next!

Ready or not, the class begins when the first child arrives.

A Thankful Attitude

What Are the Symptoms of the Gimme Syndrome?

An eight-year-old responds, "How much will you pay me?" when Mom requests her help.

A seven-year-old asks to invite more children to his birthday party so he can receive more presents.

A ten-year-old complains, "I wish we lived in a house as nice as the Garners'—AND they have three TVs!"

A five-year-old points out a multitude of toys and games she wants for Christmas.

Possessiveness and materialistic attitudes seem to be a hallmark of the twentieth-century child. The pursuit of money and possessions is glorified in many ways. Commercials, billboards, TV shows and movies all encourage children to believe that happiness can be bought.

What Is an Antidote?

What antidote can Christian teachers administer to combat the disease of materialism in their children? Knowing that in God's eyes we are all the same, rich and poor, what can we prescribe for our families and Sunday School classes?

First and foremost, we can nurture an attitude of thankfulness in ourselves and in every child. James 1:17 reminds us that every good and perfect gift is from God. We need to do all we can in our homes and Sunday School classes to help children realize that our material possessions are not really ours, but God's. As you spend time with children, pause often for brief informal prayers of thanks to God. Begin a "thank you" list at home or in the classroom. Invite your children to add to the list often. Or, read the story of the ten lepers (Luke 17:11-19) and ask your children to think about ways they can be more like the one grateful leper. Then as a family or a class, take time once a month to write appreciation notes to people who have helped you.

Make sure your children overhear your expressions of thankfulness to God and to others. If you're thankful, say it!

Second, and perhaps more challenging, encourage your children to develop a non-materialistic attitude and lifestyle.

Take advantage of teachable moments. When your family receives an income tax refund, an unexpected gift or a Christmas bonus, use the occasion to talk with your family about good use of money—some to save, some to give and some to spend. And when the occasion is a lack of money rather than a surplus, you as a family can ask God's help in determining priorities for spending and express your reliance on His care.

The children of the Israelites regularly observed their parents bringing offerings of animals, food and precious fabrics and metals to the Lord. While our gifts are often not so tangible, children need to know what and why their parents give to the Lord. Your offering of a check once or twice a month, hours of volunteer labor or use of musical talents, for example, needs to be coupled with a brief explanation. You might say, "Helping to paint the worship building is a way I give to the Lord." Or, "God wants us to use our money in good ways.

When I give this check to our church, I'm helping our church tell others about God. I'm glad to give this money because I'm so thankful for God's love to me."

Another way to help your children escape the "gimmes" is to plan ways for your children at home or at Sunday School to become aware of the extreme poverty in which millions in our world live. Show current newspaper and magazine pictures which depict the impoverished circumstances of others in third-world countries (or even your own country or community). Call your child's attention to TV news segments which highlight the needs of others. Avoid creating guilt (the "starving children in China" syndrome); simply offer information.

Then build on this awareness by providing a way for children in your home or class to act in a caring way for a needy person or family. As a family or class, plan and carry out a project to contribute to the well-being of others. Encourage your children to not only think about the needs of others in our world, but to follow your example in giving.

Consciously and unconsciously, children want to be like their parents. Your attitudes and actions now will make a difference in their attitudes toward money for the rest of their lives.

What About Christmas?

Many parents approach the holidays with a sense of dread at the overwhelming pressure to buy, buy, buy! Christmas celebrations do have a special attraction for children, and there's no point in simply wringing our hands over the way in which Christmas has become the most materialistic celebration of the year. Without diminishing the pleasure of Christmas and the joy of giving and receiving gifts, thoughtful steps can be taken at home and at church to increase the spiritual significance of Christmas for children.

The key is the attitude of the adults. If the spiritual quality of Christmas is not truly meaningful to parents and teachers, attempts to force sober observances and teachings on children will be self-defeating. Children take their cues primarily from those things that are of greatest interest to the adults in their lives.

Here are some specific ideas:

▶ At home you can set clear limits early in the season for gift-giving. Each child will benefit by realistic expectations.

▶ At church or home each person may secretly prepare a low- or no-cost gift for someone else.

▶ Encourage your family or class to participate in church, school or community giving projects.

What Is the Result?

The dictionary defines materialism as a preoccupation with or stress upon material rather than intellectual or spiritual things. Your efforts to cure the "gimme syndrome" will result in children whose value system is being changed—from a focus on selfishness to a focus on God and others.

Making Easter Joyful

Children learn about Easter in some interesting ways! They are exposed to videos (both religious and secular), photo opportunities with the Easter Bunny in the mall, traditional family gatherings, community egg hunts and ads for Easter clothing, Easter baskets and candy. This celebratory mixture is bound to confuse children! Even for adults, it's sometimes hard to separate the traditions from the truths. Jesus' death and resurrection is the single most powerful and important chain of events in human history. But it is easy to focus on the fun and yet miss the joy. Easter is far more than the trappings that surround the holiday!

Keep It Simple

Long after Easter day is passed, it's important that children understand and remember that Jesus is alive! As adults, we need to keep in mind that words and phrases that are quite clear to us often have little meaning for young children. Young children have very vague and uneasy notions about death. While this truth is vitally important to our faith, "Jesus died and rose again" is not likely to be clear or seem like a reason to be excited and happy! (*What does dying have to do with a flower? Why are you glad that Jesus died? I was sad when my Grandma died.*)

Instead of dwelling on the details of Christ's death, help children grasp the great truth of the Easter story—that Jesus took the punishment for our sin and that He did not stay dead. He is alive now! Help them understand how Jesus' friends felt: "Jesus' friends were very sad when Jesus died. They were sad because they thought they would never see Jesus again. When they found out that Jesus did not stay dead, they must have laughed and hugged each other! They told everyone they knew, 'Jesus is alive again! Jesus is living! We saw Him!'"

As you talk, show pictures (from a Bible storybook, for example) that are clear and help children understand what you are telling. Ask them open-ended questions, so you can find out what they know. This is your opportunity to clear up any misinformation children have picked up and build happy feelings about the Easter story. Reinforce true details about the story, rather than misconceptions children may have.

Keep It Focused

When a child talks about the Easter bunny, traditional activities or candy, simply smile and comment, "Those things are fun. But the biggest reason we are glad at Easter is because we know Jesus is alive!" In order to keep children's attention focused on the Easter story, avoid use of decorations that picture the Easter bunny. However, don't expect that children will be as excited about spiritual matters as they are about tangible things such as candy! Your excitement, enthusiasm and example in talking about Jesus' resurrection and love for us provide more understanding for young children than any extensive verbal explanation could!

Answers to Questions

As a child's ability to understand grows greater, he or she will ask more questions. Keep your answers clear and biblical.

Why did people kill Jesus?

Jesus was hurt and killed by angry people who did not like Him. They did not know that God sent Jesus to love and help everyone. Jesus let these angry people kill Him. He knew it was part of God's very good plan. Jesus knew He was going to die to take the punishment for our sin. He loves us so much that He was willing to do that. And Jesus knew He was going to be alive again!

Avoid graphic details of Jesus' death: these are better left until a child is older. If a child becomes frightened by talk of Jesus' death, he or she can be gently reminded, "It's OK. Jesus knew this was going to happen. He did not stay dead. It was part of God's good plan to make a very SAD thing into a very GLAD thing!"

Where is Jesus now?

Jesus lives in heaven now with God, His Father. Heaven is a very beautiful place. Everyone is very happy there. No one is sick or hurt there. No one cries or is sad.

What is Jesus doing in heaven?

Jesus is making a wonderful home in heaven for every person who is part of God's family. Every member of God's family will be with Him in heaven someday. Even though we can't see Him now, we know that Jesus has promised to be with us and care for us.

WHAT'S THE MAIN IDEA OF CHRISTMAS?

Christmas! The word itself stirs feelings of extraordinary excitement. And rightly so. During the holiday season there are reminders of the season everywhere. But let's be sure our children know what the excitement is really about.

How can we help a young child realize that Christmas is a celebration of gratitude to God for His wonderful gift of love? There are several ways you can make the biblical and spiritual aspects of Christmas meaningful and attractive to a young child.

Help children know the simple facts of Jesus' birth as they are recorded in Scripture.

▶ Tell or read the story of the first Christmas to children from Bible storybooks or from an easy-to-understand version of the Bible.

▶ Allow children to participate in assembling a manger scene. Retell the story of Jesus' birth as they move the figures, or invite children to tell the story as you move the figures.

Help children feel that Jesus is God's best gift of love.

▶ Remember that much of a child's response is a reflection of the attitudes he or she sees from you. Nurture feelings of joy, love and thankfulness in your child.

▶ In the presence of your child, give thanks to God for Jesus.

▶ Include children in your church's plans for expressing love to Jesus by caring and loving others (collect canned foods or personal care items for a rescue mission, fill a shoebox with age-appropriate gifts to be given to needy children, etc.). With your child, talk about the gifts the wise men gave to Jesus to show their love for Him. Explain that we give gifts to others at Christmas to show our love for them.

Help your child express joy, excitement and feelings of love.

▶ Show gladness as you sing about Jesus' birth.

▶ Be sensitive to moments when it is natural to talk about Jesus' birth and encourage your child to thank God in prayer for sending Jesus to be born.

Keep Santa in the proper perspective.

▶ Avoid referring to Santa as a real person. If a child talks about Santa, say "Talking about Santa is fun. But it's even better to talk about Jesus who loves us all year long."

▶ Avoid the "What do you want Santa to bring you for Christmas?" and "Be good for Santa" emphases.

▶ Keep the meaning of Christmas clear by frequently commenting on it. "Christmas is a happy time because it is Jesus' birthday. People give presents to show their love. God showed His love by giving us Jesus."

KEEP YOUR EYES ON JESUS AT CHRISTMAS

It's the most wonderful time of the year, but parties and visits to Santa can muffle the true meaning of Christmas for children. How can teachers at church reclaim this holy season for God's glory?

Remember that much of a child's response to Christmas is a reflection of what you model. Share your own feelings of joy, love and thankfulness for Jesus during this season. In class prayers, give thanks to God for Jesus. Avoid referring to Santa as a real person. It's OK to talk about Santa and Christmas gifts in the classroom, but keep the meaning of Christmas clear by frequently commenting, "Christmas is a special time of year because we remember how glad we are that Jesus was born. Jesus loves us all year long." Keep classroom activities low-key and avoid complicated art projects. Avoid the hurry and busyness of Christmas that often add to the stress in a child's life.

At the beginning of December, consider the schedule of lessons you plan to teach. Adjust your lesson plans as needed if many children in your class are likely to be absent during the holidays or if Christmas church events (children's choir rehearsal, etc.) will affect children's attendance.

Celebration Ideas

Each year, stores begin promoting the Christmas buying season earlier and earlier. In church, resist the temptation to rush into Christmas too soon. The church needs to set standards, not the commercial industry. Even if Santa has already arrived at the mall, wait to hang decorations in your classroom until the first Sunday of Advent.

Advent wreaths. In the rush toward Christmas, many Christians overlook Advent, the preceding four-week season of anticipation and preparation. Use this time to teach about Jesus' birth. Make or purchase a wreath for the class and teach the meaning of the lighting of the candles on the wreath. (Note: Information about Advent is available from your pastor, the Internet or devotional books.)

Nativity scene. Provide a nativity scene for your classroom or let students create their own scenes. Children can make their own class nativity scene by painting ready-made figures or by drawing a large butcher-paper scene. Depending on the age of your students, invite students to arrange nativity scene figures and use them in telling the story of Christmas.

Service projects. Involve children in service projects, so they turn their focus away from their personal wish lists. They can make holiday cards and cookies for homebound church members, buy toys for needy children, put together food baskets, serve at a church dinner or soup kitchen, sing carols at a senior center or host a party for younger children. If the children have a class gift exchange, set a one-dollar limit on purchases or give only handmade presents.

Creative storytelling. Since many of the children in your class may be familiar with the Christmas story, consider the following ideas to add interest:

► Read the Christmas story from Luke 2:1-20, and then read one or more contemporary Christmas storybooks. Ask children to evaluate the contemporary books by identifying which parts of the story match the biblical version.

▶ Spread out a long length of butcher paper. Let children help you draw a road from Nazareth to Bethlehem, adding scenery, buildings, animals, etc. Move toy figures to indicate the actions of Mary, Joseph, the shepherds and the wise men.

▶ Provide simple Bible-times costumes and props and let children act out the Christmas story. For another drama idea, provide paper bags and markers. Children make paper bag puppets to use in acting out the story.

TEACH CHILDREN THAT JESUS IS ALIVE!

Easter is the most wonderful and important celebration in the Christian year. However, the increasing secularization of Easter threatens to make it little more than a time to gorge on candy and cuddle stuffed bunnies. As you interact with children during this time of year, use this great opportunity and privilege to present children with the true meaning of Easter.

Some of the aspects of Holy Week, especially the arrest, torture and death of Jesus, can be disturbing to children. Emphasize the positive aspects of the Last Supper and Easter: Jesus is alive today and loves every child. Students can be taught that Jesus laid down His life because of the sins of every person and as part of God's plan to demonstrate His love for us.

Teaching the Easter Message

The trappings associated with Easter—baby animals, colored eggs, new clothes, spring flowers—can all be used to show and share joy because Jesus is living. Keep the focus of your conversation on the biblical truth that Jesus is alive and that Eastertime is when we celebrate His love for us.

If a child asks about or seems disturbed by Jesus' death on the cross, you can say, "When we see a picture of the cross or think about the sad day when Jesus died, it helps to remember that Jesus loved us so much that He was willing to let Himself be killed. The third day after Jesus died, God raised Jesus from the dead! It's good news for all people to know that Jesus is alive!"

Easter Celebrations

Depending on the age level of the children you teach and the traditions followed in your church, consider incorporating some of these Easter celebrations into your class.

▶ **Ministry baskets.** On Palm Sunday, children receive empty Easter baskets. During the week, children fill the baskets with small toiletry items or canned food. On Easter, the baskets are collected and distributed to families in need, a homeless shelter, food kitchen or residence home for youth. (Check with the organization first to get a list of desirable items.)

▶ **Flowers on the cross.** Set up a wooden cross with two rows of nail heads protruding down the front. Children decorate the cross by putting fresh flowers between the nail heads. If a wooden cross cannot be used, then draw a cross outline on a large sheet of paper. Let the children color and glue paper cutout flowers on the cross.

▶ **Easter egg hunt.** Use plastic eggs, but instead of filling them with candy, use strips of paper with Bible verses, pocket crosses or coupons for a larger prize, such as bookmarks, paperback books or music CDs. You may also fill eggs with items related to the Easter story (a small rock, a small piece of wood, a small artificial flower, etc.). Hide the eggs inside the church or on the church lawn. If the hunt is indoors, keep the hunt confined to one or two rooms. Separate children by age so that the older children in their enthusiasm do not trample over younger children. Set a guideline for how many eggs each child is allowed to collect. Invite older children to prepare the egg hunt for younger children.

▶ **Dramatics.** The events of Holy Week are full of visuals and spectacle. Provide palms and let children act out the story events of Palm Sunday. Bring in a basin of water to reenact

Jesus washing the disciples' feet. Find a dark closet to represent the tomb, and have children take the roles of the women and the angel. Use costumes and props if possible. Taking part in the Resurrection story will make a dramatic impact on children.

▶ **Flower celebration.** If the sanctuary is decorated with Easter lilies, after worship the older children and an adult supervisor can take the flowers to a hospital or nursing home. Or, several weeks before Easter, have children plant their own flower bulbs and care for the plants as they grow.

▶ **Easter sharing.** Invite children to donate good-quality used clothing to a homeless shelter or relief organization. Encourage families in the church to buy clothes, socks or underwear for needy families instead of or in addition to buying new clothes for themselves.

▶ **Worship participation.** Children learn an Easter song or skit that they present to the congregation during a worship service.

Seasonal Tips

The excitement and stress of holiday activities are often overwhelming to a child. Family routines are disrupted and commercial interest bombard children with unrealistic expectations. The child may respond in class by acting in ways that are unlike his or her normal behavior. When you see that a child is overly excited, invite him or her to help you with a quiet task. Sit beside the child and give him or her a few moments of undivided attention to help the child calm down and focus on the task at hand.

The Christmas season is full of excitement for a child but often his or her attention is focused on gifts or activities rather than the reason for the holiday. Help the children in your class focus on the true meaning of Christmas by expressing your own joy and thanks that God sent His son Jesus as the very best gift ever. Be sensitive to moments when it is natural to talk about Jesus and to give thanks to God in prayer for His best gift.

On the Sundays before Christmas, there may be frequent mention of Santa Claus and toys. Avoid discouraging such talk; rather, listen attentively and then build on the child's ideas. **That sounds like a fun gift! I like to get gifts at Christmas, too. There is one very special gift that God gave to us—He sent His Son, Jesus. God's gift is the real reason for all of our celebrations!**

Keep the meaning of Christmas clear by often commenting, **We are glad at Christmas because of Jesus. We celebrate at Christmas because we are glad Jesus is born! Jesus is God's gift to us!** It is helpful for children (and adults) to remember that the feasting and giving of gifts are all a result of the fact that Jesus Christ came to change history!

Repeat often the simple facts of Jesus' birth—for some children, this will be the first time they may have heard the story. Remember the miracles, the angels talking to the shepherds, the baby in the manger and the amazed joy of the returning shepherds. Your enthusiasm and zest for remembering Jesus will plant seeds of joy and thankfulness—and a curiosity to learn more!

Easter Sunday is often a hectic day for children. If you are teaching on that Sunday, consider providing some quiet activities, such as books, manipulative toys and puzzles for children. This gives you prime time to talk with them and a chance to repeat the real story of Easter while their hands are busy and their minds are quiet!

Seasonal Tips

Because some children get information about Jesus' death from watching television programs that air during this season, be alert for comments about programs they have seen. If a child asks, "Why did they kill Jesus?" answer simply and accurately. **Jesus was killed by men who hated Him. But Jesus knew this would happen. It was part of God's plan made long ago, so that we could become part of His family. And Jesus didn't stay dead. God made Him alive again!** Avoid emphasizing the cruel details about the crucifixion for younger children who might be emotionally overwhelmed. A child's understanding of pain and death is very limited.

Easter Sunday is often the one day of the year that many unchurched children show up at Sunday School. Plan not only to have extra materials but also an extra adult or two in your classroom. These adults should be instructed that their purpose is to get to know new children and make them feel welcomed. Be sure to provide these greeters with notepads and pens so that the names, addresses and phone numbers of new children can easily be recorded. Then call these children during the week and invite them back! It is the genuine interest of a caring adult that often is the deciding factor in a child's desire to return. Use this opportunity to reach new children by being prepared for the holiday!

As children talk about holiday activities and gifts, ask open-ended, "what do you think?" kinds of questions to determine what they do or do not understand about the reasons for the holiday at hand. If a child states something that is incorrect, simply restate the fact correctly. Then repeat the simple facts about the reason for the holiday. **We have big meals and give presents because we are glad that Jesus is God's Son. We are glad He came to take the punishment for our sins, or wrong actions!**

If you teach children for whom Santa Claus may be a big issue, comment, **It's fun to talk about Santa. But in our Bible we read that the real reason Christmas is special is because Jesus is born. We are glad! We celebrate because Jesus is born!** Don't comment on whether or not "Santa is real." With older children, you may want to give the history of St. Nicholas: that he was a generous Christian who took care of poor people.

For a quick finger-fun or singing activity at Christmas, act out the words of a simple Christmas carol such as "Away in a Manger" or "Silent Night."

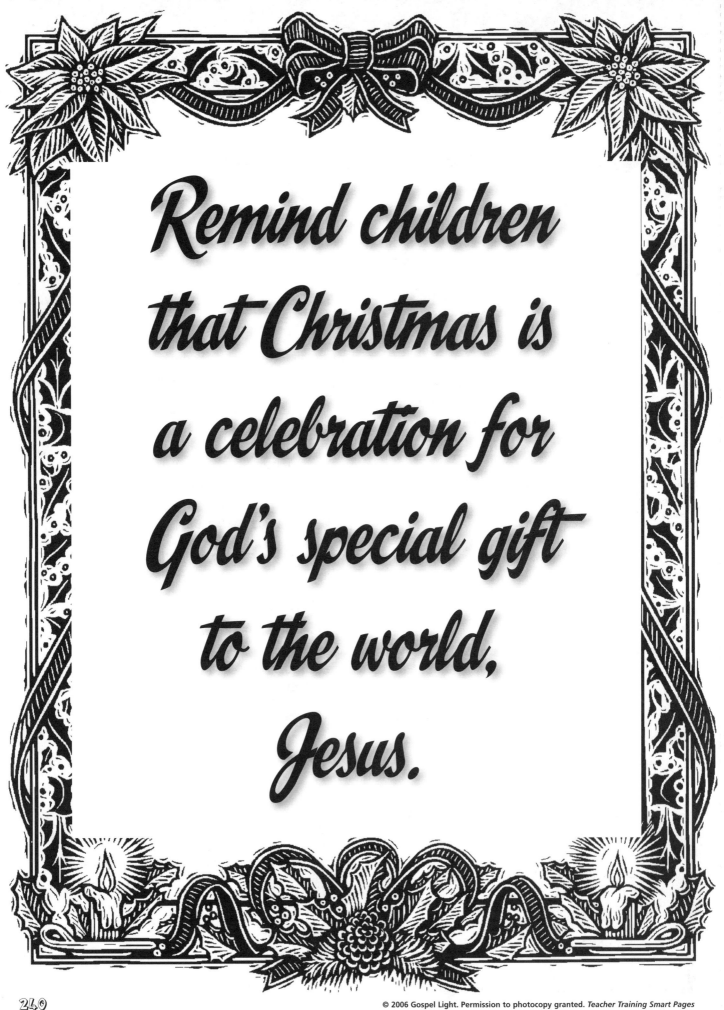

Remind children that Christmas is a celebration for God's special gift to the world, Jesus.

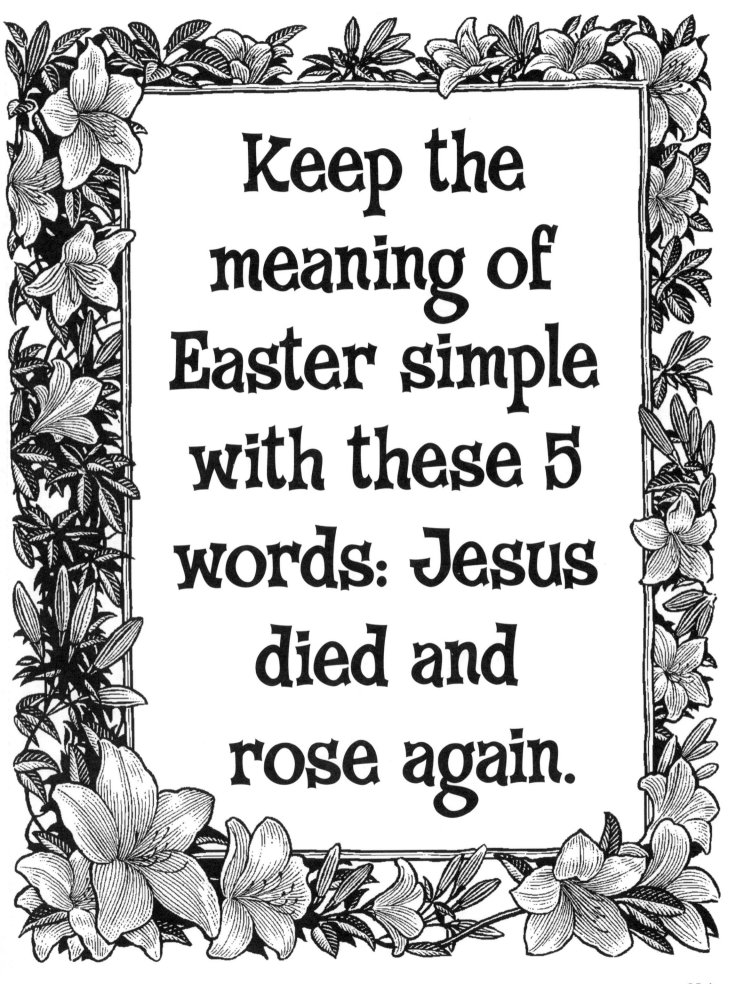

Keep the meaning of Easter simple with these 5 words: Jesus died and rose again.

CAPTURING CHILDREN'S ATTENTION

A child's time at church is limited to a few hours a week at best. In order to make effective use of these hours, develop classroom habits to gain attention, so children follow instructions quickly. Children will respond to specific attention-getting techniques when they are an established part of class routine.

Communicating with Children

Catch their eye, and then use your voice. A child responds best when directions are given specifically to him or her, not shouted across the room to everyone. Be sure the child is listening before speaking. Go to the child and bend down to his or her level. Say the child's name to emphasize that you want to speak with him or her.

Keep it short and simple. Give a clear, brief direction of what you want the child to do. Long, detailed or vague instructions will confuse a child. Instead of ordering, "We must get our coats off the table, so we can use the crayons," simply say, "John, please hang up your jacket."

Keep it positive. State requests in a positive, rather than negative, manner. Instead of saying, "Don't leave the paint bottles open and let the paint dry," say, "Jill, please put the lid back on the paint jar."

Speak naturally. Adults have a tendency to talk down to children, use a high-pitched voice or overemphasize words. Use a natural, calm tone of voice. Never yell or speak harshly. Speak softly and cheerfully. Smile while speaking!

Attention-Getting Techniques

One good way to keep attention is to follow a routine in your class—particularly for younger children who respond well to familiar patterns and predictability. If the same schedule is followed in each lesson, children will know what to expect and be ready to calm down and be active when needed.

There are two types of attention-getting signals. The first is to indicate the next activity. When children see or hear the signal, they know it is time for storytelling or games or art projects, and they can get ready for that activity. By using the same signal each time for a specific activity, children know what to expect.

▶ Play or sing a theme song for the activity. The children sing along as they gather.

▶ Start a countdown "10 . . . 9 . . . 8 . . . ." with all children seated before "1."

▶ Ring a bell, shake a tambourine, beat a drum, ring a tone chime, or shake a maraca.

▶ Clap hands in a different pattern for each activity. Students repeat the pattern as they sit.

The second type of signal is to quiet children when they are talking too much or not paying attention. Children are more likely to respond to fun techniques than to shouting. Make a game out of quieting down. Teach one of these techniques at the beginning of class and soon children will respond. Thank the children who respond first. When the signal becomes ineffective after repetition, try a new technique.

► Flick lights on and off two or three times.

► Use a silent hand signal, such as holding up (two) fingers and stop talking. Students sit down and hold up (two) fingers until everyone is seated.

► Hold up an object, such as a small toy, that is designated as the "attention grabber." Or put on a funny looking "quiet hat," scarf, gloves or sunglasses. When students see the object, they know it is time to be still.

► Thank the children who are quiet first, and then give positive reinforcement to disruptive students when they settle down. Children often disrupt just to get attention and will be calmer when you give attention to their good behavior.

► If helpers are needed for a project, select the children who are most attentive and quiet. Most children like to be selected to help and this will encourage them to be attentive. However, if the same children are selected each time, use another means to pick helpers.

► Use Simon Says instructions, such as "Simon says, 'Get a marker!' " or "Simon says, 'Stand up and find a partner!' "

► If there are other adult teachers or assistants in the room, take turns giving directions. Sometimes children stop listening when they hear the same voice all the time.

► Try not to schedule a very quiet activity, such as prayer, after a rowdy game or busy activity. Give children a chance to "cool down."

► Be prepared with an interesting lesson. Children give their attention when they are mentally engaged and enjoying the activities.

► If the classroom noise level increases, start whispering and lean in toward children. They will be likely to respond in kind.

CLASSROOM CONVERSATION

A child's education is not confined to hearing the Bible story or doing an activity—learning happens the moment the child steps into the church building. Before, during and after class, children are talking to their friends or teachers. These informal conversation times can be utilized to enforce the lesson concepts and to build a stronger bond between teacher and child. Don't dismiss these opportunities as "time fillers" or "shooting the breeze." Listen for cues and strive to guide conversation into a learning experience. Engaging a child in conversation makes class time an active, rather than a passive, learning experience.

Conversation Guidelines

Encourage dialogue. Conversation is speaking **with** someone not talking **to** them. During informal conversation, allow the child to contribute and to talk about his or her interests. Adults may feel that children have little to offer in a conversation because of their limited life experiences and education. However, children can be surprisingly perceptive and entertaining. They relish conversation when adults treat them as persons worth listening to. Taking time for conversation says, "I love you" more clearly than words.

Listen up! The best conversationalist listens more than he or she speaks. When the other person is talking, most people tend to think ahead to reply and thus miss out on what the person is saying. When a child talks, concentrate on what he or say is saying. Let the child do most of the talking.

Listen to the child's attitude and how words are said. A child may say, "I'm fine" in a way that really means, "I'm sick" or "I'm upset." A teacher who hears anger, sadness or disappointment may want to investigate further and talk with the child about his or her problems.

Children have different priorities than adults do. They may consider their pets, their favorite superheroes, their spelling tests or their games of soccer to be the most important things in their lives. Be interested in the child's world rather than judging it. Respond to the child's talk and ask questions. Children are always delighted when they know more than adults and they love to talk about their hobbies.

Watch for nonverbal clues. Some children simply don't speak a lot. They may be shy, may be frightened or may come from a family that encourages them to be quiet. They may communicate more with nods, shrugs or smiles. If a child doesn't speak much, continue to engage him or her in dialogue, even if the response is just a nod. When a child gets to know you better, he or she may begin to speak more.

Tips for Talking with Children

Be present. Stay with the children to be available for those unexpected moments. Avoid the temptation to chat with the other teachers while the children are arriving or working on art projects. Sit at the child's level so you can always make eye contact when talking to him or her. Avoid interrupting or moving away when a child is speaking. Say the child's name when addressing him or her. Such actions tell children that you value their willingness to talk.

Be prepared. Know the lesson and the Bible well. A child may arrive to class with an unexpected question about something he or she heard, saw or read in the Bible. Allow a few moments to digress from the lesson long enough to deal with the child's question. The entire class may get interested in the answer and start the ball rolling for a new lesson idea!

Find out what's happening in the children's home lives. Then you can be ready to provide comfort for a child going through a difficult time. You may want to record in a computer file or on an index card brief notes about events or concerns in each child's life. Before class, use this record to remind you of what to talk about.

Relate Bible concepts to daily life. Affirm children when they do something well and show how they are living out God's commandments. "Thanks for taking turns with the CD player, Ashley. That's a good way to obey the Bible verse we talked about today." "Luis, I saw that you helped Nathan when the markers spilled. That's what the Bible talks about doing—helping others. Thank you." Look in your teacher's manual for conversation suggestions to help link activity to learning.

Ask open-ended questions. This not only starts a conversation but also helps the teacher to evaluate the student's learning and application. Look for ways to ask questions while children are engaged in an activity or talking about themselves. "What's it like going to a new school, Brittney?" or "Nico, how was the first day of school?"

Let children discover answers themselves. Instead of giving out all the answers, let children figure out the solutions. Rather than saying, "Here are ways we can show God's love to our families," say "What can you do to show God's love to your family?" Instead of saying, "Paul saw a bright light and heard God's voice on his trip to Damascus," ask "What does this verse say happened to Paul on his way to Damascus?" Rather than telling students that Jonah was sorry for his sins, ask them "How do you think Jonah felt when he was inside the big fish?" Then help children find and read the Bible references that hold the answers!

Guided Conversation Connects the Bible and Life

Why do we need to guide conversation with young children? Don't we simply talk to them? Certainly there are many times when simple conversation is spontaneous. However, guided conversation helps children remember and recognize ways to apply the Bible truth that is the foundation for the day's activities.

What is guided conversation? Does it mean the teacher spends every minute spouting Bible verses or repeating the day's lesson focus? Talking only when a problem arises? No! Guided conversation is simply informal but planned conversation in which the teacher looks for opportunities to connect what children are doing to the Bible learning content of the session. Relating the child's activities to Bible truths helps the child understand the relationship between what he or she is doing and what the Bible says.

Step One: Know the session's lesson focus and Bible verse. This prepares you to share these ideas whenever natural opportunities and teachable moments occur.

Step Two: Listen. The biggest part of being a skilled teacher is being a good listener. When children are absorbed in an activity or are playing together, don't take a break or leave the area. Place yourself at the children's eye level, available to hear. Listening and observing provides you with helpful insight into each child's thoughts and feelings. Watch and listen for clues to their interests, how they see themselves and what things might bother them. Resist the temptation to tune a child out or race ahead mentally.

Step Three: Ask questions. Invite children into conversation that involves more than answering yes or no. Ask open-ended questions that invite the child to describe and discuss! For instance, when you see a child stacking blocks, you could say, "What do you think will happen if you put this big block on top? This little block?" Or you could say, "Tell me about your construction." Questions and comments that cannot be answered with a yes or no help children learn verbal skills, help them express their feelings and give you greater insight into their thoughts and feelings.

Step Four: Relate the child's thoughts and feelings to God's Word! You might begin by commenting on what you see. "Sheena, you helped Jake! You are obeying our Bible words. God tells us to help each other. Thank you!" You may also rephrase a child's words. "It sounds like you had a happy time with Delia, Mike. Our Bible tells us God gives us friends. We can thank God for Delia. Thank You, God, for Mike's friend Delia!"

When you identify acts of kindness or helpfulness, children then learn what it means to help each other, share or take turns. Relate a child's actions immediately, before children forget the circumstances. And use the child's name. Often, a child who does not hear his or her name assumes you are talking to someone else!

As you see children experience satisfaction, curiosity or even frustration, you are witnessing teachable moments. Children are especially receptive to new ideas at such times. Step in with a comment or question that will help the child resolve the problem; affirm a child's accomplishment with an "I see . . ." comment; answer a child's question and thank God for the child's curiosity on the spot!

With the session's Bible truths in mind, you are ready to listen, observe and comment in ways that will help each child understand more about how God's love and God's Word relate to his or her world.

MAKE YOUR WORDS COUNT!

Imagine that you are standing among giants who constantly mumble words you don't understand. That's a great deal what it's like to be a young child in a crowd of talking adults! Although we may talk at children, we find that unless we know how to talk effectively with them, they seldom hear or respond. We need to talk so that they can understand!

First, follow Jesus' example. Remember that little children need far more action than talk. When Jesus was around little children, He loved them; He didn't lecture them. Actions say more than words ever could. Young children often don't understand the meaning of all our words; our body language, facial expression and tone of voice contain most of the meaning they grasp.

How to Talk Effectively

▶ First put yourself at the child's eye level. Squat, kneel or sit.

▶ Look into the child's eyes, not only to get the child's attention, but also to say "You're important to me—I care about you." Smile as you talk. Avoid wearing that pasted-on smile grown-ups sometimes wear around children. Children need to see genuine love, not a professional manner that wears a professional smile.

▶ As you converse, show a child the same respect you would show an adult. Don't interrupt, put down or talk down to any child!

▶ Listen without passing judgment. Young children are in the process of making words work to put across their ideas. They may tell things that they imagine as if they were real. If Sean tells about his dog and you know he has no pets, say, "Sean, I bet you wish you had a dog. What kind of dog do you like?"

▶ Use the child's name often. A child may well assume you are *not* talking to him or her unless you use the child's name!

▶ Give a kind touch on the shoulder to express your love as you talk.

▶ Use these words frequently: "please," "I'm sorry," "that's all right," "thank you."

▶ Use these phrases often: "I see you . . . ," "I like the way you . . . ," "I need for you to . . . ," "It's time to . . ."

▶ If you don't understand a child's words, don't pretend you do. Instead, patiently ask the child to tell you again. If you still don't understand, invite another child to listen and help you. If you don't understand at all, say, "I'm sorry. I still can't understand, Ryan. Here. Maybe you could draw me a picture of what you want." Or you could say, "I guess my listening ears aren't working too well today! Let's try again in a minute." Be sure the child knows he or she is important to you, whether or not you understand the words.

▶ Be quick to see and point out what is good. "I see you sharing with Josiah, Kade. Sharing is a way to obey God's Word. Thank you." You've related the action to the Bible and helped both children better understand what sharing looks like.

▶ When a child refuses to cooperate, give a choice. This creates a new focus and puts responsibility for behavior back on the child. "Nathan, it's time to do something else. Would you like to play with blocks or glue pictures at the art table?" Offer choices that are perfectly acceptable to you. Don't offer more than two or three choices. Too many choices can overwhelm a young child.

What to Avoid

▶ Avoid sarcasm! Young children don't understand it but can feel belittled by a sarcastic tone of voice.

▶ Don't overexplain. Thirty seconds is about all you can expect for attention, so keep explanations short and to the point.

▶ Don't exaggerate. Part of your job as an adult is to explain how the world works in clear terms. Don't confuse the child.

▶ Don't label ("You're a lot of trouble!" "You're a handful!"). Negative words shut down open communication. Correct the behavior with positive directions and without calling the child's value into question.

▶ Don't correct what you think a child is saying or finish the child's sentence or thought. Young children need your interest and attention as they process the ways to use words.

▶ Don't use negative nonverbal signals. Sighing, looking away, glancing at your watch or making other impatient gestures tells the child clearly that you are not listening.

Remember that whenever you talk with a child, you can in some way communicate God's love to him or her. Use the opportunity!

QUICK IDEAS FOR GETTING THE YOUNG CHILD'S ATTENTION

When it's time to give directions or get children's attention, children may be told "Sit still until everyone is here" or "Wait in line until we are ready." Such methods of gaining attention and control are self-defeating if we are trying to teach kindness and respect through our own behavior. They also create negative feelings and waste valuable teaching time. There are better ways!

When You Want to Start

It's easy to establish a simple attention-getting signal for the children in your class. Choose a signal to use and introduce the signal with spoken directions. It's a good idea to practice using the signal until the children are familiar with it. Once children know the routine, simply give the signal and allow children time to respond. Always acknowledge and thank children by name who respond quickly to the signal. Here are a few signal ideas:

▶ Flick lights on and off two or three times.

▶ Slowly count aloud to five to see if everyone can be quietly looking at you before you say "five."

▶ Hold up two fingers (or hold up a different number of fingers each time) and invite children whose attention you've gained to tell how many fingers you are holding up.

▶ Sing the same song or play the same music before the same activity at each session. "By the time the song is finished, you should all be sitting on the floor."

▶ Ring a bell. (Collect several different bells. Make a game of identifying which bell you rang.)

▶ Clap hands in a pattern. Children imitate pattern as you gain their attention.

▶ Say "One, two, three—all eyes on me." (Follow this with a question: "What color is my sweater?" or "What animal do you think is on the back of my shirt?")

▶ Use a finger-play poem or other chant for children to imitate. (Change finger plays to keep interest high, but do the same one consistently for a while, so children know that finger play is a signal.)

▶ As children gather, sing a song that includes each of their names. Others will hurry to join you to hear their names sung!

While Children Listen

There are times during a circle time or story time when some children lose interest. Plan ahead for these times! When restlessness runs high, try these ideas:

▶ Ask a question, using a child's name.

▶ Whisper your words, which often generates renewed interest from children.

▶ Change the pace by leading children in a finger play, an action song or a simple imitation game to recall attention.

250

© 2006 Gospel Light. Permission to photocopy granted. *Teacher Training Smart Pages*

► If you are using a visual aid or a book, invite children to put hands on their heads when they see an item in the picture. Then return to the story without further comment.

Always phrase directions to even the most wiggly child in terms of what he or she can do, instead of what not to do. "Ryan, you need to sit on the floor. I'm looking to see if you can put your hands on your knees like mine. Thank you!"

How to Get Your Message Across

Here are some tips for effective communication with young children:

► Get the child's attention before speaking. Adults waste lots of breath saying things when no one is listening. For example, shouting across a room to a child results in confusion, rather than communication. Go to the child. Bend down so that your face is at his or her eye level. Speak the child's name. "Seth, it's time for you to put the markers in the can."

► Say the most important words first. After you've spoken the child's name, briefly state what you want the child to do. Then you may add a reason. "Karla, put your paper by the door. It's almost time for your dad to come."

► Use simple words and a natural tone of voice. Speak slowly and distinctly in a soft, yet audible, tone. Let your voice express your enthusiasm and interest. Add a smile to your words. Avoid baby talk or gushing.

► Use specific words. General terms leave a child confused, not knowing exactly what you mean. Rather than "Put the toys away," say, "Alex, your red truck needs to go here on this shelf."

ASKING THE RIGHT QUESTIONS

The art of a good discussion begins by asking effective questions. Most often, the best questions will not occur to you during a discussion but will result from good preparation. Take the time for thorough lesson preparation and for planning good questions. The best teachers continue to evaluate and refine their question-asking skills, even after years of service.

Basic Preparation

Master the material. The teacher needs to know more about the lesson than what the child is expected to learn. Although the youngest children will have simple lessons, some teachers may find that their own Bible knowledge is less than that of their older children!

If possible, supplement your teacher's guide with a study Bible, concordance and a few basic Bible study tools such as an atlas of Bible maps and a Bible dictionary. Check the Internet or your church library for these resources. If a concept presented in your lesson material is confusing or difficult to understand, ask your supervisor, the pastor or another leader in your church for help. As you participate in adult Bible studies and personal Bible study, you will find that your knowledge and understanding will grow. In class, never be afraid to let a child know that you don't know the answer to a question. After class, look for the answer and share it with the child and others in the next class meeting.

Avoid yes and no questions. These kinds of questions provide little learning and little interest for the child and only reinforce what a child already knows. Yes and no questions do little to encourage discussion and, in fact, may inhibit discussion if children are worried about giving wrong answers.

Start where the children are starting. Try to gauge where the children are in their knowledge. Many children in church today come from unchurched families and are unfamiliar with the Bible and church traditions. They may not know that the Bible is divided into the Old and New Testaments. In seeker classes, start with the basics and do not assume what the children know. Another challenge can be children with sporadic church attendance. They may be playing "continual catch-up" for the weeks missed. The challenge is to keep the interest of the more knowledgeable children while also meeting the needs of the beginners.

Developing Questions

Understanding the different types of questions can help a teacher ask the best questions for the lesson and the children.

Knowledge questions. These are questions that recall information and recite facts: What are the names of the 12 disciples? In what city was Jesus born? What cities did Paul travel to? Children are familiar with this type of question from weekday school. These questions may test what the child knows, but they do not stimulate discussion. If children give wrong information, never point it out, simply supply the correct facts. Remember that too many knowledge questions make children feel they are being grilled and may embarrass children who don't know the information. These questions also do not probe into the subject matter or help children understand how the subject matter relates to their lives.

Comprehension questions. These questions help children interpret their knowledge. Such questions ask the child to describe, explain, retell or identify. Some examples: What was different between the actions of the Samaritan and the actions of the Levite? What else could the father have chosen to do when he saw his son coming down the road? Why do you think Noah obeyed God's command to build an ark? These questions help the child move beyond just knowing the information to understanding it. Comprehension questions have no right or wrong answers, so a child can feel comfortable expressing his or her ideas.

Application questions. Bible knowledge reaches a new level when the child can apply it to his or her own life. Application questions help the child to make the lesson personal and to use the information in a new setting. These questions ask the child to apply, experiment, show, solve and describe. Questions such as What are some ways God provides for you? How can you follow Paul's example in telling others about Jesus? What are some ways we can be good stewards of the things we own? These questions move beyond "head knowledge" and into "heart knowledge."

Synthesis questions. These questions encourage children to use information in a creative and original way. Children are asked to design, create, construct, imagine and suppose: What do you think a disciple of Jesus is like? What do you think Noah and his family talked about on the ark? What would have happened if David had not trusted God when he challenged Goliath? Such questions stimulate children's natural creativity and curiosity.

Analysis questions. These questions challenge children to break apart information and examine its parts and relationships. Such questions require the child to connect, relate, arrange, analyze, compare and contrast. Some examples: Compare and contrast the actions of Saul and David. How did Joshua's actions make a difference in the lives of God's people? What factors contribute to our church's ability to worship God? These questions require abstract and analytical thinking that is most appropriate for preteens.

Evaluation questions. These questions motivate children to make informed judgments regarding the given information. The child is asked to judge, debate, decide and evaluate: Which Bible verse about honesty is the most helpful? Why? Which character in this Bible story is the best example of following God and why? Again, these questions are best handled by preteens who have developed skills in analytical thinking.

KEEP THE DISCUSSION GOING!

Children like to speak their minds! The challenge is to keep the discussion focused on the lesson, to involve all children and to prevent distracting chatter. Children's learning will be much more effective when they are involved in the process of learning through discovery and discussion rather than through sitting and listening.

Good Preparation

Write good questions before class. Good discussions occur when the teacher knows what questions to ask. Study the class material thoroughly (even if it's a familiar Bible story) and think through the discussion questions provided in your curriculum. Think of additional questions to ask as well. Avoid questions with obvious one-word answers. Discussion grows out of questions that ask for opinions, ideas, reactions, etc., not just repeating factual answers. (This means you must begin preparation well before Sunday morning!)

Minimize distractions. Children are naturally curious and are interested in everything that goes on—whether it's the lesson activity at hand or not! Evaluate the distractions in your classroom by asking the following questions: Is there noise in the classroom from the choir warming up next door? Are people walking through the hallway? Are there toys or items scattered around the classroom that the children will want to play with? Are cell phones ringing? Do parents arrive long before the class ends and stand around outside the room?

Then consider these solutions: If outside noise is a problem, play a music CD or cassette as background to cover outside noise. Toy shelves can be turned to face the wall to help children avoid the temptation of playing with the toys. Arrange chairs so children are faced away from distractions. Remind teachers (and children!) before class begins to turn off cell phones. Keep in mind, however, that your reaction to distractions is the biggest factor. If you respond in a matter-of-fact manner, children will, also.

Limit the discussion. Children are not able to remain interested during long times of discussion. Children's physical requirements for movement need to be met. It's better to end the discussion time before children grow restless. Most discussions should be tied to some physical activity, either as an introduction to the activity, as a break during the activity or as a summary after the activity.

Involve everyone. Try to involve all children in a discussion. Start by asking several easy, low-threat questions that all children are capable of answering. Seek to involve the potentially disruptive child right at the start. Children are less likely to be disruptive when they're occupied. If a child looks restless, call him or her by name and ask a question. Also ask questions of children who have been quiet. Be sure not to ask a difficult question they may not know. One reason children may not participate is that they feel they don't know the answer and don't want to be embarrassed in front of their peers.

Handling Interruptions

Get back on track. Despite the best plans, a discussion may veer off course. First, determine if the new topic is valid. Perhaps one child is overly focused on a small detail (such as how Joshua could make the sun stand still when in reality Earth moves) but the rest of the class is not interested. Acknowledge that the new topic is interesting and can be discussed at another time, and then return to the original topic. Restate the last question and if children do not respond, try another question.

If a child deliberately wants to get off the topic, use humor to return to the topic. If the children digress because they don't understand the topic or the question, use a simpler question or take time to explain the topic.

Discussion off the topic is not always cause for alarm. Sometimes a child needs to discuss a topic not on the agenda or finds an unexplored point in the topic. If the new topic will help children apply Bible truth to everyday life and will benefit the entire class, stay with it. If a child needs to discuss a special need, such as a death in the family, make time at the end of the activity for the class to offer support and prayer.

Go with the flow. Interruptions will happen. If the interruption is minor and the children are not unduly distracted, then ignore it and continue. Some interruptions require the teacher to stop and take care of matters: a child needs to leave early, an adult arrives to make an announcement or the air conditioner needs to be adjusted. Try to get the class back on track. If the class has grown too distracted, move on to another activity.

Be prepared for silence. Sometimes children will respond to a question with silence. This can be good if the children are pondering a deep question. It can be fatal if this is due to lack of understanding, embarrassment or boredom.

Give children a few seconds to think about the question. Ask for a visual signal (thumb up, fist on chin, etc.) when students think they may have at least part of the answer. Rephrase the question in case the first question was not understood. If children still are unable to answer, you might share the answer you would give and then move on to another question.

Some children may feel uncomfortable speaking in front of a large class. Divide the children into small groups of six or fewer in which to discuss the answers. Provide to each group large sheets of paper on which to write their answers. Then a volunteer from each group shares the replies with the whole class. Small groups are also good for discussing sensitive or personal topics, perhaps occasionally forming all-boy and all-girl small groups.

Sometimes children do not respond when the questions are too easy (Who are Jesus' parents?), too obvious (Does God want us to help our neighbors?), too personal (What sins have you committed this week?) or too difficult (According to legend, what are the names of the three wise men?). After class, revise the questions that failed to get a good response and use the improvements as a model for writing good questions for the next class.

Sometimes children will give the answer they think the teacher wants to hear. Write open-ended questions that are more challenging: How would you feel if you had been a shepherd who was off-duty the night the angels appeared? What do you think the blind man did after Jesus healed him? How can you defend your friend from a bully?

Guiding conversation is the ingredient that turns an interesting experience into Bible learning. As children work and play together, never assume you are no longer needed: This is your time to shine! Observe carefully and then use words to connect a child's actions to a Bible truth: **Luis, I see you helped Zane lift the blocks. Thank you for helping. God says to help each other!** Putting words to children's actions gives them a way to connect God's Word with their everyday lives.

Guiding conversation during an activity does NOT mean you need to talk during the entire time! Children will quickly tune you out if you talk too much. But it is important to talk at least once with each child during the session—conversation beyond the giving of directions. Show them that you see them and love them. When they are sure of that, they will be the more ready to hear how God loves them, too!

To talk with a child of any age: Place yourself at the child's eye level (even if it means sitting on the floor!). Talk to a child in a normal tone of voice, as respectfully as you would talk with another adult. Use the child's name often. Use gentle safe, touch. Listen actively to the child's words by repeating or rephrasing the child's words. Ask questions about what the child said. Accept the child's feelings and ideas. Make positive comments about specific actions the child does. Link those actions to obeying God's Word.

The key to guiding conversation is to move away from asking "yes or no" kinds of questions and into "what do you think?" kinds of questions. Open-ended questions don't have "right" answers, so children are not intimidated that they might give a wrong answer. Then listen! When you listen carefully to children's answers, you will discover what they do or do not understand. Then you can better help them clear up any confusion.

If you have very quiet children in your group, try initiating a conversation by using a puppet to "talk" to the child. Or, use a telephone to talk into and then offer the child another phone with which to reply.

If you are teaching children who are not yet verbal, encourage their use of language by describing their actions. **Timmy is cooking. I smell something good! Let me guess what you're cooking.**

Small-Group Discussion Tips

A great teacher spends twice as much time listening as talking to children. (Sound impossible? Begin by listening more than you talk!) Listening includes looking at the child who is talking and demonstrating interest in what was said. Respond to the specific ideas the child expressed. Your responsiveness reveals the love of God!

As you guide the discussion with children, often use words like: "Please," "Thank you," "I'm sorry," "I see," and "I am glad" in your conversation. Kind words express kind feelings. Children hearing your words will follow your example.

Adults waste lots of breath saying things when no one is listening! Get a child's attention before you speak. Go to the child. Put your face at his or her eye level. Say the most important words first, briefly. Talk with a smile and show the child the same courtesy you would show an adult

How do you decide when to step in and offer help? Well-meaning adults often interrupt a child's activity immediately when they see a better way to do something. However, it is better to observe a moment longer, watching to see how the child will solve it. If the child is becoming frustrated, it is time to offer a suggestion or question. This gives the child the satisfaction of finding a solution!

When you see children are happy, put the feelings of their experience into words. **Juan and Justin, I see you are having a good time together. I'm glad to see you are friends.** Then link the feelings with God's Word: **God gives us happy times with friends. Thank You, God!**

What do you do when a child gives a wrong answer? First ask, **What do you remember about that part of the story?** to see if he or she misunderstood something. Use the Bible to verify the answer. **It says here that he was 120 years old.** Using the Bible not only helps children to know that the answers are really there but also validates the child's efforts to answer.

Few things so effectively communicate the significance of God's Word than the attitudes of the adults in the classroom! When children can tell by your enthusiasm that you love and value God's Word, they will also come to value it. Use the Bible often in your conversation (especially the day's memory verse) and link it to the actions you see in the classroom. **Denis is giving the markers to Ella. That's the way we share. God's Word says to do good and to share. Thank you!**

Small-Group Discussion Tips

If you are surprised by a child's reply to a question, ask the child to tell you more so that you are sure you understand what he or she is saying. Don't judge the answer (not even by facial expression). This will help even the quietest child to feel more secure sharing ideas. When children's ideas are treated with respect, they are more ready to hear your ideas!

Children often give answers that they think the teacher expects to hear. To get deeper answers ask instead **What do you think a kid your age might say about that? Do about that?** By asking children to tell how another child might respond, the pressure is off the child to give the "good" answer and discussion can be taken to higher levels of honesty!

Instead of telling a child exactly what to do, try posing a question that will help him or her think of an answer. **What is a way we could help clean up?** This challenges children to develop thinking skills and responsibility.

When talking to a child whose attention often wanders, try placing a hand on the arm or shoulder. This tactile grounding can sometimes help them to keep focused—and it sends loving message to a child who is sometimes moving too much to be kindly touched!

It's estimated that only about 30 percent of any message a person sends actually comes from the words he or she uses. Most of the meaning comes through tone of voice, facial expression and body language. Your warm smile, quick arm around the shoulders or pat on the arm gives positive reinforcement of the words you say.

To create a climate where good discussion will flourish, keep small groups to no more than eight children. Otherwise, direct involvement become difficult and the quality of the discussion and of the relationships diminishes.

TALK ABOUT WAYS YOU SEE CHILDREN PUTTING GOD'S WORD INTO ACTION.

TO CREATE A CLIMATE WHERE GOOD DISCUSSION WILL FLOURISH, KEEP SMALL GROUPS TO NO MORE THAN EIGHT CHILDREN.

HEARING DISABILITIES

A child with a hearing disability is as intelligent and aware as a hearing child. Hearing disabilities can vary widely and include children who have partial hearing loss in one ear or a loss that can be corrected with a hearing aid. Some children are skilled at reading lips and others can only speak through American Sign Language (ASL). Talk to the child's parents to determine how much the child can hear and comprehend. Consider asking an adult helper to assist regularly with the child.

Methods of Communication

Speech. Interview the parents to determine the child's level of function with speech, too. If the child has some hearing capacity, you may be able to communicate through speaking. But remember to let the child choose the ways to communicate that best suits him or her. Avoid shouting at the child. This draws unwanted attention and distorts the words. Speak naturally and enunciate clearly. Do not talk too rapidly, but at the same time, avoid speaking too slowly or drawing out words. If you normally talk very softly or have a high voice, you may need to speak up a little. Exaggerated facial expressions or speech will not be understood. Look directly at the child and let him or her see your lips moving, especially if the child can read lips. Avoid turning away or covering your mouth when speaking. Keep your hands still, as unnecessary gestures are distracting. Do not use baby talk or talk down to the child. Use complete and grammatically correct sentences. Ask the child to repeat what he or she heard to ensure understanding.

The child may have hearing loss in only one ear. When speaking, face the child but stand toward the side from which the child hears best. The child may need to turn his or her ear toward the teacher instead of making eye contact.

Music. Even a deaf child is able to feel music by touching a stereo speaker or feeling the beat through the floor. A child may pantomime the words instead of singing. However, some children need or want the volume of music turned up very high. Music that is too loud will be uncomfortable for the rest of the class and surrounding classrooms. Ask the parents how much the child can hear and at what volume. If the child needs loud music, perhaps he or she can use a portable cassette/CD player with headphones.

Games. Children with hearing disabilities can play along with the rest of the class. If the child cannot hear a whistle, buzzer or bell, use a flashlight or hold up a stop sign as a signal. Explain the instructions clearly and demonstrate the game, so the child is not confused when the game starts. Written instructions may be useful, too. Make sure the players do not depend on only verbal cues to play the game. The other children may need to use hand signals to direct the child who cannot hear. Include hearing impaired children's ideas into the activities so that they feel they are contributing members of the group.

Love. Communicate to children who are hearing impaired that God loves them just the way they are. Don't oversimplify or trivialize their disabilities. Think of ways to encourage them that don't require listening. Nonverbal communication (a touch, a hug, a smile, etc.) is a great way to demonstrate God's love!

Tools for the Hearing Impaired

Imagination. Pretend you are in a foreign country where you don't speak the language. You would likely use your hands, your feet, facial expressions, draw and point as much as possible. Don't be afraid to use whatever communication method gets a positive response!

Sign Language. The child may use American Sign Language (ASL) as the principal form of communication. Learn some basic requests and words in ASL. Training books are available, plus many schools offer ASL night classes for adults.

Teach some ASL words to the entire class. Better yet, have the hearing-impaired child teach the other children! Most children love to learn ASL. This will not only help the children to speak to the hearing-impaired child but also will make the hearing-impaired child feel included because the entire class is signing. The class can learn to sign simple prayers or short Bible verses.

ASL has a different grammatical structure than standard English for faster speech and fewer hand motions. A child who cannot hear regular speech may not be aware of how standard English is supposed to sound. Do not be surprised if his or her spoken or written sentences are grammatically incorrect. Accept the child's speech as his or her gift to the class. Instead of correcting the child, repeat the statement back with proper grammar.

Hearing Aids. A child with a partial hearing loss may be able to use a hearing aid. Today, such devices are incredibly small and effective. The other children may not be able to see the hearing aid. However, a hearing aid may not be able to fully restore all hearing loss. Even with a hearing aid, the child may not be able to listen to one voice if there is a lot of other noise in the room, such as other children talking or music playing. Continue speaking clearly and directly to a child with a hearing aid. If there is a lot of surrounding noise, stand directly in front of the child to speak.

Sometimes the child may need to stop and adjust the hearing aid if he or she is trying to hear someone speaking softly or the surrounding noise is too loud. If the child is working with the hearing aid, stop talking to the child and wait for him or her to finish.

At times, a hearing-impaired child may turn off the hearing aid or pretend not to hear. This may be due to sensory overload or problems with the hearing aid. Observe the child to determine if he or she simply doesn't want to be involved with the class. Talk with the parents to determine how they handle similar situations. Use positive reinforcement to increase the behavior you want to see. As you model appropriate behavior and establish trust, you can expect hearing-impaired children to behave as respectfully as other children.

PHYSICAL DISABILITIES

At one time or another you will likely encounter a child in your class who is physically disabled. Sometimes the disability is mild and the child can fully participate in all activities with minimal assistance. Other disabilities require more attention. Some disabilities are temporary, such as a broken leg, while other impairments are permanent. The most important thing is to focus on what the child can do instead of what the child cannot do. Get the child involved in classroom activities as much as possible instead of letting the child sit idly on the sidelines. If a particular activity is totally unsuitable, find an alternate activity that will allow the child to remain in the group and study the same material.

Types of Physical Disabilities

Allow all children with special physical needs to participate at their own level. Ask their permission, if possible, before helping them complete any project. Consider asking the parents of a child with a disability to come and tell about the disability and/or show appropriate visual aids or videos to help children understand the disability.

Arms and hands. Some children have limited use of their fingers on one or both hands, or they may have only one hand or arm. They may be able to write, color or paint if an adult puts the pen in their hands or bends their fingers. If they cannot operate scissors, precut materials for them. If they need assistance holding a book or turning pages, they can set a book on a small podium while they stand or you can tape pages together in one long strip.

Legs and feet. A child may need a cane or walker to move around, or he or she may be confined to a wheelchair. Recent federal legislation requires that all public buildings must be handicapped accessible. New churches are built to code with wheelchair ramps, elevators and accessible restrooms. However, some older church buildings were constructed with many stairs and narrow hallways and may be accessible in only a few areas. If a child cannot easily reach the classroom, move the class to an accessible room. Check to see that nearby restrooms are also accessible. If an elevator or stair climber must be used, be sure the child can safely operate the device or that an adult is present to assist.

Children in wheelchairs can still participate in games and may be quite mobile and quick. They may be able to move while carrying an object in a lap, one hand or a chair basket. Allow them to participate as much as they are willing and able. Make sure there is sufficient space in the playing area for wheelchairs to maneuver. Make clear rules that other students are not to grab, touch or push the wheelchair without permission. A wheelchair is a tool, not a toy. However, if the child is willing, others can learn a lot from having a turn using the chair.

Facial features. Some children were born with facial deformities and others have had their features changed through injury, disease or fire. Children with cancer may need to wear a medical mask or they may lose their hair as a result of chemotherapy. Other children may react by staring or by avoiding. Teach by modeling for your class that God loves each person no matter how we look. Treat the child with respect and dignity. Emphasize to the other children what abilities everyone in the class shares. Look into the child's eyes when speaking to him or her. The class will likely imitate your attitude.

Assisting the Child with a Disability

Plan appropriate activity. Find out the limits of the child's endurance. Most children have no problem with a typical one-hour class session. However, some children with special abilities tire easily. If the child is to be involved with an all-day event or an overnight camp, allow the child time out if needed. Have a quiet, private place where the child can rest. Do not make a big issue over rest time but allow the child to leave the group quietly. Some disabled children also require daily medications. Have a qualified medical professional or the child's parent present to safely administer all medicines.

Use an assistant. If the child suffered a recent injury, he or she may need help with simple daily tasks, such as holding a pencil or tying shoes. Recruit an adult assistant who can help the child while the teacher leads the class. However, children who have lived with a disability for a long time have learned ways to handle most tasks and compensate for their limitations. Allow the child to do as much as he or she can do without tiring or excessive strain. Be patient, as they may require more time to complete a task.

Solicit the parents' cooperation. Speak with the parents about the best ways to assist the child. Have the parents sit in on the class to gauge the activities where the child may need assistance. Get information about the disability from the child's therapist or school.

Speak to the class. The other children may have questions. They need to feel comfortable learning and playing with a classmate who has a disability. Allow the child to explain as much as he or she wishes, but the class does not need to know private details about the medical condition, what caused the disability or how the child handles personal functions.

Be loving and understanding. If the disability is from a recent accident, if it is permanent or if it is likely to be terminal, the child may be upset, depressed or angry. Show love and compassion consistently. Make your class an emotionally safe place for a child to ask hard questions and express his or her feelings. Allow the child time to deal with feelings. Give the child time and private space to talk about his or her feelings. The child may blame God or be upset with God, especially if a loved one was lost in an accident. Do not argue with the child. Assure the child that bad things happen in the world and God still loves him or her and is working something good out of the situation.

SPEECH DISABILITIES

A teacher may encounter a child in class who has difficulty speaking. Such children cannot pronounce words correctly, or perhaps they do not use proper grammar or sentence structure and their sentences are unintelligible. This can be frustrating if you feel that you are not able to understand what a child is trying so hard to communicate. Talk with family members to gain knowledge of the situation. Be patient with yourself and with the child to help establish communication.

Types of Speech Difficulties

Physical disabilities. Some children have problems with speech due to a birth defect, physical defect, injury or disease to the brain or neurological speech functions. Some examples include apraxia, cerebral palsy, cleft palate or mental retardation. In most cases, the speech difficulty cannot be cured but can be managed.

Learning disabilities. The speech of some children will develop slower than that of their peers.

Baby talk. Some older children may continue to speak below their age level, such as "Me want pencil" or "Go potty." This could be a learning disability but may also be an emotional problem. Be sure to consult with the family for more information. The child may feel that baby talk is a good way to get attention or special treatment. Encourage the child to speak properly by rephrasing the request. "Tiffany, do you want to use a pencil?" or "Do you need to use the restroom?" Invite the child to repeat the sentence correctly with you without turning it into a challenge.

Stuttering. A child may stutter only on certain words, because he or she is experiencing a growth spurt or because he or she is nervous. If the child stutters, be patient and loving. Avoid the temptation to finish a sentence for the child or show annoyance. Invite the child to choose a way to communicate that better suits him or her, such as writing or drawing. Respond by narrating what you see for immediate feedback ("I see. You meant the other dog. Now I understand!"). If a child believes that you are not annoyed by his or her speech, the child will become comfortable speaking with you, even if it is difficult. Often, stuttering decreases as the child feels accepted.

Understanding. Some children may not understand what is said to them, such as English as a second language (ESL) students or students with cognitive disabilities. They may seem to disobey a request because the words make no sense to them. Always phrase directions positively, so the child hears exactly what he or she needs to do. Speak directly and calmly to the child. Repeat the request clearly. If necessary, pantomime or act out the request. If the child is learning English, learn basic words in the child's native language and use them until the child is more comfortable using English.

Tips for Communication

Get help. Enlist another adult who is aware of the situation to help the child.

Consult with the parents. Find out if the parents have any special techniques that they use to communicate with the child. Also consult the child's therapist or specialist who can share ideas on communication with the child. Keep updated on changes in the child's condition or treatment.

Preserve the child's dignity. Most children feel awkward that they are "different" and cannot speak as well as the other students. Avoid drawing attention to problems or treating the child as abnormal. Rather than saying, "Let's wait for Tom to write out a question," say "Hand me your question when you are ready, Tom." If the child feels he or she cannot participate in class discussion, allow the child to ask questions privately and encourage the child to say as much as he or she is comfortable saying. As you create a safe and accepting environment, some children will gain confidence to practice and improve their speech.

If another student makes fun of a child's disability, simply comment, "We show respect to everyone in our class." If the teasing continues, speak to the offender privately about the need to respect others. Teach a parable about tolerance to the entire class without pointing out the disabled child. Establish a safe and nurturing atmosphere so that the student is comfortable speaking without fear of ridicule.

Repeat for clarity. When the child has spoken, repeat the statement for confirmation. "Do you want a Bible?" "Are you saying that Daniel was brave when he was in the lion's den?" The child can confirm the statement with a nod. You have demonstrated that you understood the words. Don't pretend to understand unclear speech. If necessary, ask the child to show, draw or write what was meant. The child will only feel more frustrated if you give a vague answer in reply or do something other than what the child asked.

Be honest. If the child's speech is not intelligible, admit it. "Roy, I didn't quite understand. Could we try again?" If the statement is not clear, ask the child to point or act out what he or she wants. Invite the child to show, draw or write what was meant. If you still cannot understand, tell the child that you're sorry you can't understand and that you will ask the child's parents for help in getting to know what the child is trying to say. The child knows that you are making an honest effort at communication.

Be patient. Children may become frustrated or angry at their limited speech ability. Assure the child that you are glad to have him or her in class and that what he or she says is important. You may also admit to feeling frustrated at the difficult communication! But continue to use every available avenue of communication. As you work with a child over time, you will grow accustomed to the child's speech and be able to discern the child's best communication style.

Visual aids. A child can indicate his or her needs by pointing to a picture. Keep flashcards on hand with pictures of items a child might need: a glass of water, a bathroom door, pencil or a question mark. An older child may be able to read and write without difficulty. Such a child may want to write out requests or point to words in a book that spell a question.

Sign Language. A child can communicate his or her wants through simple hand signals, point to an object, point to the bathroom door or make motions to indicate "drink" or "eat." If the child has extreme difficulty with speech, recruit another adult to be a child's regular aide during the class session. Spend time with the child, parents and the aide to learn better ways to communicate with the child.

Visual Disabilities

Visual disabilities come in degrees of severity. A child may be totally blind or partially sighted. In the latter case, the child may be able to see somewhat if he or she wears glasses or holds items close. Speak with the parents to determine the extent of the child's abilities. Encourage a partially sighted child to use his or her vision as much as possible so that the child can develop independence and confidence.

A student may come to class with an undiagnosed vision problem. If a student insists that he or she cannot read the chalkboard from a distance, holds books close to the face for reading or is hesitant about walking into a crowded hallway or crossing a street, the child may have a vision problem. Mention your observation to the child's parents so that an optometrist can be consulted if needed.

Communicating with the Visually Impaired

Speak normally. Blind children are not deaf. Some people have a tendency to raise their voice when speaking to a blind person. Use a normal speaking tone, but enunciate words clearly since the child cannot see lips or facial expression.

Identify speakers. When greeting the child, say your name, even if the child recognizes the voice. Say the names of new children or those who are talking.

Explore the classroom. On the first day of class, give the child a guided tour of the room, so he or she will know the location of furniture, supplies, closets and restrooms. Older children may pace out the room to learn the layout. If possible, arrange for the child to arrive early, so he or she has plenty of time to explore. Keep furniture and supplies in the same place each week so the child can find them. Keep the floor clear of trash and objects so that the child does not stumble.

Use touch. A hand on the shoulder or a gentle hug is a good way to show love. When guiding the child, do not grab his or her arm. Tap his or her hand and let the child hold your fingers. Do not pull a child, but gently walk alongside the child at the child's pace.

Treat the child normally. There is no need to pamper or isolate a child with a disability. Such children have adapted and can deal with their abilities. The child will be happy to be included in all classroom activities. Allow the child to do as much as possible within his or her capacity. If necessary, let another child serve as a buddy if the child needs extra guidance. Always consult the parents for more ideas when you have difficulty.

The child can participate in many games if instructions are clear and easy to remember. Put raised bumps on objects so that the child knows what to pick up. Playing the game in pairs allows a child with a visual disability to participate.

A partially sighted child can make art projects and follow clear verbal directions if you describe the process step-by-step. Make an art project with him or her and let the child feel your hands as you create together. Describe the actions you see and the materials you use with words the child can understand. A child with a visual disability may enjoy art projects that he or she can feel, such as threading yarn through large holes or working with textured fabrics. Talk to the parents about the child's capabilities. With some imagination, alternative art projects can be designed if needed.

A child with a visual disability is expected to behave with the same courtesy as a sighted child. Expect cooperation and respect as you are cooperative and respectful—the same as for a sighted child.

What to say. A sighted person can still say "see" or "look" to a blind person. Some will say they are having a "look" when they feel an object.

Other students may have questions about the disability. Encourage the child to answer questions if he or she would like. If the child feels uncomfortable say, "Everyone sees differently. Julie doesn't see the way we do." The other children will grow comfortable around the child with a visual disability if you are confident and do not treat the child anxiously or differently. Encourage interaction so that the other children will become more comfortable and confident in dealing with the visually impaired child.

Tools to Help a Child Who Is Visually Impaired

Large print. A partially sighted child may be able to read large-print materials. If the child does not have a large-print Bible, perhaps the class or church can donate one to the child. The American Bible Society sells large-print New Testaments and Bibles in several versions. A photocopier can enlarge existing activity sheets, or retype activity sheets into a computer and print out sheets with large print.

Braille and audiocassettes. Some charitable organizations provide free Braille Bibles and Scripture portions to the visually impaired. The Bible is also available in audiocassettes, CD-ROMs and mp3 downloads.

Three-dimensional teaching aids. If the class is discussing an item such as a scroll, clay tablet, animals or well, make a sample from clay or play dough. The child can "see" the item through touch and learn more than by simply hearing a description. Sighted children will also enjoy touching and looking at the object!

Canes and guide dogs. A child who uses a cane and/or guide dog has been educated on how to use such aids, so you will not need to help the child with these items. Instruct your class that the cane is a tool, not a toy. Likewise, a guide dog is working and is not to be petted unless the child gives permission. Guide dogs are housebroken and trained to be calm around strangers, so you do not need to worry about the dog's behavior.

Teaching Children with Special Needs

Society places a high value on both appearance and achievement. For this and many other reasons, including a child with a disability in class can cause some people to cringe inwardly, unsure of how to react or what to say. But a child with a disability is as loved by God as any other! Including a child with a disability in your class is a tremendous opportunity for the other members of the class to put God's love into action.

If you are unfamiliar with the condition of a child with a disability, you may be uncertain about how to best help him or her. Here are some general guidelines and strategies to help you become prayerfully prepared. Expect to be greatly blessed as you discover the gifts God sends through that child! With skills and understanding, you can minister effectively both to a child with a disability and to the other children in your class.

The foundation. Provide space on the children's ministry registration form for registering parents to indicate a child's special needs or medical concerns. If parents indicate that their child has a need, set up an interview with the child's parents to learn more about the child's situation and how best to meet the child's needs. Take complete notes and share the information only with those who need to know. If the child is enrolled in a public school, it might be appropriate to ask parents to share their child's IEP (individual education plan) developed by the school staff to outline ways they help the child learn best at school.

Also invite a parent to attend class with the child the first few times. The parent can demonstrate the most effective ways to help the child. Then your help will be understood by the child and consistent with help the parent gives at home.

The challenge. One challenge when any child who is different enters a classroom is distraction. A child's disability or behavior may cause others to focus on that child to the exclusion of everything else. To prevent distraction, some churches train and then assign an aide to accompany each child with a disability. Each aide works with only one child during a class session so that the child can participate fully while keeping distraction to a minimum.

The structure. For many children with disabilities, a consistent routine provides structure that will help them function best. During the first few class sessions, establish a routine and follow it consistently. As you get to know the child, you can then adjust the routine to accommodate the child's strengths and learning styles. Use the learning-center approach (centers well staffed with adults) to give all children the chance to work at their own levels of ability.

TEACHING THE CHILD WITH ADD/ADHD

Although ADD and/or ADHD affect only 2 to 5 percent of school children, this small percentage translates into more than 2 million children in the United States alone. You may have a child in your class who has been diagnosed with ADD/ADHD. If you are not a professionally trained educator, however, you may know little about these disorders. With patience and good teaching skills, most ADD/ADHD children can be taught successfully in your class. Place a priority on developing a good relationship and ongoing communication with the parents of children with ADD/ADHD. These parents may need the support of the church in many ways (child care, access to trained counselors, prayer, etc.)

What Is ADD/ADHD?

Attention deficit disorder (ADD) and hyperactive disorder (HD) are two types of attention deficit disorders. Often the terms are used interchangeably. Children who have both types of disorders are ADHD. Research has shown that ADD and ADHD are biologically based and not a result of poor parenting or not learning to obey. These children will not grow out of these disorders. More than half of the children with ADD/ADHD will continue to exhibit symptoms as they mature.

Children with ADD/ADHD may have difficulty focusing on and completing tasks. They may be easily distracted and may not listen when a teacher talks to them. They can be forgetful, inattentive to detail or careless with objects. These children find it difficult to follow instructions or organize tasks. They act impulsively and sometimes recklessly.

Sometimes called hyperactive, children with ADD/ADHD can seem like fast-running motors that never shut down. They might squirm, fidget in their chairs or find it difficult to sit for a long time. They sometimes prefer to run around the room. They talk nonstop, blurt out statements and interrupt when others speak. They find it hard to take turns or wait in line. ADHD children might find it difficult to work quietly. If ADD/ADHD is left untreated, the child may be unsuccessful in school, at work and in getting along with others.

More boys than girls are diagnosed with ADD/ADHD because the symptoms are less visible in girls. Because girls with ADD/ADHD may not be treated as often, they may drift through school with mediocre grades and few friends and not live up to their potential.

Only a trained professional counselor or physician is qualified to diagnose a child with ADD/ADHD. Neither a teacher nor a pastor can assume that a rowdy child has or does not have these disorders merely by watching his or her behavior. If a child exhibits the symptoms of ADD/ADHD to the extent that your class activities are regularly disrupted, your supervisor may wish to talk gently with the parents to ask for their advice on how to better meet the needs of the child. No child should be labeled with this disorder without a qualified diagnosis.

How Can I Teach the ADD/ADHD Child?

Medication. Many, but not all, ADD/ADHD children take prescription medicine as part of their treatment. Such medicine, however, only relieves the symptoms and does not actually cure the disease. This medicine is not a tranquilizer that makes the child compliant, or a magic cure-all. Teachers and pastors are not qualified to prescribe or handle these drugs.

If medication is required, the parent or a qualified medical professional should administer the dosage to the child.

A child may show some side effects, such as loss of appetite, sleep problems, moodiness or fatigue, when ending the medication or changing the dosage. Because some parents do not medicate their children when their children are not in school, you may see these side effects during class.

Student attention. Part of a child's treatment is training the child how to concentrate and pay attention. In addition to the tips included in this article, consult the parents, a health specialist, educator or reference books for additional information on teaching the ADD/ADHD child.

You may wish to also enlist the help of another adult who is willing to be trained in helping the ADD/ADHD child. During class, the adult mentor stays near the child and is ready to offer one-on-one direction as needed. In some cases, it may prove helpful to have the adult provide patient and loving one-on-one guidance rather than pressing to have the child try to fit in to what the other children are doing.

While the following teaching tips are useful when teaching all ages, these tips are particularly important if you are teaching children with ADD/ADHD.

▶ Provide colorful posters, markers and chalk as well as a variety of visual aids.

▶ Use sound and music to signal to the child when it's time to listen.

▶ Speak clearly and look for visual cues that the child is listening.

▶ Use words the child will understand. Be specific.

▶ Draw a square around information on a chalkboard, poster or white board to show the student where to look. Use a flashlight to draw a child's eyes.

▶ Use a variety of storytelling techniques including props, first-person stories, skits. Avoid having any presentation extend too long. Be brief and change to a new activity at the first sign of restlessness.

▶ Try to eliminate or soften outside sounds that could distract a student: a loud air conditioner, street noise, hallway traffic, music or talking in a nearby room.

▶ Keep room decorations attractive but simple. Take away all unnecessary materials and furniture that could distract the child. Erase the chalkboard or white board after the information has been presented.

▶ Cover all but a few lines of a book page as the child reads it so that the child is better able to concentrate on a few lines at a time.

▶ Avoid lag time. Have materials and multimedia prepared for quick use. If the rest of the class is doing an activity that requires a significant amount of time, have alternate activities on hand for the ADD/ADHD child to do when his or her attention wanders.

▶ Let the child sit close to you and away from doors and windows. Make eye contact when speaking. Surround the ADD/ADHD child with well-behaved children.

▶ Maintain a regular class routine. ADD/ADHD children do not cope well with change. Give choices within appropriate boundaries.

▶ Before a child begins a task, be sure the child clearly understands the directions. Don't embarrass the child but do have the child repeat back or write down the instructions for clarity. Encourage the child to ask for assistance if he or she gets stuck. Keep projects simple, with a minimal number of directions. Give simple instructions, one at a time, and repeat instructions if necessary. Show patience and understanding when a child is unable to remain focused on a task.

▶ Give age-appropriate rewards for completing tasks within a reasonable time limit. ADD/ADHD children may work slowly and may grow frustrated if they cannot keep up with the pace of other children's work. Be available to give assistance and encouragement if the child gets stuck.

Being diagnosed with ADD/ADHD is not an excuse for the child to misbehave. Establish class rules ahead of time and talk about the consequences of not following the rules ("If you want to play this bowling game, you need to wait in line for your turn"). Redirect children's behavior in a fair, kind and calm manner. Avoid confrontation, ridicule and criticism. Do not announce to the entire class when the child needs to take medication or that the child has ADD/ADHD.

Most of all, give plenty of positive reinforcement and affirmation when the child does well. Show love and affection with more than words. Children will pick up your caring feelings by seeing your facial expression and actions.

Special Needs Tips

Challenging children who are antagonistic is a special task. Perhaps the child does not have a diagnosed "disorder" but he or she seems negative and moody. Provide choices in activities. Be sure the child knows you accept him or her, even with the negative feelings. Let the child know you are on his or her side with a comment like **Donna, you seem bored. Let me know if I can help you do that another way.** When a child is loved and accepted, the mood is likely to improve!

You may have a child in your class who needs help focusing his or her attention on the task at hand. Children who fidget, blurt out answers, interrupt conversations and react physically when excited may not have a "diagnosed disorder" but are simply kids whose impulse control is not yet well-developed. They may also have trouble with waiting for a turn, following directions or may do something dangerous with no consideration of consequences. Help this child by: Diminishing distractions by putting the class into small groups; maintaining eye and physical contact (a hand on the shoulder or arm) while speaking to him or her.

As a rule of thumb for any child who comes to your class lacking a physical ability, always make it a point to interact with the child. Focus on the senses he or she does have and the abilities he or she displays. Build on the child's favorite way of relating. For example, if he or she chooses to be involved with music, encourage the child's participation and give him or her more encouragement during that time. **I know Kendra really likes to sing this song!** Help the child to understand that everyone is different and everyone is gifted in his or her own way.

Kids in your class may make insensitive comments about others' differences. "I run faster than her because her legs are funny." What do you say? Rather than let it drop into an embarrassed silence, rephrase the child's observation. **Yes, Cinthy runs and walks differently than you do.** Then explain in simple, factual terms. **Her right leg is a little shorter than her left. So she wears a special shoe. Running is harder for her than for you.** Then remind children, **God makes each of us different. He has something different for Cinthy to do in the future than He has for you. And that is good! It's OK to ask questions but it is not OK to say things that can hurt a person's feelings.**

If you have a child in your class whose behavior is largely negative, be alert to notice, acknowledge and encourage any positive behavior. **Chad, I see you picked up two crayons. Thank you!** Catch that child doing good so that there is a positive base to your relationship. Often, a child who is a "problem" has never learned to garner positive attention. Giving this child a special job (especially if it is something he or she does with you) is another good way to build relationship that can result in significant behavior change!

If you have a child in your class who has special needs, it is valuable to make a visit to the child in his or her home. You can see how the parents teach the child, and how the child lives at home. This will help you to better plan for the child in class. It will also give you a good basis for relationship with the parents so that if there are questions, you will feel comfortable asking.

Special Needs Tips

If you have a partially sighted or a blind child in your classroom, follow these guidelines to help the child feel comfortable: Talk to the child as you would any other child. There is no need to avoid the words "see" or "look." Many visually impaired people see objects by looking at them very closely. Others with less sight are able to see an object by feeling it. When speaking specifically to the child, use his or her name. Allow the child to move as close to the materials as he or she needs to. Allow the child to explore materials by touch and in demonstrating how to do an activity, bring your hands close to the visually impaired child or place your hands on the child's and repeat the action. Make use of verbal cure: describe pictures, explain activities, talk about what you see happening, etc.

Children who have not had experiences with disabled people are unsure of what to do and are sometimes afraid. Talking about their fears helps children to feel more comfortable around disabled people. Let children discuss things that would be difficult about having a disability. **What might be difficult to do during recess? At lunchtime? How would it be different to go to and from school?**

The more children think about this the more comfortably they will relate to disabled people. Always emphasize that disabled people are people with the same feelings and experiences that everyone else has.

Have children take turns to wear a blindfold or to close eyes while another child acts as guide and walks beside the non-sighted person; children then switch roles so that both may experience being without sight.

Bring a wheelchair or walker to class. If possible have the person to whom it belongs talk briefly about his or her reason for using the equipment. A short and appropriate explanation is sufficient for children and emphasize what the person can do or an interest he or she has. **Roger's legs don't work the same as ours, so he uses a wheelchair to move around. He plays basketball really well from his chair!**

Remember that your responses and reactions to any child with special needs will be the most powerful teaching most children will ever get on this important topic. If you are able to model respect, compassion and acceptance, the children in your class are likely to follow your example!

The child who is hardest to love needs love the most.

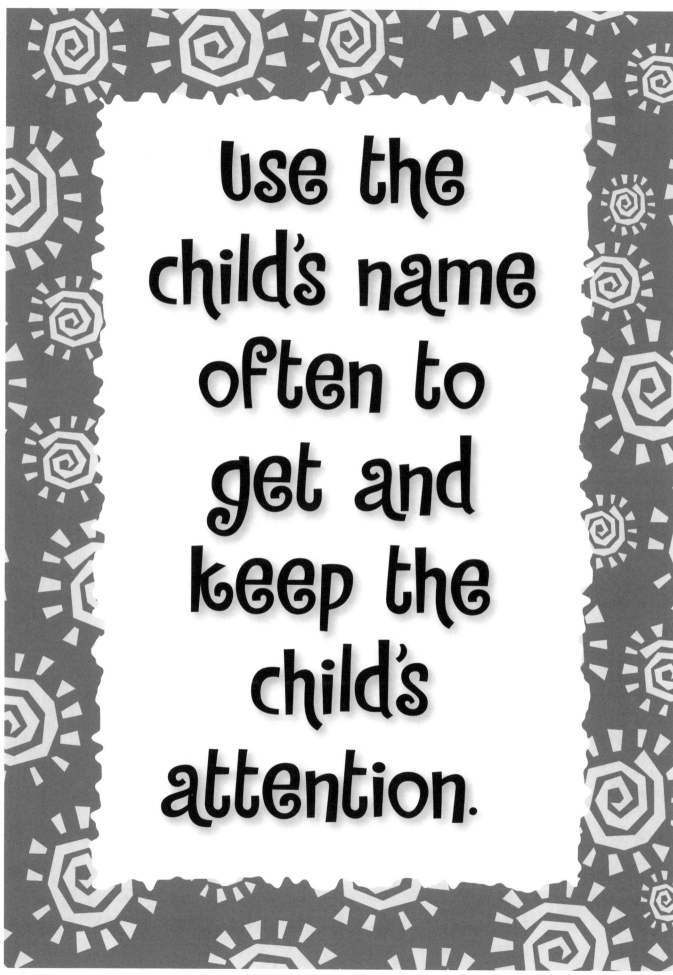

Use the child's name often to get and keep the child's attention.

Teaching Theology to Children

We humans first learn through what we experience. As children, we begin as concrete thinkers; that is, we understand what we see, touch, taste and experience. It is through living (not listening!) that we come to understand what life is about. As we gather more experiences, these experiences create a unique frame of reference by which we then process and understand new ideas.

We cannot see God. We cannot experience the kind of life people experienced in Bible times. So how then is it possible for children to learn about God or understand the Bible concepts of salvation, sin, prayer, love, faith and patience? Although those who study children say that until around 12 years of age children are not fully able to think in abstract terms, it is during this same "pre-abstract" time of life that most people report having begun a personal relationship with Christ! So the ability to absorb and act on abstract ideas is related to the work of the Holy Spirit, to a child's developing ability and to a teacher's ability to make those abstract concepts understood.

To teach an abstract idea most effectively, it is best to link it to a child's previous experiences and insights. The child then builds understanding of how the abstract information relates to his or her life. This process develops mental "hooks" upon which he or she may "hang" the new information. This means the information is more likely to be categorized, understood and remembered! Jesus taught this way through His parables: He began with experiences and items that were familiar to His hearers. Then He incorporated (new) abstract ideas in ways that His hearers could absorb and understand.

The biggest pitfall in teaching abstract concepts is our adult inclination to use words that we ourselves often don't understand! Terms like "the presence of Christ" or "communion of the saints" need to be put into words that can be understood by anyone. (This is often as big a difficulty for new adult believers as it is for children.) If we cannot put the idea into plain words, it is time to use the Bible, a children's dictionary and a children's Bible resource to find simple and direct words that will describe the idea. Using curriculum written for the age of child you are teaching will also help you gain language that is clear and direct. This method works with any term or concept you present. Think through what the words mean; use words that mean what they say. Avoid symbolic language, which often confuses rather than clarifies ideas; be simple, clear and direct. (You'll probably find yourself telling parables of your own to help children gain the hooks they need to hang onto new ideas!)

Because the ability to absorb abstract ideas is a unique developmental process, some younger elementary children will understand abstract ideas such as "being kind as Jesus was," especially when the teacher links the idea to children's life situations and gives examples that help them understand. When children indicate interest in becoming members of God's family, avoid using terms such as "Jesus in my heart" or "born again." Because many children do still think quite literally and concretely, it is better to talk about "joining God's family," helping a child begin with something familiar and understood—a family—to gain understanding of the abstract concept of salvation.

This ability to think in abstract terms develops at a unique pace all throughout childhood. While older elementary children will be far more able to talk about the overall concepts and principles of Bible stories and Bible verses, do remember that even at this age, they have a far more limited frame of reference than what their sophisticated exteriors may indicate!

Each of us moves through our path of intellectual development in as much of an individual way as we do in any other area. God is tirelessly at work to bring us into closer relationship with Himself and knows each of us intimately. Whatever the individual point of completely understanding the abstract, never forget that we present Jesus most effectively to children when our actions speak louder than our words: We teach God's love by showing it! As we listen, encourage and make each child feel loved and cared for, God's love is communicated in concrete, tangible ways through our joy, excitement and loving actions that create an *experience* of the *abstract* that teaches any child at any age!

THE VALUE OF CHILDREN

The most striking thing about Jesus' encounter with the little ones in Matthew 19:14 is not that He interrupted an adult meeting to take time for some children. Nor is it surprising that He physically picked up the children and loved them. The remarkable part of this incident is Jesus' words. Most adults would have said something like "Let the little children come to me, and don't prevent them, for some day they will grow up and become important."

Jesus saw something in childhood besides the future. He recognized worth and value in the state of being a child, for He told the waiting adults in the crowd that children are important for what they are right now—"For the kingdom of heaven belongs to such as these."

We adults always seem to be looking to the future. This push for preparation robs childhood of much of its essence, as parents and teachers urge little ones hurriedly through the present in search of a more significant future.

The Future—Now

"I know it's hard for a three-year-old to sit quietly and listen, but I have to start getting him ready for later when he will have to sit still."

"If he's going to be a success in life, he'll have to go to college. And to make sure he can stay ahead in school, I'm going to teach him to read before he starts first grade if it kills us both!"

"If a child is going to grow up with an appreciation for the great hymns of the church, you just can't start too young to teach them."

These and many similar statements are used repeatedly by parents and teachers who are earnestly concerned about helping young children get ready for future roles and demands. However, these well-meaning adults sometimes actually do more harm than good, because in their long-range view of growth they have lost sight of the value in just being a child.

Children are more than people in transition, waiting for some future date of real meaning. The qualities that come from being young are not flaws or imperfections; rather, childhood is a marked and definable stage of development.

You may think, *But an adult has so many capabilities and accomplishments far beyond those of a child. Surely the years of productive and responsible adulthood are more significant than those of infancy and early childhood.* But what adult experiences could replace the laughter of children that gladdens the hearts of all who hear? How many hours of labor would it take to equal a little girl's smile? What a sterile world this would be were children not present to add their unique joys and sorrows!

The Value of a Child

Has any parent ever seen more deeply into him- or herself than when holding a newborn child and looking into that child's eyes? All the writings and research of humankind couldn't provide the insights that come with observing the experiences of a child starting out on his or her own unique adventure. The child's fresh enthusiasm for everything seen, the child's honest questions and powerfully simple logic—all combine to peel the scales from our encrusted adult eyes.

What is the value of a child—as a child? Incalculable!

This is no plea for attempting to stop the progress of maturation. This is simply a call to recognize that just because a phase of life is brief and is replaced by another more sophisticated, we should not rush past it; for if we bypass the unique stages of childhood, we strip each succeeding developmental stage of some of its finest ingredients. The best preparation for any phase of life is the proper completion of the previous one. The second coat of paint must always wait for the first to dry. Harvest never begins when the first green shoots appear in the spring. Human life has an aching void when childhood is squeezed away.

Is this what Jesus had in mind when He took a small child in His arms and said, "I tell you the truth, unless you change and become like little children, you will never enter the kingdom of heaven" (Matthew 18:3). Is there a place in our homes and churches for children to be children? Do we wholeheartedly accept them as they are, not as we wish they were? Do the rooms and materials we provide sound out "Welcome!" to a young learner? Are the adults who surround young children deeply sympathetic and understanding of what these special years are all about?

Or do we merely see little ones in terms of their potential, enduring them until they get old enough to really matter? Is the church's objective in providing children's ministries a means of attracting their parents or of getting ready for the church of tomorrow? Is our goal to train young children to act like miniature adults because their noisy spontaneity might somehow mar our sacred corridors?

W.C. Fields wrung many laughs from his famous line, "Anyone who hates dogs and kids can't be all bad." But have you ever met a person who wanted to live in a world where everyone shared Fields's dislike of children?

It's far better to follow the Lord Jesus' pattern with children. His loving response to children lets us see into His heart's feeling of the worth of a young life.

Childhood is not a disease to be cured or endured. It is a God-ordained part of human life with value and significance that continually enriches the experiences of those who may have forgotten what it is like to see the world from a fresh, unspoiled point of view.

How Young Children Learn

How do you learn? How do you acquire information or develop opinions? Perhaps you do this by reading a book, by listening to a lecture or by talking with someone else. Much adult learning is by means of words—the symbols by which we are able to communicate.

However, learning in early childhood is different from learning as an adult. The mind of the child is not yet capable of handling ideas expressed only in words. The young child does not have the ability to give real meaning to a word unless the word is a very familiar part of experience and evokes ideas and feelings from memory.

Through the Senses

While we cannot know all that occurs in the mind of a young child, we do know that information enters the mind through the gates of the senses—seeing, touching, smelling, tasting and hearing.

Firsthand experiences are the hard core of learning for young children. Efforts to produce learning must involve as many of the child's five senses as possible. Watching videos, sitting in large groups to sing songs and drawing on coloring pages are activities of limited value, as they involve only portions of the child's senses. Quality Christian education requires much more. Building with blocks, exploring natural items and participating in art and dramatic play are activities of great value, as they often engage the total child.

By Repetition

Repetition is a necessary and natural part of a young child's learning. A child who feels happy and satisfied with a learning experience will want to repeat it. Songs and stories become favorites only when they are enjoyed over and over.

By Practice in Play

The child also needs opportunities to practice behaviors that reflect Christian values. Repetition through play strengthens habits, attitudes, knowledge and understanding. Children learn because they are doing. And for young children, doing is play.

Play does not sound very educational or spiritual. But play is a child's full-time occupation: It is the activity through which the child learns best. Adults often distinguish between work and play. Not so with young children! Blocks, crayons, dolls, play dough and toy cars are the tools children use in play. They are tools by which children can also learn Bible truth when guided by alert teachers.

By Imitation

From infancy the child continually picks up ways of doing things from observation of others. A teacher's role, therefore, is not just to do "teacher things" but also to participate with children in the midst of their activity. If you show kindness by sharing a crayon or marker, children will learn to share. If you thank God for making the colors in a fabric collage children are gluing, they will learn to pray in the midst of daily activities.

By Connecting Words to Actions

Children have limited vocabularies and experience. This combination results in a limited ability to understand and combine concepts. When you and a child are building a house with blocks, you may think, *I'm glad I have a house to live in. God shows His love for me by providing a house!* The young child, however, may only think, *I like the way this house looks!* You must provide words that help the child respond to the activity and relate God to the event. Once this relationship is made, the child is able to think about God the next time he or she builds a house. Without your words, the activity would be simply another of many fun play experiences.

Most efforts to teach young children focus on the things adults want children to know. While accurate information is important and is expressed through words, words and facts are very imperfect vehicles for the learning child. In order to see long-term results for your efforts, all dimensions of a child's learning must be involved. Your role is not merely to transmit truth; you must also demonstrate truth in practical everyday activities.

Make a Difference in the Lives of Young Children

If you are like most teachers, you want to feel like you're making a significant difference in the lives of the young children you teach and care for. As a busy person who has chosen to be involved in ministry to children, you want to know that your time will be well spent. Sometimes, however, either from a lack of awareness or from misguided priorities, a teacher may miss the opportunity to effectively nurture young children. Instead of being a teacher who helps young children begin to build a lifelong foundation of faith, a minimum of Christian Education is given. You want to feel you are doing more than babysitting or filling time.

The goal of this article is to help you focus your teaching so that you will see significant benefits and results in the Christian growth of preschoolers. Consider this key question: What are the ways in which young children learn and grow in their understanding of who God is and how His Word gives direction for everyday life?

The Big Picture of Learning

Examine your ideas about learning. It's generally assumed that learning follows four steps:

Gain new information.

Come to understand the meaning of the new information.

Develop attitudes and beliefs about that meaning.

Put the information into practice.

With young children, however, a great deal of learning occurs almost in reverse:

Experience something that is true.

Accept that experience as true.

Repeat the experience often enough so that the truth begins to be understood.

Hear words that describe that truth, giving the truth a new richness and resulting in additional understanding.

As this cycle repeats itself over and over, a child's learning and understanding grow in significant ways.

This cycle of learning applies to education in all areas of life, including Christian education. Therefore, an effective early childhood ministry gives teachers the tools to help children learn through everyday experiences coupled with the words of Bible truth. Such a ministry will truly make a difference in the spiritual nurture of children.

The Hallmark of Christian Education

The hallmark of Christian education for preschoolers is active play experiences that engage each child with loving Christian adults. Play is not only the way the young child learns about objects, people and relationships; but it is also the best way for a young child to learn about God and His love. The Christian faith we share with children must be more than mere words or information. It is not enough for the young child to hear God's Word or even to memorize it. The child must live it. A child is not yet able to listen to explanations about the concepts and beliefs of Christian faith: the child must play with materials. In order to learn effectively, the child uses all of his or her senses—seeing, touching, tasting, smelling and hearing.

Therefore, we can best help children learn Bible truths by providing active play experiences that a teacher connects to Bible stories and verses through comments and questions. As teachers use words to describe ways children are putting God's Word into action, the child's play takes on the qualities of Bible learning. The combination of words and actions, frequently repeated, expands and clarifies the child's thinking. This kind of active learning cannot be rushed. It takes time! Early childhood programs that allow for significant active learning time provide the most benefit to young children.

DISCOVERY LEARNING

Children learn best by what they do, not what they hear or see. So wise teachers choose activities that reinforce the focus of a lesson. But how does a teacher select the best activities for the class? How does the teacher lead students to gain the maximum amount of learning from these activities?

Selecting Learning Activities

Suitability. As you look at activity ideas in your curriculum, ask yourself, *Is the activity appropriate for the age, number of children, interest and skill level of my class?* While young children may enjoy using puppets, they may not be able to actually make puppets. Older children may feel that some activities are too childish. Because of their learning styles, the students may enjoy doing certain activities more than others. Inner-city churches may have different challenges than suburban or rural congregations. An effective curriculum will provide you with varied activities from which to choose so that you can customize your lesson to the needs and abilities of your class.

Don't let having a small classroom or limited budget prevent learning from taking place. Rather than focusing on limitations, think of ways to creatively use the available resources. Instead of buying expensive maps of Israel, ask a church member who has visited there to share slides and photos of the trip. If there is no money for art supplies, ask church members to donate paper and markers. If a classroom is too small for games, make arrangements for the students to use the fellowship hall or an outdoor patio.

Teachability. Does the activity support the objectives of the lesson? Or is the activity only a fun time filler? While children love to have fun, and your classroom should provide times of fun, it is also necessary to provide a good balance of activities that help students discover how to apply the Bible concept to their daily lives. Does the activity clearly present the teaching objectives? If the activity is too complicated, if it hides or distorts the teaching objective, find another activity that requires less explanation. Look for activities designed to help students learn to use the Bible and Bible reference tools.

Life-related. Your lesson should have one Bible truth for the students to grasp, and student learning should connect that truth to everyday life. For example, the lesson may focus on obeying God by being honest, so an effective game activity will help each student to name situations and ways in which to show honesty.

Leading Learning Activities

Tell the purpose. Tell students *why* they're doing an activity. They may see the activity as a fun thing to do, but use your conversation to point students toward a higher purpose: "We're going to make a 3-D mural of the Israelites escaping from Egypt to help us remember we can trust God to take care of us."

Give clear directions. Children grow frustrated if they don't understand what to do. Explain clearly what is expected and how students can accomplish their tasks. Write directions on a chalkboard or large sheet of paper for reference. Have supplies nearby and organized.

Let children work at their own pace. Once the project is explained and students begin working, avoid micromanaging. Avoid the temptation to "do it for them" and let children proceed at their own pace. Let students make choices and mistakes. Allow students the freedom to ask for help instead of anticipating their needs. Have additional activities on hand or books to read for students who finish quickly instead of making the slower students rush.

Use guided conversation. Use comments and questions during the learning activity to help students connect the activity to the lesson's Bible truth. "I see you've drawn a comic strip of a way to show patience at home. What is a way to be patient at school?" or "Thanks, Nathan, for helping clean up the spilled glitter! That's what the Bible tells us to do."

Summarize what was learned. Near the end of the session, ask students to summarize what they learned about today's Bible truth. "What was one important thing learned by the boy who shared his lunch?" If students cannot answer the question, then more learning is needed. Ask additional questions, or tell an example from your life to extend students' interest and learning.

Share learning with others. Information is best used when it's passed on to others. Teaching is the best way to learn. Encourage students to share what they learned in class with their parents and friends. Let students lead an activity for a class of younger children. Students can share their learning by giving short talks to the congregation during worship or a church event. Children who are shy about public speaking can write statements for other students to read. Artwork can be displayed during an open house.

THE BUILDING BLOCKS OF LEARNING

We may think of learning as a result—"something" intellectual that was gained from a lesson, such as "Billy knows the alphabet." However, we need to recognize that learning may not always occur in a series of definable steps. Especially in children, the learning process is not always in a neat, sequential order. The steps may be simultaneous or in any order. In fact, the younger the child, the more likely it is that these steps will be taken in reverse order! Although learning can't be reduced to a formula, we need to be aware of the God-given ways in which we learn so that we are prepared to teach in ways that will make learning effective. Below are the major steps in the process of learning and ways each step fits into the process.

1. Listen: Give Attention/Receive Information

Learning is most efficient when a person realizes there is something to be learned. And that something must be of interest or value to the person for focused attention to be given!

Most commonly in Christian education, a teacher says something to gain the interest of the learners. But in no way is this first step limited to listening! Catch a learner's curiosity with a poster on the wall or a question on the chalkboard. Involve as many of a learner's senses (hearing, sight, smell, touch, taste) as possible to gain interest and attention.

While hearing and sight are the most common ways we present, far too many teachers approach the whole learning process as if this step were the only one! They feel they have succeeded if learners simply paid attention to what they had to say or show. (Never forget, either, how often a learner may pretend to pay attention while not mentally engaged!) However, after a learner has listened or looked, he or she has taken only the *first* step in the learning journey.

2. Explore: Examine Life and the Word

Having his or her interest caught, the learner has received information that is valued. The next step is to investigate further. To learn effectively, humans need to actively pursue new or expanded insights. A teacher needs to relate the learner's experiences and insights to the new information.

A wise teacher guides this exploration in the direction of the current lesson. This way, learners examine their already-understood life situations in the light of the Word of God. Each week a teacher helps learners see commands, examples, principles and answers that apply to the child's life situations.

When a teacher actively involves learners in connecting God's Word to issues they care about, this increases the learner's understanding and retention of the passage being investigated. This approach also develops the vital ability of using the Bible themselves, instead of merely listening to someone else report about it. Even nonreaders can be guided to begin exploring Bible truths for themselves by posing a question before presenting a Bible verse or story and asking students to listen to the reading for the answer to that question.

3. Discover: Find the Truth

The wise teacher plans for learners to make some discoveries for themselves. No matter how excited a teacher may be about discoveries he or she has made, it's more effective to let those same exciting discoveries be made by the learners themselves. Learners who are prepared through listening and exploring are ready to discover for themselves what the Bible says. Discoveries that learners make on their own will be remembered longer and have more impact than insights simply handed down from the teacher. The "light goes on" and the learner is filled with excitement when he or she has discovered a truth on his or her own. That truth now becomes "owned" by the learner!

4. Apply: Respond to the Truth

Somewhere in the learning process, learners need to confront the personal implications of God's truth. The point of a lesson is not to discover interesting bits of historical or theological information but to recognize that the Bible is speaking directly to people. It is one thing to recognize that God is love; it is another to recognize that God loved the world; it is yet another to recognize that God loves *me*.

Taking Scripture personally does not happen automatically. Through prayer, questions and guided activity, the teacher is used by the Holy Spirit to cause students to see themselves as characters in the story—the people to whom God is speaking.

Provide appropriate activities to stimulate learners' awareness and thinking about a topic to be considered. Children often think best when their bodies are in motion! When choosing activities, consider the life experiences of the children you are teaching: the younger the child or the more limited his or her life experience, the more he or she needs concrete, multisensory, firsthand experiences (experiments, construction, games, drama, art, etc.). Concrete activity can build understanding of seemingly simple concepts (sharing, being kind, helping, giving thanks, etc.) when a teacher who is aware of his or her goal guides conversation toward the lesson goals and points out ways children are applying Bible truth during these activities.

5. Assume Responsibility: Apply the Truth

This step is the crown of the learning process, the point where God's truth not only makes changes in a person's heart but also works itself out in actions. God's truth has been given to produce growth and change in us. Learners take in information about what God said and develop an understanding of what that information means. They must then go on to understanding what it means to me personally and finally to ways I can *respond* to what I have learned, to what I understand and to what I have personalized.

Not every class session can end by carrying out a major new spiritual commitment, but each class can nudge learners to look beyond the class time and think of ways to put God's Word into action in the coming week.

USING BIBLE LEARNING ACTIVITIES EFFECTIVELY

As Christians, we have far more to teach children than facts and words. It's not enough for a child to hear us read from the Bible or even for a child to memorize it. Words alone are the least effective way humans learn! When we hear words only, we must build a mental image based on previous information. Because a child's knowledge and experience is so limited, he or she is not likely to gain a real understanding through hearing words alone.

For an idea to make any sense to a young child, he or she must DO something with it. And the word that describes most of what a young child does is "play." However, a young child is not yet able to play with *ideas*. So a child must build understanding through playing with something he or she *can touch*. That's the reason for hands-on activity. Firsthand activity (or play) is a young child's most effective way to learn! Young children can learn Bible truth effectively through active play experiences. As a child draws, plays a game, builds with blocks or holds a doll, natural opportunities arise for the teacher to link the child's actions to what God's Word says. When we describe the ways children are putting God's Word into action, we turn play into Bible learning. Play then takes on a greater purpose!

For instance, during a simple beanbag toss game we can comment, "Ainsley, you gave Josh a turn to toss the beanbag. Thank you! That is a way to be kind. Our Bible tells us to be kind." As we effectively link a Bible truth to Ainsley's actions, she now has a concrete example of a way to be kind!

Providing repeated opportunities to think and talk about Bible truths creates more and more of those mental building blocks. As you participate with children in an activity, it's important to watch for opportunities to acknowledge and encourage children you see acting in ways that you can relate to the Bible truth.

A Bible learning activity is different from a craft. Crafts, while offering enjoyable experiences to children, are usually limited in the amount of Bible learning that can occur because the focus is usually more on following directions than on the total process that the child experiences. A meaningful session for young children should provide more Bible learning activities than crafts. The list on the next page will help you distinguish whether an activity is a craft or a Bible learning activity. (Obviously, most Bible learning activities that involve art will have some characteristics of crafts, and some craft projects can be guided in ways that engage children in active Bible learning.)

Busy Hands Mean Open Minds

When children are fully involved in an activity they enjoy, we have the privilege of seeing them simply being themselves. When we observe them, we understand more about how they think. Also, children whose hands are busy are often eager to talk. Ask open-ended what-do-you-think questions. Avoid questions that have one-word answers. This chance to listen helps us determine what a child does or does not understand. Then we are able to respond in ways that truly meet that child's needs!

Watch for moments when a child experiences curiosity, expectation or frustration. In that moment of heightened interest, a child is most receptive to a new idea or the security of a familiar truth. Remember the words "acknowledge" and "encourage" as your conversational cornerstones. For example, when Kim's block tower is finished, he looks around with satisfaction. He's eager to know you see him and share his joy. "I see you finished your tower, Kim. It looks very strong. God has given you good hands and a good mind. You're a good builder!"

Choice Creates Interest

Children are usually more content to stay with an activity they have chosen, rather than one they have been assigned. When you provide several learning activities (each led by a teacher) that appeal to different learning styles and interests, discipline problems often diminish and children enjoy finishing what they began. The child who is absorbed in an activity he or she has chosen is in a prime position for learning!

Some children find it difficult to begin an activity when they first arrive. They need help in learning to choose. Allow the child to move at his or her own pace. "Liam, when you're ready, you may build with blocks in the corner with Mr. Sanchez or glue these pictures with me. Watch for a while if you like."

When we provide a choice of several activities, we should not expect young children to stay focused on one activity for more than a few minutes. The younger the child, the shorter the attention span; again, this is part of helping a child learn. When the child moves back and forth between activities, remain quietly observant for ways you can connect his or her activity to the Bible truth being taught.

A child needs to use every sense—tasting, touching, smelling, hearing, and seeing—to learn effectively. This is why it's important to provide activity choices that may not appeal to you personally. When we give children activity choices that involve as many senses and learning styles as possible, we send them the message that we want them to choose, learn and enjoy! It's another way to show the loving acceptance Jesus modeled.

BIBLE LEARNING ACTIVITY OR CRAFT?

Bible Learning Activity

► Children explore, create and discover with the provided materials.

► Teacher talks informally with children, asking questions and guiding the conversation toward the Bible learning aims; children talk with each other as well as with the teacher.

► Focus is on the process (including the use of materials), group interaction and the connection to the Bible truth.

► Children choose from two or more activities and choose how they want to complete the activity.

► Small groups work with one activity at a time and move freely from one activity to the other.

Craft

► Children follow predetermined pattern.

► Teacher gives instructions with little opportunity for children to talk.

► Focus is on the product.

► Only one project is offered and children are expected to produce a similar result.

► Children all work on the same project at the same time.

Spiritual Formation Tips

Young children need many firsthand experiences with a variety of things to begin to be aware of the wonder of His creation. However, when a child examines a flower, the child needs an adult who is conscious of the reality of God to help him or her know, **God made the flower. God made everything—even you and me!** Your brief but thoughtful comments add to the child's growing awareness.

Some skills a child needs to acquire are obvious, such as tying shoes and talking. Another dimension of the growth process is not so apparent. Each child needs to learn skills in developing godly attitudes and actions toward others. As with other skills, obedience to God is learned by doing. Children need opportunities to practice these developing attitudes and actions. When you put words to these actions, they understand how obeying God works in the real world!

One of the exciting aspects of teaching is the chance to encourage spiritual growth. Children are naturally curious and eager to learn. However, for a child to be able to be open to new ideas, he or she must have a way to make sense of them. The new idea is best understood if there is something that can attach it to the things the child is already familiar with. This is known as a mental "hook." When you talk about how Elena's dad shows love to her, for instance, you provide a mental hook upon which she can then hang an understanding of how love is shown through kindness.

We have the best news in the world to share with children! So how do we "translate" the good news of Jesus' love to a young child? A younger child (and an older one, too) learns best through experience. This means that words must be accompanied by deeds or the words mean very little! The deeds? Listening to a child, giving moments of undivided attention without interruption; replying with a kind word, a comforting hug, a smile; using the child's name often, enjoying his or her efforts. While those may not sound very theologically brilliant, they are the very stuff of Jesus' loving acceptance of the children who came to Him!

Remember that the younger the child, the greater the need for hands-on experiences. These are the best way young children learn, repeating the experiences to lay a foundation for understanding. Younger children are not yet able to think about ideas; older children become more and more able to think about and talk about ideas and feelings. Expect children younger than upper elementary level to think in literal, not abstract, terms. Know that each child develops this ability at his or her own pace.

For instance, first and second-graders may be baffled by God's nonphysical nature. However, they will generally accept the concept of God being omnipresent when the significant adults in their lives (parents and teachers) communicate this belief by their words, attitudes and actions.

Spiritual Formation Tips

How did you learn to ride a bicycle? Like every child, you learned by doing it for yourself. You needed adult help and encouragement. But with repeated attempts, you were soon pedaling down the sidewalk. In the same way, learning Bible truths is not complete when a child hears or even memorizes God's Word. He or she must do it! Direct, first-hand activity is the child's most effective way to learn. Guiding children at church helps them learn best through active experience.

Don't hesitate to make the effort to help your class do service projects. These projects are effective ways to help children actually obey the Bible and recognize that God's Word leads His people to act!

The fact that children may often sit quietly in school is not by their choice. And it may not be the best way for them to learn. That is all the more reason to do our best to make our classes a place where every child can learn—joyfully! Many children younger than about nine years of age are really not physically able to sit still for long periods of time. This is not due to some deficiency; it is simply that children were made to learn by doing, moving and experiencing! Providing a variety of experiences that involve both minds and bodies result in the best learning.

If you are leading a small group activity from which children come and go, expect to repeat the conversation about the words from the Bible again and again. This may seem boring to an adult. But for children, this is an effective way to learn! Children have had very little experience, so repeating an experience, embellishing it, trying it a different way, all help the child to integrate new information into what he or she already understands.

When you provide Bible learning activities, you are giving children the opportunity to apply Bible truths to everyday living in a variety of ways. The activities may also help a child review and reinforce Bible story information. But the goal is to involve the whole child in the activity: this results in decreased discipline problems, greater learning of Bible truth and better retention of the information that was reinforced by doing!

Before the child can be ready to play with ideas, the child must play with materials.

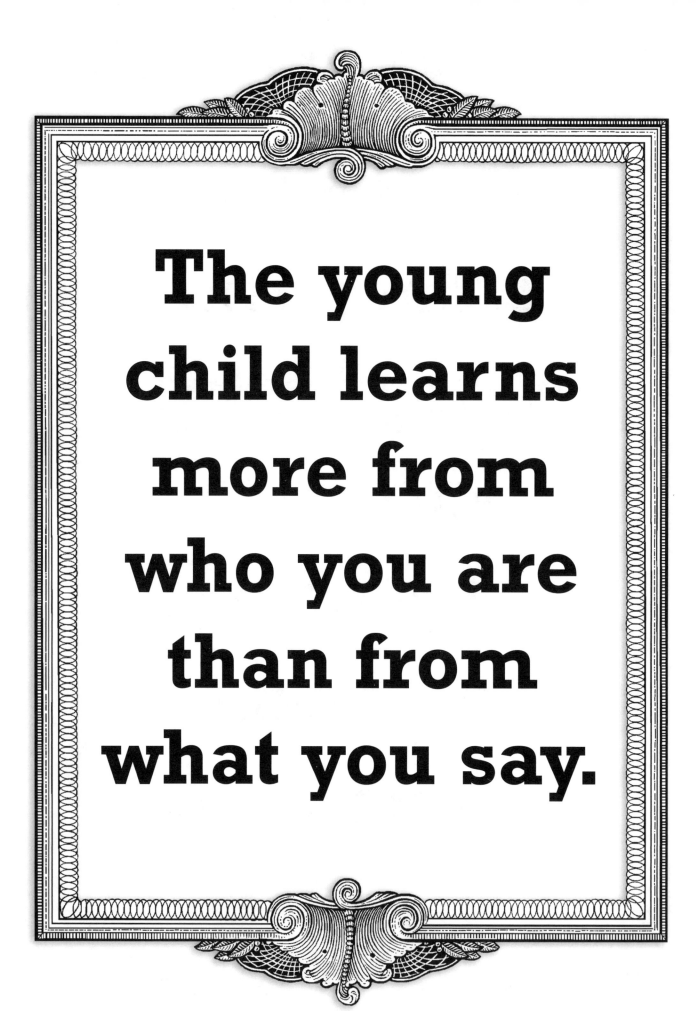

The young child learns more from who you are than from what you say.

EFFECTIVE STORYTELLING

Everyone is a storyteller. Storytelling is how people communicate important, heartfelt information. Whether it is a promotion at work, moving into a new house, getting engaged or a child's hitting the winning Little League home run, we all love a good story—and when we are "full of" a good story, we're eager to tell it!

Storytelling is how the Bible was written. For centuries, stories of the patriarchs and matriarchs were handed down from parent to child. After the resurrection and ascension of Jesus Christ, His followers preached about Him through telling His stories until the New Testament Scriptures were completed. When a teacher tells a Bible story, he or she is continuing in the grand tradition of the ancient storytellers who passed on God's Word. It's a responsibility and a privilege.

Tips for Telling a Story

Know the material. Study the story. Understand the main theme, know the central characters, research the setting if needed and be able to answer questions about it. (Remember how important it is to be "full of your story!") As you read the story, focus on finding the answers to these questions: Who is the main character(s)? Where does the story take place? Does this setting need to be explained to the students? What elements of this story (characters, objects, feelings, actions, etc.) are similar to the experiences of your children? How does this story illustrate the lesson aims? What one Bible truth do you want children to remember and use during the week?

Additional questions to ask: What is the conflict in the story? Every good story has a conflict and a problem to be solved (Joseph is in jail, the soldiers are chasing the Israelites leaving Egypt, Paul is arrested, the lame man can't get into the pool, etc.). How is the problem solved? How is God involved with solving the problem? How are the characters' lives changed?

Use words familiar to the children. Rephrase Bible passages that children may not understand. Avoid talking down to children. Use modern language, not "thee" and "thou." Consult a children's Bible for easy-to-understand vocabulary if you have no curriculum resources.

No need to memorize. It is not essential to recite the story exactly as written in the Bible or your curriculum manual. While you should always have your Bible open to the story reference, storytelling is more interesting and spontaneous when the teacher doesn't read from a page. Telling rather than reading makes the presentation more natural and exciting. Reading the story from a book keeps your face buried in the pages and unable to look at the children. This is why preparation is essential: The better one knows the story, the less one needs notes. Know the plot points well enough to get back on track if the story digresses.

Practice, practice, practice! Many people feel uneasy about storytelling simply because they have little experience speaking to a group. Skills and confidence are built by repetition. Practice the story at home in front of a mirror. Tell it to your own family. Record the story on tape and listen back for improvements. One can always erase a bad tape!

Be bold. Bring the story to life through dramatic gestures, movement, and facial expressions. "Larger than life" and "over the top" are good rules when telling a story. Feel free to emphasize words, be expressive, even look silly. Vary your voice—loud in some spots and soft in others. Some people use different voices for various characters, although this is not essential.

Be confident. Have faith in the story. Bible stories are powerful because they contain God's Word for today's people. Be enthusiastic. Think about how excited people get when telling about their children or accomplishments. Carry that same energy into biblical storytelling. If you are "full of" and interested in the story, the children will be, too! Maintain eye contact with children.

Be relevant. Show why the story is important for today. The Bible is not a collection of 2,000-year-old fairy tales that are read for entertainment. Draw parallels between the story and children's lives. In the Joseph story from Genesis, discuss sibling rivalry and family relations in the children's homes. For Noah and the flood, ask how students might feel if they were teased for doing the right thing.

Involve Children in Storytelling

Children learn by doing! Incorporate the children into storytelling. This is particularly beneficial for children who already know the story and may feel bored by retelling.

Act it out. Have students pantomime or dramatize the story as it is told. Students may use puppets, hold up pictures or put felt figures on a flannel board. If a student already knows the story, let him or her tell the story for the class or assist you with the telling. Invite a student to retell the story in his or her own words. Play "What happened next?" with a child who is familiar with the story: "And Moses came down the mountain. What happened next, Jake? What did he see?"

Sound effects. Have children make appropriate sounds when they hear a cue word. They can make animal sounds when they hear an animal's name. They can gurgle for "river," stomp their feet for "walk" or "march" or say "grumble grumble" when characters are tired or hungry. Look through the story for repetitive words or ideas and think of sounds the children can make. This keeps children alert and listening so as not to miss a cue.

Use the Bible. Have students look up the story in the Bible. This familiarizes students with the books of the Bible and shows that the stories are not made up. Even young children can find chapters and verses with some help and even locate the name of a Bible story character.

Research. Older children look up unfamiliar words in a Bible dictionary, locate cities in a Bible atlas, and read more about characters in a Bible encyclopedia. Let the children find more information on the Internet or dramatize the story by making a video.

Storytelling Tips

Stories told informally that apply to immediate circumstances have the greatest impact in the lives of younger children. As children work on a project, feel free to retell details of the story. Don't fear that younger children will be bored with a retelling during activity time. Children's favorite stories are the ones they know best. If someone comments, "I know that story already!" then include that child in the retelling. **Dane, it sounds like you should tell us what happened next in that story! Which part of this story do you like best?**

When telling a story, you are teaching not only the facts of the story but also the feelings. Express the feelings of the story through your voice. When you talk about something being heavy, for instance, let your tone and your actions reflect the hard work it takes to lift something heavy.

To read a book to children, seat yourself at the children's eye level. Sit on the floor on a low chair so that children can look at the book and at your face comfortably. Hold the book to one side of your face and read by looking from the side. Turn your face forward often to maintain eye contact. Pace your words so that children can both look at the picture and absorb your words. Change the pace and tone of the story by speaking in a higher, faster voice as you describe action or in a soothing, lower tone as you describe quieter parts. If a child interrupts and you cannot respond at that point say, **Levi, we'll talk about that after we finish the book.** Be sure to keep your word!

Having a picture or an object to show children as you tell a story is a great attention-getter. However, children often complain, "I can't see!" Always hold the picture or item high enough so that everyone can see it and if it is possible, pass around the object or picture so that children may have a closer look. After the story time, be sure to place the picture or object where children may look at it again.

Use pictures not only to illustrate a Bible story but also as an attention-getting item by asking children to find items in the picture, colors or shapes. Invite them to find the tallest, shortest or widest item. Children will enjoy the game and you will have gained everyone's attention.

Encourage children to tell details of a story that they already know. Once you have told the story briefly and see that most children are familiar with it, bring out the costume box and encourage them to choose characters and act out the story!

When you practice telling a story, do it before one of your own children or a neighbor's child. See what parts of the story don't seem to be interesting or what words leave the child puzzled so that you can better prepare.

Consider dressing in costume to tell a Bible story. You'll find that children respond very differently to you when you are "in character" and will often ask questions that would not be asked of the teacher!

Young children need friendships with their teachers more than they need polished story performances.

A Teacher's Vision

Why We Teach Kids

Adults send messages to kids all the time—by their behavior.

Sometimes these messages discourage kids,

demean their worth or diminish their hope.

But a Sunday School teacher who arrives week after week

to faithfully love and look at, smile and listen to kids,

sends messages through behavior, too. Those messages say:

"You are important to me and to God. I choose to spend time with you."

"Your opinions and feelings matter to me because who you are matters to God."

"You are valuable—not someday, but now. You are not a problem to me.

You are God's gift. I am glad you are here!"

Where else in the world can a disheartened kid find such affirmation?

What better way could a lonely kid

find the welcome, acceptance and love that is in Christ?

This is how God's kingdom comes—week after week, building life upon life.

To become faithful givers of such cheerful loving and patient teaching,

we must surrender ourselves to the love of God in Jesus Christ.

Only He can empower us to love unselfishly, consistently and genuinely—

so that what we do sends the message that is truly from His heart.

Then our behavior will say that even without monetary compensation,

without applause or appreciation, we choose to love them

purely because we value them for who they are,

because we know Jesus loves them

and because we know

eternity would not be complete without their shining faces.

GET PREPARED TO TEACH

When we finish a class session, we might say to ourselves, *Whew! Glad I don't have to do anything about this again until next week!* It's a far more common feeling than most of us care to admit! But that attitude can keep us from doing what we need to do most: nurture relationships with children and involve them in life-changing Bible learning. To do this, a teacher's work needs to be ongoing.

Any person can run into a classroom, throw a few materials together, keep children from hurting themselves for an hour or so and send them on their way. But is this effective teaching? The attitude expressed by the adult in the above example says to children: "This is something anyone can do. You kids won't know the difference. You aren't worth preparing for." Because children so easily absorb an adult's unspoken attitudes, they will soon conclude that indeed this is just another situation where the teachers are nice but where the children are not very important.

Most of us have an owner's manual for every gadget we own. We seldom read these, assuming that we can figure things out on our own. Sometimes that works. But when it comes to the short and precious time we have to teach God's Word to children, we need to know the ground rules that will take teaching from humdrum to high-energy!

Prepare yourself. One terrific teacher says, "Begin preparing for the next class session as soon as this session is over. Look at the next session while the manual is still open! When you know what is coming next, you have time to think things through, collect materials you otherwise wouldn't have thought of and can be relaxed instead of harried."

Prepare the Bible content. Don't assume that you know the story. During the week, block out an hour of time during which you will read the Scripture and the teacher's devotional and pray for the children in your class. Familiarize yourself with the age-appropriate version of the story from the lesson. Your goal is to be able to tell it, without being tied to the teacher's guide. Maintaining good eye contact is essential to keeping children involved.

Prepare the environment. Look at your classroom both when children are in it and when it is empty. Ask yourself, *What kinds of clutter collects in this room? Where are the bottlenecks where children can't move freely? What items distract children?* Take time to eliminate clutter, rearrange space and make the room a place that is inviting and involving, not just cluttered. If you share a room, meet with those who share the space to work out ways to keep the room functional and inviting.

Prepare the materials. Ask yourself, *What are some things that might happen if the children have to wait while I collect supplies for this activity? What could result if I don't have materials ready for group time?* It can be very difficult to refocus children's attention when they have waited for an adult to prepare materials. Being prepared is the best way to improve wandering attention!

During the week collect materials and prepare them for the activities you have chosen. Stack materials in the order of use. If your church has a supply room, plan to arrive early enough to gather needed materials before going to your classroom. When you arrive in the classroom, it's easy to place the stacked prepared materials in the area of your classroom where they will be used.

Prepare to arrive early. If you've taken the steps above, you have only some simple setting up to do when you arrive in the classroom. You've eliminated that panicky feeling of needing to do a lot of preparation in a hurry. It's important to remember that no matter what your class's stated starting time, class begins when the first child enters the room. Arriving early to set up materials is well worth your commitment.

One veteran teacher points out that this first 15 minutes or so after you enter the classroom has the most potential for doing the very thing we are called to do as teachers: nurture relationships and involve children in life-changing Bible learning. Children need to be the priority, not our preparations.

Have at least one or two activity centers prepared by the time the first child arrives. This gives even early arrivals a choice of activities. If you still have some setting up to do, make helping you one of the choices you give as a child enters the room. (Yes, this means you must be ready for church half an hour earlier. Commit to it as part of your ministry!)

Prepare ways to interact. We quite often can picture what *we* will be doing during a given part of the class session. But a good question to ask is, What will the children be doing during this time? Be familiar with the discussion questions provided in your curriculum. Have a couple of backup ideas in mind (a simple game or an open-ended art activity) in case something you have planned doesn't work well. When children are involved in an activity, it is never time to sneak away to do something else. This is another prime opportunity to build relationships and involve children in understanding God's Word.

Take one more tip from a veteran teacher: We have very little time to impact children with the good news of God's love. Being prepared makes us ready to do this with a loving, relaxed attitude that reflects His love and care to the children we teach!

Spiritual Preparation for Teaching

Passing on the living Word of God to the next generation is the most important and daunting task a teacher can do. Most new teachers approach teaching the Bible with trepidation. "I don't know much about the Bible!" "I haven't been trained in teaching methods or in theology!" "I haven't done this before!" "I'm not good enough!" "What if I say something wrong?"

Some of God's greatest heroes didn't feel up to the task, either. When Moses heard God's call, he complained that he had no credentials, he didn't know enough, he worried about failure, he didn't speak well, and finally in desperation, he begged God to send someone else! Does this sound similar to modern-day excuses?

Such fears can be relieved through Bible study and spiritual growth. God does not give you tasks without His promise of help. Daily personal devotional time will strengthen you for your work.

Personal Bible Study

Study the lesson. This may sound obvious, but study the lesson's Bible story. While you may not present all that you learn to the class, studying the passage will equip you to teach, answer questions and apply the lesson to your own life. Begin your study early in the week so that you have time to reflect on what the lesson passage is saying to you.

Some teaching curricula have devotionals and study aids in the teacher's manual. Take advantage of these gifts and use them in your personal study time. The Bible is not so mysterious that only the super saints can understand it. God wants His Word to be known! Come to Bible study with assurance that God will open His Word and make it clear.

Establish a regular time and place. Try to establish a regular time and place for study. If one tries to fit in study "when there's free time," there usually isn't any. You may need to wake up a few minutes earlier, stay up a little later at night or refrain from taking on one more activity. Even when people feel they can not fit lengthy uninterrupted study time into their schedules, it is important to make this time a priority. A short time every day might be great for some teachers!

In a busy family, a person may be hard pressed to find quiet time. Use your children's nap time or school time as study time. The working person may squeeze in study during a lunch hour or study in a quiet office before or after other employees arrive or leave. Some people may be able to concentrate on the train or bus going to work!

Clear the air. Some people like to begin study time with confession. Remember that through Jesus' sacrifice all sin is forgiven and all things are made new. Say a brief prayer of confession and then move forward with confidence because of God's grace.

What's the point? Begin by reading through the lesson passage several times for meaning. If an overly familiar story seems dry, read a different translation.

Determine the main concept of this passage. First, what did God tell the people of that era? Second, what is God saying to me today? When reading about Jesus telling a rich man to sell all that he owned and give it to the poor, God may be telling you to be more generous with your time or possessions.

Meditate. Spend some quiet moments reflecting on the main point. Perhaps reread a verse that was especially meaningful. Think of ways to apply the main point to situations in your daily life. After reading, write your thoughts in a journal or practice being quiet so that you can hear God. You may find it helpful to keep a prayer journal or underline a special verse.

After considering the message of the passage for your own life, look at the lesson aims to see the suggested focus for using the lesson with children. Begin to pray that God will help you guide your learners toward that goal. Most of all, remember Jesus' promise that the Holy Spirit will guide you into all truth. Invite God to lead and teach you.

Get the background. The Bible was written in another time, place and society with many customs different from today's customs. The various books were written for specific purposes and persons. The Bible makes more sense when one knows how and why each book was compiled. Find information on the Internet, or invest in a good Bible dictionary, commentary, maps and reference books. Read what scholars say about the passage. Look up Bible characters, place names, and unusual words or customs. It is usually not necessary or even useful to share all that background with children. Simply look for insights that help you better understand the passage.

Other Growth Opportunities

Adult study groups. Take advantage of adult Bible studies provided outside of the Sunday morning educational hour. Some adult studies meet in homes on weeknights for casual discussions; others are formal lessons taught by a lay leader or the pastor. Many churches offer short-term courses. If there are no classes available, contact the pastor or education direction for assistance in participating in or starting an adult Bible study.

Corporate prayer. Take advantage of prayer groups, prayer chains and special worship services of prayer and praise. Use the time to pray for the students, other teachers, the unchurched in your community and for yourself.

Retreats or seminars. An all-day Saturday seminar or weekend retreat is a great pick-me-up for the burned-out teacher. Take time away from the demands of work, family and church to relax and be refreshed at a retreat center or campground. Ask your supervisor to recommend opportunities for Bible study conferences or retreats.

TEACHER'S ROLE

Your role in children's ministry may well be a child's only or primary source of Christian education. The majority of adults who are active in church began as children in Sunday School. This is where children learn the Bible, and most important of all, it's the place where many children encounter God and make a personal commitment to Jesus Christ. Whether you teach in Sunday School, Saturday-night service or midweek program, you are following in the tradition of Jesus who taught the little children.

It's been said that the Church is only one generation away from extinction. The Church will continue to survive and grow only when the children and youth receive a solid foundation in faith. Therefore, in this important ministry, do all you can to arrange a warm and open learning environment, present the gospel and show Christian love.

In-Class Responsibilities

Before class. Arrange with your supervisor for room repairs and replace furniture if needed. Decorate the room with appropriate posters, pictures and learning aids. Have the needed amount of student books, Bibles, name tags and learning supplies on hand. Contact your supervisor when more curriculum or supplies are needed.

Be punctual and dependable. Keep track of the schedule and know when it is time to teach. Arrive 10 to 15 minutes early so that learning materials are in place before the first child arrives. Arrange for a substitute (or follow the approved procedure in your church) as soon as possible if an absence is unavoidable.

Prepare the lesson with reading, study and prayer. Plan learning activities with other teachers and assistants. Try new teaching techniques and ideas.

Warmly greet the children as they arrive and learn their names. Assist them with coats, if needed. Show the restrooms to visitors. Start each child on a discovery activity as the class begins.

During class. Present engaging learning activities with enthusiasm. Give attention to students who may not be interested or who learn more slowly. Be sensitive to the needs of children with learning or physical disabilities or those who may feel uncomfortable in the group.

Use all the teaching tools provided with your curriculum to fulfill the lesson objectives. Plan to share personal examples to help connect the Bible story with the children's lives. Encourage teamwork, sharing and honesty among the children. Help children plan specific ways to apply the lesson's Bible truths to their daily lives, so they can grow in their Christian faith.

At the end of each lesson, evaluate student learning and progress. Use the lesson aims provided in your curriculum to help you know if lesson goals were accomplished. Adjust future learning plans to make better use of your class time and to better meet the needs of your students.

Love each child and listen to his or her joys and concerns. Model God's love and enthusiastically show your love for God and His Word.

Out-of-Class Responsibilities

Follow up on visitors and absentees with e-mail, postcards and phone calls.

Engage in daily personal devotion time of prayer, Bible study and meditation. One who leads other to Jesus must first be walking with Christ. Regularly pray for each child and your co-teachers. Pray also for guidance and wisdom in teaching. Participate in an adult class, Bible study or prayer group for personal enrichment and regeneration.

Pray for other teachers and assistants and make suggestions of possible teachers to your supervisor. At least two adults should be present during any class session. This way, one adult can handle an emergency while the other adult continues the lesson.

Participate in teacher training events, workshops, seminars and retreats. Ask if the church will provide teachers with subscriptions to Christian education magazines or provide teacher resource books for the church library. As experience is gained, assist rookie teachers as they enter the ministry.

Get to know the children, their families and their school life. Find out their interests, sports, hobbies and needs. Identify unchurched families and encourage their participation in church life. Assist the church in promoting and publicizing the education ministry. Provide news updates and articles for the church newsletter and letters to parents.

Some teachers may feel overwhelmed at the many tasks asked of teachers. Take heart! Many of God's great heroes felt the same way. Moses, Gideon and others hesitated when God called them to do great things in His name. When God calls, God prepares. Jesus promised His disciples that when He left them, they would not be alone. God sends the Holy Spirit to all believers for guidance and support. God gives His grace to teachers who seek Him and who strive to accomplish His will among children.

Ten Commandments for Teachers

One

Understand that teaching children is a holy calling of eternal value; pray for each child and ask for loving wisdom as you prepare. (Being prepared says you care.)

Two

Get down at a child's eye level; show love and welcome by your touch, words and smile. Teach respect by showing respect. (Your actions will teach far more than your words.)

Three

Make suggestions more often than you give commands; phrase directions positively. (A child must know what he or she *can* do in place of what he or she *cannot* do.)

Four

Be a teacher of great vision: See the most active, the most difficult or the most withdrawn child not as a problem, but as a person to be loved into God's family. (Remember and repeat often that God loves and has good plans for each one.)

Five

Give acceptable choices and set reasonable limits; stick to them and keep your word when you make a promise. (Limits foster a child's sense of security.)

Six

Realize that your interaction is always needed, even when children are absorbed in an activity. (Stay nearby to guide conversation: listen, show love and ask open-ended questions to help children understand and apply Bible truths.)

Seven

Be quick to see, describe and thank a child for right actions. (Describing a child's actions helps the child put meaning to concepts like fairness and kindness.)

Eight

Remember that children learn by doing, and provide active ways to learn. (Have several activities ready when the first child arrives, so children may choose.)

Nine

Know what is typical behavior for children and guide the child toward desirable behavior. (Children are not always able to see how their actions affect others.)

Ten

Remember how easily children absorb our attitudes and how watchful they are of our actions and reactions. (Our attitudes and actions will either affirm or deny the truth of our words!)

HELP! I'M A NEW TEACHER

When most of us were recruited as early childhood teachers, we thought the job mainly consisted of keeping little ones from hurting themselves or each other, providing snacks, singing songs and telling a Bible story. But as we teachers grow in understanding, just as our little ones grow in learning, we can see far more accomplished! Read the following guidelines for teaching young children. Remember, though, that your prayers for the children in your class are the best preparation of all!

What to Expect

▶ Young children learn by doing, not sitting. Play is their work. A fidgety class needs active ways to learn. Have several activities ready and let children choose where to begin. Discipline problems will decrease! Use the conversation ideas in every lesson to link the Bible truths to what you see children doing. "Hannah, I see you are drawing blue circles. God made your hands so that you could draw!"

▶ Young children have a very limited grasp of ideas that we as adults take for granted. They need for us to relate big biblical ideas (such as being kind or accepting God's love) to what they know or do. "Christie, you shared the dough with Josh. That is being kind!"

▶ A young child is not yet able to understand how his or her actions affect others. Guide the child toward desirable good behavior. "Seth! Hitting hurts! Until you remember not to hit, you cannot play with Justin. Right now you need to play with the blocks or look at books."

▶ Small children quickly absorb our attitudes! If you think a child is a problem, your attitude will show it. (And the child will probably become a bigger problem!) Pray for each child. Treat each one with the same kindness and respect you would show an adult.

What to Do

▶ Follow Jesus' example. Little children need far more action than talk. When Jesus was around little children, He loved them; He didn't lecture them. Actions say more than words ever could. Focus on the children. Listen to them. You are the living example of God's love to each little child!

▶ Get close. Put yourself at the child's eye level. Squat, kneel or sit. Before you talk, look into the child's eyes. You'll get the child's attention as well as send a message: "You're important to me. I care about you."

▶ Be positive. Tell a child what you want him or her to do, not what to STOP doing. "Marina, dough belongs on the table. Please pick it up off the floor. Thank you. You may use this cookie cutter."

▶ Be quick to see and point out what is good. "I see you sharing with Josiah, Kade. Being kind is a way to obey God's Word. Thank you." You've not only related the action to the Bible, but you've also helped both children better understand the concept of kindness!

▶ Give a child a choice. Even if a child is upset, giving a choice creates a new focus and puts responsibility for behavior back on the child. "Nathan, would you rather take turns with the blocks or glue pictures at the art table?" Whatever choices you offer, be sure that either choice is perfectly acceptable to you.

How to Prepare

▶ The job of preparation begins during the week prior to each class. Pray for yourself and the children in your class. For each lesson, read the Scripture for the lesson, even if it is a story with which you are familiar. Then in the teacher's guide read the summary of the lesson content and pay special attention to the goals of the lesson. Scan the overview chart to see the activities that are offered in the lesson and how each activity will help you meet the goals of the session. Choose the activities you will prepare and collect any needed materials.

▶ To prepare Bible learning activities, read the instructions for each activity to understand what the children will do to complete the activity. Think through how the activity will work in your space, with your materials and your children. Then become familiar with the suggested conversation which will help you connect children's actions to the lesson's Bible story or verse.

▶ To prepare for the telling of the Bible story, practice telling the story as written in the lesson so that you become familiar with the words and phrases appropriate for young children. As you tell the story, show the flannel figures (or other visual aids) to illustrate the story action, and keep your Bible open to the appropriate Scripture reference. Remind children that your words are from this special book of God's messages to us. State clearly that the stories in the Bible really happened.

▶ If a student activity page is provided with your curriculum, look at how it is to be completed and become familiar with the conversation suggestions. Teachers who are ready to talk with children about the Bible story and Bible verse make a big impact on the child's learning. Plan to complete your page in class as a demonstration for children so that children can work on their pages with a minimum of instruction from you.

Teacher's Role and Preparation Tips

Early in the week before each class, take a few minutes to read the Scripture upon which the coming lesson is based. Then write the Bible verse and lesson focus on an index card. Place the card where you'll be sure to see it during the week. This technique will help you to focus your thinking so that by class time, your conversation will naturally and easily guide children through the lesson. As your understanding is enhanced, children's understanding improves!

Coming ready and coming early to your classroom communicates to the children you teach that they are important, that what you will be doing in class is important and that as you took time to prepare for this class time, you thought about and prayed for them during the week. That's a powerful message to deliver—and you haven't yet spoken a word!

If you teach alone, limit the number of children who are at an activity by limiting the number of chairs at that table. There may only be as many people around the table as there are chairs. Other children may play with individually-based items such as skill toys or puzzles.

Is your classroom sending the messages you want your children to know? If your room reflects order, friendliness and some degree of spaciousness, the child can enter and feel comfortable. Is the room neat and clean? Is it light and colorful? Can children find and return the materials they need? Is there space to move about without bumping into furniture? Are pictures at children's eye level? Even in a shared classroom, take time to personalize it for your own group.

The shortcut to becoming a great teacher? Spend much more time listening to children than you do talking to them! Ask open-ended, "what-do-you-think?" questions and then really listen to the answers. You'll find out what children really know and be better able to help children understand.

To the point when teaching what is meaningful to children: Keep it brief. Attention spans are short. Avoid symbolism. Literal minds are at work. Ask questions. Let the child tell what he or she thinks.

Be sure that each child in your group hears at least one specific and honest encouragement from you sometime during the session. Avoid pointing out what a child does wrong; instead, notice and acknowledge those things children do right! This shows unconditional love and acceptance: when you show you want to see every child feel successful, your model will influence the children to imitate you!

In your conversation, use often-used words like, "please," "thank you," "I'm sorry," and "that's OK." Not every child lives in a home where kind words express kind feelings. Hearing your words gives children good words to make their own.

As you model love, remember to use not only your voice but also your face, hands and feet! Love moves us to speak, to look at a child at eye level, to give a loving side-hug or pat on the shoulder and walk to where a child is instead of speaking across the room.

Sometimes, a child may not want to participate in an activity. Allow the child to watch for a while, then invite him or her to join the activity. **Audra, it's OK to watch while we play. Let me know when you're ready to join us.** Never pressure an unwilling child to participate. As you accept each child's individual differences, you show God's love.

When doing art projects with children, learn to avoid making value judgments about the child's art. Never tell a child that his or her work is right or wrong—a child's art just IS. Strange as it may sound, even positive value judgments such as "That's cool!" or "How cute!" can be just as damaging; after all, if the child draws a picture of fighter planes next time, they will feel you don't like him or her if you don't say, "That's cute!" Focus instead on the lines and colors of the work. **James, tell me about your work. I see lots of green.** If a child can tell about his or her work without fear of criticism, he or she will be much more likely to talk freely next time. Even a simple comment such as, **I see you put people in your picture** can signal to a child that you are interested in the work and want to know more about it.

As you model enthusiasm for God's Word, for an activity, the children you are guiding are likely to reflect your enthusiasm. Such positive feelings and ideas build interest and relationship!

When children are busy working, it is never time to take a break or talk to another adult! Rather, it is time to stay nearby as an interested observer. This gives you the chance to watch to see if a child is having difficulty, if an activity is too easy or too difficult or whether you can listen and respond to a child's ideas. Don't walk away from great opportunity to meet a child in his or her teachable moment!

You may be reluctant to use rhythm or music activities. However, these are some of the most unifying and relationship-building activities you can do! Even without a musical instrument or a recording, most children are eager to sing or to do a rhythmic stomp-and-clap pattern as they repeat a Bible verse. Your enthusiasm and interest will be the most important factor! Musical perfection is not required.

When giving directions, avoid saying "Don't." Children rarely hear that word and instead hear the rest of the message, often doing exactly what you thought you told them not to do! Instead, phrase directions positively. "You need to put the crayons away" instead of "Don't drop the crayons!" will produce better understanding and results! When a child has complied, be sure to acknowledge him or her. **Josh, you did just what I asked. Thank you!**

Make sure your classroom is a place where every child feels accepted and loved, regardless or performance or behavior. Your classroom should be a safe haven from bullying, name-calling and cliques. Make it a rule that "No one can say, 'You can't play.'" Your modeling of loving and accepting behavior will influence the children you teach to do the same.

While teaching young children, position yourself strategically. By sitting on the rug instead of in a chair at the edge of their activity, you make it easier for several children to share your attention. You might have one child sit near you, be able to pat another and still read to a third.

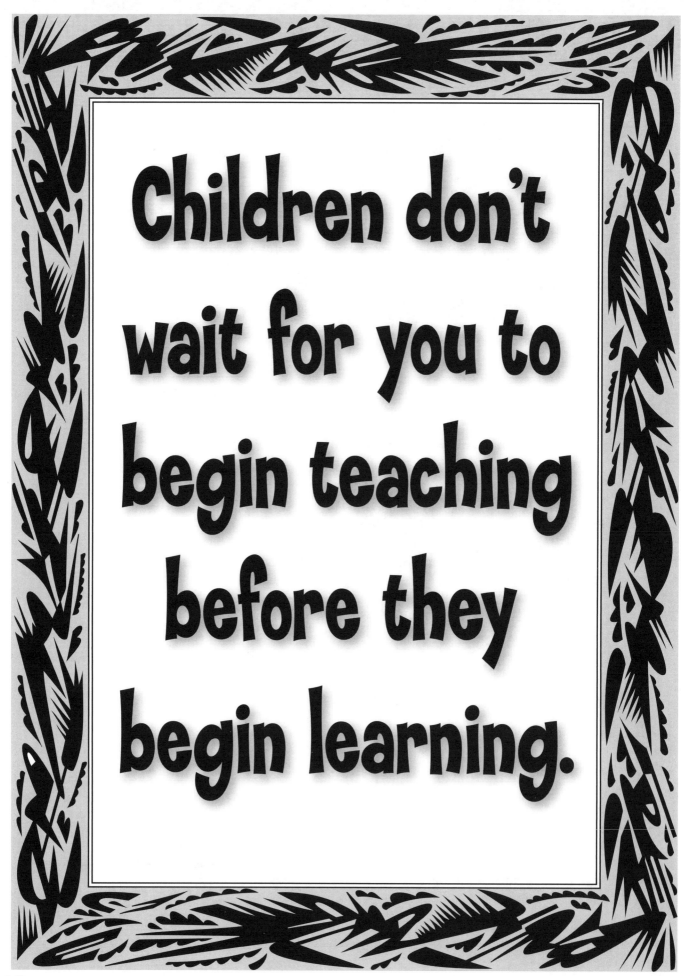

Children don't wait for you to begin teaching before they begin learning.

314

5 BASIC GUIDELINES FOR TEACHERS

1 Always have two teachers in every classroom.

2 Greet every child with a smile and a safe, loving touch.

3 Place yourself at a child's eye level to talk with him or her.

4 Use a child's name often to ensure attention.

5 Use positive discipline (tell children what they may do, not just what they may not do).

Be a skilled teacher by being a skilled listener.

Helping Kids and Parents During a Divorce

Practical Help

Parents who find themselves suddenly single are overwhelmed with the magnitude of change in their lives. They often need help finding day care, getting a new place to live or a job that fits a new set of needs. Call the family members to simply find out how things are going, to offer your help with yard work or childcare. If it's possible, make a home visit or invite the family to your home for dessert. Such simple expressions of interest and encouragement show love in practical ways to everyone involved. And as the family stress level becomes more manageable, a child's situation improves.

If your church or community offers support groups for families in divorce or other family difficulty, provide those contact numbers to family members. Volunteer to go with them the first time. If the child in your class is old enough to attend a group for children, provide contact numbers for programs focused on children of divorce. Giving them a place to talk about their feelings and finding out that others have had similar feelings will greatly help.

Staying in Touch

It's possible that a child will no longer be in your class every week due to family issues. Be sure to get complete contact information for both parents (or others with whom the child stays). Whenever the child is absent, save take-home papers and notices; mail them to the child, along with a personal note.

It's also possible to reach out to the parent who does not bring the child to church. Send duplicate notices to that parent about upcoming events; call that parent occasionally to report something positive you observed in his or her child. Once a parent knows you have no agenda but care about him or her, you may find that the parent feels safe to bring the child to church out of a desire to provide consistency in the child's life.

Simple Ways to Help During Class Time

Tommy walks in, red-eyed and sniffling. Tamara comes in holding her stomach and says her head hurts. Tino bolts into the room, grabs another child and starts shouting. This is children's ministry?!

These are children under stress. It doesn't matter if you know the source of the stress; know the symptoms. Realize that a stressed child is not likely to be ready to participate "as usual" during class.

If you teach mainly younger children (under 6 years of age), keep a "stress stash" handy: dough and dough tools; a water table, sand table or tub of beans; old fabric to tear into pieces (which may then be used to glue onto an art project).

When a distressed child enters, offer one or two of these options. If the child later wants to join in class activities, welcome him or her. But for this child, allowing him or her to play quietly might be the best way to show God's love.

Offer similar activities to older children, but you might want to ask the child to do the activity as a favor to you: tear old fabric into pieces, sharpen crayons or pencils, sort out broken crayons, test and sort markers, etc. Also, offer art materials for drawing. Invite the child to join class activities when ready.

If you can, provide one or two age-appropriate books that might help a child in distress. Place them where children may look at these books as interested.

We're often encouraged to reach out to those who need to know God's love. Families in distress are people in critical need of God's love and your acceptance and help! Make the most of the opportunities presented as you love and teach children who are living in different, difficult or stressful family situations.

Questions and Answers About God

1. What does God look like? How big is God? Is He as tall as my dad?

No one has ever seen God, so we don't know what He looks like. The Bible does talk about Him sometimes as if He looks like a man. That helps us be able to think about Him.

No one has ever measured God because God doesn't live in a body. He is a spirit. And, he can be everywhere at once. He can be with you in your house and with me in my house. While some people are pretty tall, they can only be in one place at a time. But God is so great He can be with us all the time.

2. Where does God live?

God is everywhere, all at the same time. No one understands how He does that, but we know it is true.

3. How does God take care of me?

God made the whole world with everything in it that we need to live. And God planned for us to have families and friends so we can help each other.

4. Does God get angry? (Usually asked after the child has done something wrong.)

God loves you so much that He always wants you to do what is best so that you and everyone else will be happy. When you do something that isn't the best, God is sad, for He knows you won't really be happy.

5. How did Jesus make the blind man see?

Jesus loved the blind man so much that He wanted the man to be able to see. Jesus made the man able to see because He loved the man. We don't know how Jesus made the blind man to see, but we do know that Jesus always used His power to show His great love.

6. Who made God?

The best answer to your question is in the Bible, the book that God gave to people to help us understand some things about Him. There's a place in the Bible where God says, "Before me no god was formed, nor will there be one after me" (Isaiah 43:10). That means that no one came before God. And He will keep on being God forever; there will never be a time when He isn't around. That's really hard for me to understand, but I'm glad to know that God is so much greater than I can even imagine. Otherwise, He'd be a pretty weak god.

7. What did God start with to make people? How did God make cars?

The Bible tells us that God used dust or clay to make the first person, and then breathed into him to make him alive. How did God make cars? God made people and people make cars.

8. Why does God allow terrible things to happen to good people? Are those people being punished for sin? What will happen to bad people? When will God punish them?

When God made people, He didn't plan for terrible things to happen. God made the world perfect! But God also made people so that we can choose to love and obey Him or not. God doesn't force anyone to obey Him. Because all people who have ever lived have sometimes chosen to disobey God, our world isn't perfect any more. Sometimes very bad things happen.

Because we live in this world that has both good and bad in it, we experience some of both. The good news that the Bible brings is that God has promised to always be with us, even in the middle of the worst things we can imagine! He has even promised that no matter what happens to us, He will bring something wonderfully good out of it.

Sometimes people do very wrong things that hurt others. When people are hurt, it's normal to feel like we want God to punish whoever did the bad thing. We need to remember that God still loves the people who did bad things. He loves us all so much that He sent Jesus to die, to take the punishment for all the bad things we've done. Jesus even taught us to love our enemies, the people who have done bad things to us. That is very, very hard for us to do, but God has promised to help us be able to love just as He has loved us.

9. What happens if I'm angry at God?

God knows that sometimes everyone feels angry—even at Him. When we feel angry at God, we can tell Him how we feel and ask His help. God understands our feelings and He promises to keep loving us, no matter how we feel.

10. Why doesn't God answer our prayer to find a job/home/food?

We know that God hears our prayers, but sometimes we don't understand why our prayers aren't answered the way we want them to be or when we want them to be. It's normal to wish that God would give us the good things we ask for right when we ask. Even when we don't know why God doesn't answer our prayers for (food), we can depend on God to be with us during a hard time. It really, really helps to know God is our friend who is with us when we are afraid or sad or hungry. And God has given us people who love and care for us during hard times.

TALKING WITH CHILDREN ABOUT DEATH

When a child in your Sunday School experiences the death of a family member, a neighbor or even a pet, questions—expressed and unexpressed—are sure to arise.

"How does it feel when you're dying?"

"What's a funeral like?"

"Why do people have to die?"

During the difficult time after a death has occurred in a child's family, parents and other relatives may be unable to adequately respond to a child's questions and comments. While there is no substitute for the love given to a child by his or her parents, a caring Sunday School teacher may minister to both the child and the family by being available to talk with the child or by giving a parent some appropriate comments to use in explaining death.

Conversation Tips

In conversing with children, don't be afraid to admit you don't know all the answers. You may want to preface a sentence of explanation by saying, for example, "I know it's hard to understand exactly what heaven is like. But the Bible has told us that in heaven we are with God."

Avoid telling a child that God "took" or "called" someone to heaven. Rather than comforting the bereaved child, such an explanation can make the child angry or fearful toward God for depriving the child of someone special.

Once the immediate crisis has passed, continue to acknowledge a child's questions or feelings of grief. Sometimes all that is needed is a simple statement of understanding. For example, "Jeremy, your grandpa died recently, didn't he? I'm sure you miss him. God knows when you feel sad and He understands how you feel."

Often a child may volunteer information about a death that has occurred in his for her family. Sometimes that information will be shared when a seemingly unrelated topic is being discussed. Take time, however, to respond to the child's comment. Your interest and understanding will create a bond between you and the child and will build a foundation for future conversations about significant concerns a child may face.

Questions and Answers About Death

1. What happens when you die?

When a person or animal dies, it means the body has stopped working. Our bodies wear out, like your toys wear out after you use them for a long time. After many years our bodies get tired and can't keep working. Sometimes people get sick and the disease hurts their body until it can't work anymore. Everyone will die sometime. Most people die when they get old. When you're old, you get sick more easily. It's harder for your body to get well.

2. Where do you go when you die?

After a person dies, the part of a person that thinks and feels keeps living. That part of a person is called the spirit. A person who is a member of God's family begins a new life with God in heaven.

3. Why does God let people die?

When God made people, He didn't plan for them to die. But then the first people on Earth disobeyed God. That is called sin. And then sin—and death—became a part of our world. When someone dies, it reminds us how much we need God and His love.

4. What is heaven?

Heaven is the place where God lives. And all the people who were members of God's family here on Earth live there, too. The Bible tells us that in heaven we will always be with Jesus and God. In heaven there is no sickness or death and no sadness. You can go to heaven someday, too. God has prepared a wonderful home in heaven for every person who loves Him and becomes a member of His family.

6. What will happen to me now that (Grandpa) has died?

In one form or another, this is the most urgent question the child needs to have answered. The child is deeply concerned about the void that has been left in the absence of a loved one. Reassure the child about the ways that void will be filled by people who love the child just as (Grandpa) did. "Everyone who loved (Grandpa) will miss him. But we can all keep loving each other just as we did when (Grandpa) was alive."

7. Why do people have to die?

Our bodies aren't made to last forever. No one knows for sure when he or she will die. Most people live many, many years. Thinking about dying can be sad or scary. The important thing to remember is that God cares for you every day.

8. Why do little children die?

Because of sin, our world is not a perfect world. Anyone can get sick and die, although most of the time people do not die until they are old. Only heaven is perfect. There is no disease, sickness or death in heaven. But God is with us while we're on Earth and helps us when we are sick.

9. Does it hurt to die?

Sometimes people die quickly and sometimes it looks like falling asleep. No matter what happens to us, however, we know God is with us and loves us and takes care of us.

10. I thought mean things about someone. Is that why he died?

No, people don't die because of what others think or say. People die when their bodies get so sick or hurt that they don't work anymore.

11. Will my pet be in heaven?

The Bible doesn't say if our pets will be with us in heaven. However, the Bible does tell us that God loves animals. God cares for the animals, and He even knows when a little bird falls to the ground.

TALKING WITH CHILDREN DIFFICULT FAMILY SITUATIONS

Many children we teach live in family situations other than a happy, functional two-parent family. Parents may be legally separated; they may be in the process of divorce or have been divorced. Other parents may have a boyfriend or girlfriend, be about to remarry or be in a new marriage; that marriage sometimes brings other children into the home. Others may live with grandparents or other relatives, in foster homes or in single-parent homes where there has never been a second parent.

Best Words Forward

As we talk with children about families, keep in mind the situation in which each one lives. Set aside opinions of any family situation so that you are able to treat each child with genuine love and interest.

Show that you care about each child. Often, children in difficult circumstances do not recognize or may suppress their feelings. Make sure children know that your classroom is a safe place where they are loved and accepted as they are. Don't expect to play the part of a therapist but do let a child know that you consider yourself a close and caring friend.

Speak positively about home as "the place where you live, where people love and help each other." It's important that we see and express positive ways in which family members love and help them. Remembering that most children have no voice in their family arrangements, focus on positive aspects of life as it is. I'm glad you get to see your dad next weekend, Janey. I bet it will be fun to go to the park with him!

When appropriate, describe the families of children whose stories are in the Bible: Esther was an orphan reared by a cousin. Daniel was taken from his home by force and lived far away. Samuel lived with Eli instead of at home with his parents. Timothy seems to have been reared by his mother and grandmother. The goal of pointing out these details is to help children see that they are not the only ones to whom family difficulties have come.

Be sure to point out the in the midst of different or difficult family situations found in Scripture, God did great things. He cared a great deal about these people in difficulty and proved that He can always be trusted. Remind children often of these things: You are not alone; God is with you; you can talk to God about your situation because He is eager to hear and able to help. After all, God can change a situation—or can change us through the situation!

Questions and Answers About Families

1. What is divorce?

When two people love each other and want to be a family together, it is called marriage. When people who are married decide not to be a family together anymore, it is called divorce. When people get married, they are very happy. But when people get divorced, they are usually sad, because they could not make their life together what they had wanted it to be.

2. Why does Megan have two houses? Two dads? Two moms?

Megan's mom and dad used to be married. Then they divorced. Because they both love Megan very much, she lives some time in both of their houses. After their divorce, her

CHILDHOOD/ELEMENTARY

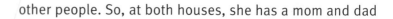

other people. So, at both houses, she has a mom and dad

who is married to someone's dad. It's like she is one step away
... or birth mom. A stepmom loves and helps take care of her hus-
... the children are at their house. In the same way, a man who marries
... led a stepdad.

Trauma

There may be a child or children in your class who are in the middle of a family crisis such as an illness, a death or a divorce. Expect these children to act out, to say angry words or to withdraw into younger behavior than you have seen before.

Use every opportunity to comfort dren who are upset through using their names often, giving extra eye contact and smiles and listening attentively to what they say. Younger children will need a seat on your knee or beside you.

When a young child seems disturbed or sad, simply ask, **You seem to be feeling sad. I'm sorry. Can I help you?** Let the child know you care about his or her feelings. Even if the child is too young to talk about a situation, a brief hug and prayer is in order. **Dear Jesus, Jenna is sad. Please help her. Thank You for loving her. In Your name, amen.**

When a child comes into class and blurts out, "My uncle died yesterday" or "My parents are getting divorced," don't take a business-as-usual approach. Set aside the program for the moment. Ask the child if he or she wants to share this information with the class. If not, take a few moments to pray with him or her alone. If the child is willing to share information, briefly explain, **Chad's uncle died. He is very sad** or **Cherie's parents are talking about getting divorced. Cherie is feeling very scared.** Invite the class to gather around the child and then simply pray a simple prayer (or invite older children to pray sentence prayers). **Dear God, Chad is very sad. Please comfort his family and help him to know You are with him, even when things are very sad. Thank You for loving Chad and his family. We love You. In Jesus' name, amen.** In your prayer, avoid making value judgments of the situation. Focus on supporting the child in need. This can become one of the most important things you do for a child in crisis! Follow up with a card or note during the week to say you are praying for the child and family.

When a child is living with a divorce situation, pay extra attention to that child if at all possible. Quite often, children feel pulled, ignored and rejected. Your consistent interest and patient love may do more than you will ever know. If the child comes only every other week, either mail the weekly materials to the child or save the materials the child missed to give later. This small act of inclusion makes a child feel like he or she belongs and is missed by the church family!

...uma
...ct of
..., give
...rojects
... to use
puppets... ...e experi-
ences can give ... ...t for their
feelings. Be nearby to listen, to ask
questions and to help children ultimately know that God loves them and
that He is in control.

There are many very frightening images that children see on television or from movies. These may or may not be seen as "pretend" but may all be accepted as real. If a child seems overly fearful, ask a few "what do you think?" kinds of questions to see if you can pinpoint the source of the fear. Listen more than you talk. Pray with the child, focusing on God's love and His ability to keep us safe and to turn very bad things into very good things.

If appropriate, take time to talk with parents of children who seem to be traumatized. Make a home visit or invite the family over for dinner. It may be that all of them are traumatized and need loving support! Be sure that children in your class know that no matter what happens, you love them and are on their side and more importantly, that God loves them and brings good out of bad situations.

When a national tragedy occurs (hurricane, terrorist attack, etc.), create an open dialogue with children so that they can openly speak about their feelings on the tragedy. Knowing that others may feel the same way they do can bring comfort to distressed children. Pray with the children acknowledging God's ability to comfort us when we are sad.

EVERY ACTION SENDS A MESSAGE THAT GOES BEYOND WORDS.

More Great Resources from Gospel Light

The Big Book of Bible Story Art Activities for Ages 3 to 6

Young children will love hearing favorite Bible stories as they enjoy creative art activities. Instructions for making puppets, collages, chalk art, friendship bracelets and more are provided to help children create Bible story art. Reproducible, perforated pages.

ISBN 08307.33086

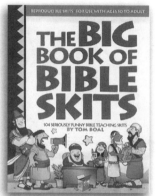

The Big Book of Bible Skits
Tom Boal

104 seriously funny Bible-teaching skits. Each skit comes with Bible background, performance tips, prop suggestions, discussion questions and more. Ages 10 to adult. Reproducible.

ISBN 08307.19164

The Really Big Book of Kids' Sermons and Object Talks with CD-ROM

This reproducible resource for children's pastors is packed with 156 sermons (one a week for three years) that are organized by topics such as friendship, prayer, salvation and more. Each sermon includes an object talk using a household object, discussion questions, prayer and optional information for older children. Reproducible.

ISBN 08307.36573

The Big Book of Volunteer Appreciation Ideas
Joyce Tepfer

This reproducible book is packed with 100 great thank-you ideas for teachers, volunteers and helpers in any children's ministry program. An invaluable resource for showing your gratitude!

ISBN 08307.33094

The Big Book of Christian Growth

Discipling made easy! 306 discussion cards based on Bible passages, and 75 games and activities for preteens. Reproducible.

ISBN 08307.25865

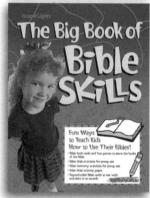

The Big Book of Bible Skills

Active games that teach a variety of Bible skills (book order, major divisions of the Bible, location references, key themes). Ages 8 to 12. Reproducible.

ISBN 08307.23463

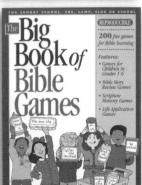

The Big Book of Bible Games

200 fun, active games to review Bible stories and verses and to apply Bible truths to everyday life. For ages 6 to 12. Reproducible.

ISBN 08307.18214

The Big Book of Bible Games #2

150 active games—balloon games, creative team relays, human bowling, and more—that combine physical activity with Bible learning. Games are arranged by Bible theme and include discussion questions. For grades 1 to 6. Reproducible.

ISBN 08307.30532

Gospel Light
God's Word for a Kid's World!™

To order, visit your local Christian bookstore or www.gospellight.com